By

The America-Israel Friendship League promotes a continuing friendship between the peoples of the United States and Israel to the end that a lasting peace may be achieved in the Middle East thereby helping to preserve Democracy and Freedom.

Publication of this volume was made possible by the generosity of the America-Israel Friendship League-Hon. Herbert Tenzer, President.

In the Face of the Nations
Israel's Struggle for Peace

by Yosef Tekoah

Edited by David Aphek

 SIMON AND SCHUSTER *New York*

Published by Simon and Schuster
A Gulf + Western Company
Rockefeller Center, 630 Fifth Avenue
New York, New York 10020

SBN 671–22240–6 Casebound
Library of Congress Catalog Card Number
Designed by Irving Perkins
Manufactured in the United States of America

1   2   3   4   5   6   7   8   9   10

Library of Congress Cataloging in Publication Data

Tekoah, Yosef, 1925–
    In the face of the nations.

    1.   Jewish-Arab relations—1967–1973—Addresses,
essays, lectures.   2.   Jewish-Arab relations—
1973–   Addresses, essays, lectures.   3.   United
Nations—Israel—Addresses, essays, lectures.
I.   Title.
DS119.7.T42   327.5694′017′4927   75-42326
ISBN 0-671-22240-6

In memory of my parents, who
taught us to love Zion

Contents

Foreword

BY YITZHAK RABIN

Prime Minister of Israel

For the Israeli diplomat there are few overseas postings that are more challenging and more testing than the United Nations. The Israeli Ambassador to the United Nations must be more than a competent orator; he must be, in the first instance, a profound articulator of the Jewish story, capable of interpreting his country's policies in the context of Jewish historical experience. That experience is ancient, often bloody and invariably lonely, for the Jewish people have walked alone through two thousand long years of tortuous exile before regaining independence more than a quarter of a century ago. Only in the context of that story of former homelessness and helplessness, climaxed by the terrible carnage of the Holocaust, can one understand Israel's ongoing struggle for equality and security within the family of nations.

Between January 1968 and July 1975 Ambassador Yosef Tekoah served as the spokesman of Israel at the United Nations. From my perspective in Washington, where I served as ambassador for much of that time, his task seemed unenviable. I never had illusions about the United Nations when it came to a fair hearing for Israel, and I quickly learned that Yosef Tekoah, as our ambassador there, shared my thoughts. Simply, we faced, and continue to face, an overwhelming, inbuilt, automatic parliamentary disadvantage. By their mere numbers, our adversaries are able to muster votes, not on the merits of any particular issue, but by the sheer size of the blocs they command.

9

For Israel, therefore, it has always been a question of striking in the UN the right balance between respect for the principles of the international organization and realism in the assessment of its actual role. Yosef Tekoah demonstrated that balance with skill and conviction.

In his addresses before the Security Council and the General Assembly he brought the power of truth made more potent by incisive reflections on the Jewish past. A convincing debater and patient negotiator, he carried into the lobbies of the international forum many years of diplomatic experience. This goes back to the early years of Israeli independence when I first met him in his capacity as the diplomat responsible for Armistice Affairs. He saw service as ambassador to Brazil and then as ambassador to Moscow, where he worked tirelessly for the right of Jewish emigration to Israel, a struggle that continues to this day.

His statements before the United Nations constitute an important contribution to an understanding of the basic issues of the Israel–Arab conflict. In their collective they convey the tenacity with which Israel has been seeking peace with its neighbors and leave no doubt of Israel's resolve to pursue that goal despite the obstacles. This is the central theme of Israel's policies inspired by an ancient prophetic heritage which the UN speeches of Yosef Tekoah project with fearless integrity.

Introduction

BY YOSEF TEKOAH

Former Ambassador of Israel to the United Nations

Few nations feel as profound an affinity to the ideals of the United Nations as the Jewish people. The vision of universal peace is deeply rooted in the Hebrew Prophets. The concept of a family of nations upholding the values of justice and morality is a cardinal tenet of the Jewish faith. So are also the principles of human rights.

The struggle against Nazism in World War II out of which emerged the United Nations was for the Jewish people everywhere, including the Jews of the land of Israel, a life-and-death struggle. The tragedy of the Holocaust has left a marked imprint on many a provision of the United Nations Charter.

It is perhaps this special affinity that has caused disappointment with the United Nations to be particularly strong among the Jewish people. Jews are saddened by the deterioration of the United Nations, the disregard for basic Charter principles which accompanies many of the United Nations actions, the abysmal powerlessness of the United Nations to handle international conflicts equitably and effectively. To the Jewish people this development is a betrayal of values which constitute an integral part of Jewish civilization and Jewish experience.

To Jews this betrayal is reflected in the granting of United Nations observer status to the PLO murder organization which carries on a neo-Nazi policy of denying to the Jewish people the rights of all

11

nations, and directs its campaign of sanguinary atrocities against innocent and defenseless Jewish civilians. The betrayal of basic United Nations precepts is further expressed by the fact that the Arab States which have, throughout the years, violated their obligations under the United Nations Charter toward Israel are in a position to suggest Israel's suspension from United Nations organs, and to force through the General Assembly a resolution desecrating the Jewish people's national liberation movement—Zionism.

The parliamentary domination of the United Nations by the Arab States, together with their automatic supporters, and the subsequent disabilities imposed on the United Nations role in the settlement of international disputes have brought about a drastic curtailment in the Organization's involvement in the peacemaking efforts in the Middle East. Security Council Resolutions 242 of November 22, 1967, and 338 of October 22, 1973, remain the basis for endeavors to attain agreement and ultimate peace between Israel and the Arab States. However, in recent years the United Nations has been relegated to a secondary and purely supporting role, such as providing international peace forces to supervise the cease-fire established in the wake of the Yom Kippur War of 1973 and embodied in the separation of forces and interim agreements reached since then between the parties to the conflict. The parties have also entrusted United Nations representatives with the essentially formal responsibility of chairing Israeli-Arab meetings, joint committees and conferences such as the Geneva Conference and the joint commission created by the Egypt-Israel agreement of September 4, 1975.

Nevertheless, the United Nations continues as the central world political arena where governmental views are aired and delegates of member States try to preserve a modicum of international thought and action. Until recently the United Nations was even more than that, as far as the Middle East situation is concerned. After the Six-Day War of 1967 the Arab States regarded it as a crucial battlefield and attempted, time and again, to compel Israel, through United Nations debates and resolutions, to abandon its demand for genuine peace and security.

They have failed. Their ceaseless onslaught on Israel in the United Nations has, however, turned the confrontations in the Security Council and in the General Assembly into memorable contests of historic significance and lasting impact. In the course of these confrontations, all aspects of the situation were examined. The fundamentals of this situation have not altered. This book attempts to present the Israeli view on these fundamentals as formulated in the din of battle in the United Nations and in other public appearances during almost eight years of service as Israel's representative to the international Organization.

My gratitude goes out to my long-time colleague and friend, David Aphek, who has given of his time to edit the book, and whose superior knowledge, skill and dedication have been of invaluable assistance in the work of the Israeli delegation as a whole, and in particular to me personally, throughout my years at the United Nations.

Thou shalt not follow a multitude to do evil.
—EXODUS 23:1

I Self-determination for the Jewish People

1 The Covenant of the Land and the People

After the Six-Day War, Arab spokesmen put forward the concept of "a secular Democratic Palestinian State in which Jews, Muslims and Christians will live in peace." Arab delegations at the United Nations began to promote this slogan in the Twenty-fifth Session of the United Nations General Assembly (1970).

The following statement was delivered on December 1, 1970, in the Special Political Committee in reply to Arab representatives who had suggested replacing the existing State of Israel by a "secular, democratic Republic."

At the dawn of time, when peoples, states, civilizations and religions were still in a formative stage, a nation was born destined to preserve its identity and survive through the ages till our days. It was a time when, in most parts of the world, the concept of community was confined to the tribe or the city; the political unit was based on loyalty to a king or emperor rather than on ethnic affinity. It was then that the Jewish people emerged as a nation distinct not only in its political personality but also as a separate cultural and religious entity.

For more than a thousand years this people maintained its sovereignty over the land of Israel. When the Roman Empire conquered nation after nation, the Jewish people stubbornly resisted, clinging to its independence, its faith and civilization, and was the last people in the Mediterranean basin to be subdued, in A.D. 70.

Part of the nation was uprooted by the conqueror and carried away into bondage in distant lands. Those who remained continued to resist and to rebel again and again. In the year 132 they succeeded in restoring their independence for several years, only to be crushed once more by the Romans. The conquerors tried to suppress Jewish sovereignty even by erasing the name of the country and renamed it Palestine. The Jews refused to give up their struggle. In the year 352 they rose again in revolt against Roman rule. In 614 they raised an army which together with Persia put an end to the domination of the Roman Empire in the Holy Land.

Thereafter waves of invaders swept across the country. First came the Arabs, who ruled till 1072, then the Seljuks and after them the Crusaders. The latter took Jerusalem in 1099 and massacred the Jews of the city. After the Crusaders appeared the Mamelukes and, in 1517, the Ottomans, who remained in power for four centuries.

The Jewish population dwindled under the impact of massacre and exile. However, the land remained a center of Jewish life and learning, producing works of great national and cultural significance.

In the meantime, the Jews exiled to foreign lands preserved their identity as a nation and remained bound to their homeland by the civilization and religion of which they were bearers. Their faith, culture, customs, food, and even their clothing made their lives a continuation of the existence in their homeland. They celebrated holydays based on the history of the land of Israel or on climatic and agricultural seasons which prevail in it. Forbidden by their faith to intermarry with non-Jews, they remained a distinct people transmitting their national heritage from generation to generation. Persecuted by their neighbors on account of their Asian origin and Oriental civilization, the Jews knew and felt that they were strangers and that their home remained in Israel. Through the centuries they strove to return to it, individually, in groups, in mass movements. Day after day, three times a day they prayed that they might go back to the land of their fathers and reestablish their independence.

For the attachment to their nation, for the bonds with their homeland they paid with their lives. The Crusaders butchered them in all parts of Europe. The Spanish Inquisition burned them at the stake. They were slaughtered in the Russian pogroms, and gassed and annihilated by the millions in the Nazi holocaust. Yet they never surrendered, never abandoned their heritage, always remained a nation proud of its identity, linked to its land by a myriad bonds.

During this time the land of Israel stood desolate. Its successive conquerors saw in it occupied territory. It never became a separate sovereignty again. The Arab and other Moslem rulers never considered its ancient capital Jerusalem even as an administrative center. Those of the conquerors who settled in the land were few, their populated localities sparse. They never saw themselves as being different from the inhabitants of neighboring lands. They never produced a national culture of their own. They never aspired to be regarded as a separate political entity.

Travelers who visited the area described it always as a dying land. The Frenchman Volney, who toured Palestine in 1785, wrote that it was "desolate." A. Keith, writing some decades after Volney, commented: "In his [Volney's] day the land had not reached its last degree of desolation and depopulation." By 1883 Colonel Condor, author of *Heath and Moab,* called Palestine "a ruined land." Mark Twain was shocked by the land's "desolation" as described in *Innocents Abroad.* In the nineteenth century there were only about 150,000 settled inhabitants and an equal number of nomads.

Indeed, until the mass return of Jews at the end of the last century and especially since after World War I, the picture of Palestine is one of a wasteland inhabited by clusters of impoverished peasants in debt to absentee landlords residing in Beirut, Damascus or Cairo.

The population began to increase and the country to develop only with the beginning of organized Jewish return a century ago. In 1922 the Arab population was 565,000. By 1947 it grew largely by Arab immigration from abroad to 1,200,000, an increase of 100 percent. During the same period Egypt, for instance, saw its population increase by 25 percent only. In Transjordan, which was lopped off in 1922 from western Palestine and was closed to Jewish immigration, the Arab population remained static.

In information bulletin No. 6 of 1962, the United Nations Relief and Works Agency reports:

A considerable movement of people is known to have occurred, particularly during the Second World War years when new opportunities of employment opened up in the towns and on military works in Palestine. These wartime prospects and, generally, the higher rate of industrialization in Palestine than in neighboring countries attracted many immigrants from those countries, and many of them entered Palestine without their presence being officially recorded.

Thus it is clear that the majority of the Arab inhabitants of Palestine at the time Israel attained its independence were immigrants who had come from neighboring Arab States in a migration that paralleled the arrival of Jews in the country.

In these circumstances, it was not surprising that Arab nationalists did not regard Palestine as a separate national or political personality. As late as May 1947, Arab representatives informed the United Nations in a formal statement: "Palestine was part of the Province of Syria. . . . Politically the Arabs of Palestine were not independent in the sense of forming a separate political entity." In 1952, the well-known Arab statesman and scholar Charles Malik wrote in the quarterly *Foreign Affairs*: "Greater Syria was dismembered, the southern and northern parts being put under different administrations." On May 31, 1956, Ahmed Shukairi, the founder and head of the Palestine Liberation Organization, announced in the Security Council that "it is common knowledge that Palestine is nothing but southern Syria."

This has been the traditional Arab view of Palestine. As recently as October 17, 1966, the representative of Syria, Ambassador Tomeh, declared in the Security Council: "We as Syrians consider Palestine to be and to have been historically, geographically and from every point of view a part of Syria . . . When we speak of Palestine we feel we are speaking about part of our country."

Indeed, the Arabs never looked upon Palestine as a land with a distinct political personality, or upon its inhabitants as a separate people. Throughout history, it was only in the eyes of one people and one people alone, the Jewish people, that the land was different and

separate from other lands, that it was the cradle of its national
aspirations.

In history this has been recognized by the Arabs themselves. The
Koran states with reference to the Jews: "Enter, O my people, to the
Holy Land which God hath destined for you."

The Arabic name for Jerusalem, El Quds, is derived from *el-Maqdes,* which is the Arab form of the Hebrew *Hamikdash,* meaning
the Holy Temple, the Jewish Temple.

On March 23, 1918, Sherif Hussein, the ruler of Mecca, published
an article in *Al Qible* in which he said:

. . . we saw the Jews from foreign countries streaming to Palestine . . .
The cause of the causes would not escape those who had the gift of a
deeper insight; they knew that the country was for its original sons
[*abna'ehi-l-asliyin*], for all their differences, a sacred and beloved homeland.
Experience has proved their capacity to succeed in their energies and their
labors . . . The return of these exiles [*jaliya*] to their homeland will prove
materially and spiritually an experimental school for their brethren [i.e.,
the Arabs] . . .

Emir Feisal, the father of modern Arab nationalism, declared on
December 12, 1918, in an interview with Reuters:

The two main branches of the Semite family, Arabs and Jews, understand one another, and I hope that as a result of an interchange of ideas
at the Peace Conference, which will be guided by ideals of self-determination and nationality, each nation will make definite progress towards the
realisation of its aspiration. Arabs are not jealous of Zionist Jews and intend to give them fair play . . .

On January 3, 1919, Emir Feisal signed on behalf of the Arab
Kingdom of Hedjaz the celebrated agreement with Dr. Weizmann,
representing the Zionist Organization, in which provisions were made
for cooperation between the Arab State and Jewish Palestine.

On March 1, 1919, Emir Feisal wrote to the future U.S. Supreme
Court Justice Felix Frankfurter:

We Arabs, especially the educated among us, look with the deepest sympathy on the Zionist movement. . . . We wish the Jews a most hearty welcome home . . . We are working together for a reformed and revived Near East, and our two movements complete one another. The Jewish movement is national and not imperialist . . . Indeed I think that neither can be a real success without the other.

The attitude changed with a change in Arab leadership. The facts of the situation did not alter, but the policies of certain Arab leaders did. Brotherhood and cooperation were replaced by hostility and violence. Enmity toward Jews was so extreme that in later years some of these leaders became Nazi sympathizers and collaborators, and spent the war period in Berlin advising Hitler and Eichmann on the genocide of Jews. Arab leaders who today invoke human rights and seek the support of African and Asian States had no inhibitions about associating themselves with the Nazi policies and actions regarding Africans and Jews.

At first they openly spoke in Nazi terms of annihilating the people of Israel and throwing the Jews into the sea. Since 1967 they have tried to conceal their destructive objectives by less bloodthirsty terminology.

Thus we hear more and more frequently that their aim is the establishment in Palestine of a "secular, democratic State." What is not always mentioned is the fact that this idea is contingent on the elimination of the Jewish State and the denial to the Jewish people of Palestine of its rights to self-determination and freedom. After Israel ceased to exist, some of its citizens who would be allowed to remain would be permitted to dwell as a minority in a Palestinian State in which they would be presumably as safe and happy as the remnants of Jewish communities in Egypt, Iraq or Syria.

Before 1967, the Palestine Liberation Organization was ready, at least on paper, to allow those Jews who had entered Palestine before 1948 to remain in the country after the destruction of Israel was accomplished. Now, according to the Palestinian National Covenant, as amended by the fourth Palestinian Council in Cairo in July 1968, such rights will be accorded only to those Jews who were in Palestine in 1917. Only those will be allowed to live peacefully on the ruins of the State of Israel.

Thus, despite semantic adornments, the aim remains the same as in the past—the destruction of a member State of the United Nations, the elimination of the Jewish people's rights to liberty and self-determination, the uprooting and exile of most of Israel's Jews.

The methods, as well, remain unchanged. As in the decades prior to Israel's independence and in the years which followed the establishment of the Jewish State, terror against the civilian population continues to be the main form of warfare against the people of Israel. The attempts to describe as resistance to military occupation the same terror activities which Palestine has known since the twenties is no less hypocritical than the attempts to depict as an effort to establish a unitary democratic Palestine the desire to destroy Israel and annihilate its people.

The more extreme of the Arab Governments and their representatives in the United Nations accompany these policies with incessant distortions and with vilification of the Jewish people. The history of the Jewish people is falsified beyond recognition, its religion abused, its culture deprecated. The Jewish people is portrayed in fact as a nonpeople.

Thus, a fantastic proposition is put forward alleging that the conversion to Judaism of the Khazar King and four thousand of his nobles in the Volga region, about eight hundred years before the first Jews began to arrive in Russia by way of Germany, Poland and Lithuania, turns the entire Russian and even European Jewry into descendants of the Khazars. To this is attached the claim that for some inexplicable reason these alleged descendants of the Turkic Khazars abandoned their own language and chose for their vernacular a Germanic dialect, Yiddish.

No less absurd are the references to Israel as a foreign European State, though it is common knowledge that the majority of its citizens are Israel-born and almost half of them are Jewish refugees from Arab lands and their families. Besides, it is an irony of fate that Jews, oppressed and discriminated against by Europeans for being of Semitic Asian stock, should be vilified as Europeans by their own Semitic brethren.

Freed of distortion, acrimony and abuse, treated in a spirit of mutual respect and understanding, the problem of Jewish and Arab rights in Palestine becomes a tractable one.

There are a number of basic, undeniable facts:

1. The reestablishment of Jewish independence in Israel, after centuries of struggle to overcome foreign conquest and exile, is a vindication of the fundamental concepts of equality of nations and of self-determination. To question the Jewish people's right to national existence and freedom is to deny the central precepts of the United Nations.

2. Throughout history, only the Jewish people saw the land of Israel as a distinct political entity, as the center of its national existence and of its civilization. All other inhabitants who settled there, after the Jews had been uprooted by foreign invaders, regarded themselves and the country itself as integral parts of larger entities, political, national and religious.

3. The Arab inhabitants of the land have always considered themselves to be part of the larger Arab nation which has vindicated its rights to self-determination and independence in fourteen * sovereign Arab States, with several more on the way to achieving independence.

4. Within the area of Palestine itself, the aspirations of the Arab people to sovereignty have been adequately met by the international community. In the period of the League of Nations, Transjordan was cut off from the West Bank, closed to Jews and established as a separate Palestinian Arab entity.

5. The existence in Palestine of one rather than two Arab States does not alter the fact that the Arab population of Palestine exercises its right to political independence within a sovereign Palestinian Arab entity. On January 14, 1963, King Hussein declared that "Jordan is Palestine and Palestine is Jordan." Mr. Anwar Nusseibi, a former

---

* Today there are twenty sovereign Arab States, all of them members of the United Nations.

Jordanian Defense Minister, who now lives in Jerusalem, stated on October 23, 1970: "The Jordanians are also Palestinians. This is one state. This is one people. The name is not important. The families living in Salt, Irbid and Karak maintain not only family and matrimonial ties with the families in Nablus and Hebron. They are one People."

It is clear, in the light of these facts, that the rights of Jews and Arabs in Palestine to national existence are not irreconcilable. The Arabs exercise them in the Arab State, the Jews in the State of Israel. The Arabs are free, of course, to decide on the name, political structure and unity of their State. However, they cannot claim that only their rights are valid, that equal rights should be denied to the Jewish people in its historic homeland, and that instead of finding accommodation between the two peoples the rights of the Arabs should supplant the rights of the Jews.

It is no secret that the Arab delegations are seeking to obtain support for the untenable thesis that only Arab rights should be respected, that Israel's rights should be denied, that warfare pursued with the avowed aim of Israel's destruction should be approved and assisted. It is no secret that the Arab delegations are preparing resolutions which reflect such views. Not only would such resolutions be contrary to the principle of equality of states and nations, but, by accepting the position of extreme Palestinian groups which reject Israel's right to independence, they would undermine the ability of Israel and the Arab States to reach agreements on a just and lasting peace as called for by the United Nations.

It is to be hoped that the Arab Governments and all member States will weigh most carefully whether to allow the introduction of such complicating factors at this crucial stage of the Middle East situation. The hopes for peace are all too fragile to be further endangered by disregard for the rights of one of the parties to the conflict.

2 For the Sake of Jerusalem I Will Not Rest

I

Following the proclamation of the State of Israel in May 1948, seven Arab armies invaded the newly born state in order to destroy it by force of arms. In the subsequent fighting, the Jordanian legions seized the eastern parts of Jerusalem, including its historic walled Old City, which contained religious shrines sacred to Christians, Moslems and Jews. For the next nineteen years—until 1967—Jerusalem remained a divided city, cut in half by barbed-wire barriers and walls.

The question of the reunification of Jerusalem in June 1967 has been the focus of bitter controversy between Israel and the Arab States in the course of several debates in the United Nations Security Council. The following statement was delivered on May 3, 1968, in a Security Council meeting convened at the request of the Jordanian Government.

Ever since the Roman conquest in the first century of this era, history seems to have reserved a distinct destiny for the Hebrew people, my people: oppression, denial of rights, martyrdom. The Prophet Jeremiah said:

. . . the children of Israel shall come, they and the children of Judah together. . . .

All that found them devoured them; all their adversaries said, We are not guilty . . .

We have survived through defeat and enslavement by Imperial Rome, through the rebellions against the foreign conquerors, through the centuries of dispersion of the people and occupation of the land by a succession of invaders, through the massacres of the Crusaders, through the autos-da-fé of the Inquisition, the pogroms, the blood libels, the holocausts. We have survived and regained our national freedom and reestablished our sovereignty in our land. Yet, Jeremiah's prophecy is not of the past; some still try to devour us and then say, "We are not guilty." In certain parts of Europe the Dark Ages are not over for the Jewish people. In the Arab States the spirit of the Damascus blood libel is still alive. This is the spirit that shapes and guides Arab policy toward Israel. This is the spirit that dominates the Arab attitude in the United Nations. Today they have chosen Jerusalem as the object of their blood libel—Jerusalem, sanctified and revered as Rome and Mecca are.

There is an old Hebrew saying: "Ten measures of beauty came into the world; Jerusalem received nine measures, and the rest of the world one. Ten measures of suffering came into the world; Jerusalem received nine, and the rest of the world one." However, whether in bliss and beauty or in suffering, Jerusalem has always remained Israel's eternal capital.

By the time it was conquered in the year 70 of the present era by the legions of Rome, Jerusalem had served as Israel's capital for more than a thousand years. Though defeated, the people of Israel refused to be subdued, and in the year 132 rose in revolt against the Roman invader. Jerusalem was freed and the nation's leader, Bar-Kochba, set up his government in the capital. He struck coins inscribed "Jerusalem" and "Year 1 of the Liberty of Israel." He succeeded in holding out for three years until the weight of the Roman cohorts overcame the Jewish people again.

Then followed a long period of Roman and Byzantine rule. In 614 the Jewish population helped Persia to dislodge Byzantium, and for a while Jews governed Jerusalem again. Then, in the year 638, Jerusalem was captured by the Arabs who had come from Arabia. Jerusalem was under Arab domination till the year 1077, but the Arab conquerors never made it a seat of government, not even of provincial administration. They ruled the area from Damascus, from Baghdad, from Ramle. In 1077 the Seljuk Turks conquered the land and the city of Jerusalem. It never returned to Arab rule again except for the nineteen years of grim Jordanian reign in part of the city.

In 1099 the Crusaders succeeded in wresting Jerusalem from the Turks. They put the entire Jewish and Moslem population to the sword. They maintained their power, except for a brief interval during the time of Salah ed-Din, until 1244, when they lost out to the Tartars. These were followed by the Mamelukes, who, in turn, were conquered by the Ottoman Turks in 1516.

Like the Arabs, neither the Mamelukes nor the Turks ruled from Jerusalem. Under the Mamelukes the seat of provincial government was Gaza; under the Turks, Acre. In 1917 the Turks were ousted from the land of Israel and from Jerusalem by the Allied forces, which included a Jewish Legion fighting under Israel's colors.

Jerusalem has never ceased to be part of the Jewish saga. It was no more Arab by virtue of the Arab conquest than Turkish when the Turks occupied it or British when the British ruled in it. Arab annals record the Arab conquest of Jerusalem. Jewish history is permeated with the memories of Jerusalem's defense, the desperate attempts to preserve its Jewishness, the destruction of the Temple, the fast and mourning that the Jewish people have observed ever since on the ninth day of the month of Ab.

Jerusalem's name is Hebrew: Yerushalem, the City of Peace. One cannot separate Jerusalem from Hebrew history, martyrdom and redemption. However, it is with profound respect that we recognize the universal interests in Jerusalem. Jerusalem is venerated by three great religions, and all three share in the city's glory. The people are the city, and the Jews have never left Jerusalem. Even after the most sanguinary of massacres they came back to it—the heart of Judaism—again and again, to heal the city's wounds and rebuild its ruins.

Jerusalem repaid the love and loyalty of its people. It remained forever faithful to it. It served as the capital of one nation, and one nation alone—the capital of the Jewish people.

Since statistics of Jerusalem's population have become available it has been evident that Jews have for generations constituted a majority in the city. In 1844, of a total population of 15,510, there were in Jerusalem 7,120 Jews, 5,000 Moslems, and 3,390 Christians. In 1876 there were 12,000 Jews, 7,560 Moslems, and 5,470 Christians. In 1896 the Jewish population rose to 28,112, the Moslems numbered 8,560, the Christians 8,748. The number of Jews in Jerusalem reached 40,000 by 1905, in a total population of 60,000; the number of Moslems declined to 7,000. In 1910 there were 47,400 Jews, 9,800 Moslems, 16,400 Christians. By 1931 the Jewish inhabitants of Jerusalem numbered 51,222; there were 19,894 Moslems and 19,335 Christians. In 1948 Jerusalem was a city of 100,000 Jews, 40,000 Moslems and 24,000 Christians. On the eve of last June's hostilities, 200,000 Jews, 54,903 Moslems, 12,646 Christians resided in Jerusalem. Today Jerusalem, a living city again in its freedom and unity, is the hearth of more than 200,000 Jews, about 60,000 Arabs, and 6,000 of other nationalities.

What precept of law, what tenet of justice, what principle of morality would deprive Jerusalem's citizens—Jews and Arabs alike—of their rights to the happiness and beauty and inspiration of their city as a whole? Why should those who have treasured Jerusalem for three thousand years as their chiefest joy be shorn of the fullness of it? Why should Jerusalem's Jewish and Arab inhabitants be despoiled of their heritage in the city's unity? Does a conquest in defiance of the United Nations, a nineteen-year occupation unrecognized by the nations of the world including the Arab States themselves, give Jordan the right to oppose Jerusalem's revival in integrity and radiance? Does the presence of 54,000 Moslems and 12,000 Christians, in addition to the more than 200,000 Jews, necessitate a bisection of the city's body?

King Solomon's Biblical judgment between the two contesting women cries out to us through the ages. Could a real mother ever agree to have her baby cut in two? Could a people ever accept that its eternal capital be divided? There are many cities in the world with large national or religious minorities. Have such communities ever claimed that their cities should be artificially divided and separate public services set up for them?

Jerusalem has existed for thousands of years, and it was only during the brief nightmare of Jordanian occupation that part of it was carved out and wrested away from the city and its people. A crime that the world witnessed in silence, a transgression that brought death and destruction, terror and desecration to Jerusalem—how can Jordan now come and demand approval of it? History, justice and faith will never pardon the nineteen years of darkness, profanation and ruin in eastern Jerusalem.

In preceding meetings of the Security Council I have described fully the Jordanian reign of vandalism. The ruins of the Jewish Quarter, the tombstones torn up on the Mount of Olives, the grim tragedy of the humanitarian institutions on Mount Scopus, the hundreds of dead and wounded in 1948, in 1967 and in the intervening years—all these will not allow us to forget. Nor can Jordanian distortions, born in hate and bloodthirst, distort the reality of today. The entire world knows what the Jordanians were preparing to bring down upon the Jews of Jerusalem had the fortunes of war gone differently. The orders to the Jordanian Army, such as those to the Reserve Battalion of the 27th Brigade, to kill all Jews in captured areas are a matter of public record.

The textbooks teaching Arab children that it is a virtue to hate and kill Jews; the school posters, the newspaper cartoons showing how to do it; the blood-chilling cries broadcast over the radio, "Kill! Kill! Kill! Butcher! Butcher the Jew!"—all this will forever be remembered, not only by my people but by humanity as a whole.

Let not the Jordanians come now and speak of Israeli behavior in terms of the sanguinary bloodbath they were preparing for us. The facts are there for all to see. Let others bear witness.

In the January 1968 issue of the Franciscan Order's publication *La Terre sainte* we read:

We must voice our opinion on the taking of Jerusalem . . . It is not true that a massacre of innocents was the price for the safety of the Holy places. In Paris, too, during the Liberation on August 25, 1944, there were people killed—women, children, unfortunate civilians—but no one dared say that spilt blood has saved Notre Dame or Montmartre. . . . Every war has its horrors, its victims—and on both sides . . .

The mayor of Hebron, Sheikh Muhammed Ali Jabari, a former Minister of Education of Jordan, proclaimed on July 30, 1967:

I swear by Allah that no Israel soldiers harmed any of our residents . . . Before the war began we expected a mutual slaughter between our people and the Israel army. You can imagine how pleasant was our surprise on the 8th of June when we discovered that the victorious army was a well-organized, disciplined body like the armies of the West.

The situation soon after the cease-fire was described in the report submitted by the Secretary General in September 1967. The findings of the Secretary General's Special Representative, Mr. Ernesto Thalmann, based on a visit to the area as far back as last August, include the following:

. . . the Personal Representative was struck by the great activity in the streets of the city. . . .

Uniforms were few and weapons fewer. . . . The picture of the crowd in the Old City was dominated by the tourists. Arab and Jews were mingling . . .

Most of the hotels had reopened. Before dawn and during the day the muezzin could be heard, as well as the church bells.

The Arab personnel of the Old City was absorbed in the equivalent departments in the Israel municipality. . . .

It was reported that from the time that access from Israel to east Jerusalem had become free, the shopkeepers there had been unusually active, selling at the rate of 2 million Israel pounds a day in the first month and at a steady rate of 1 million Israel pounds a day at present. . . . Service establishments were reported to have greatly increased their activities. The workshops, after an initial period of dislocation, were said to have all reverted to routine and normality and to be going through a process of adjustment to the new marketing conditions. . . .

The Personal Representative was told that the policy will be to pay Arabs employed in Israel enterprises salaries equal to those received by their Israel counterparts. As regards Arab enterprises, salaries would be calculated according to the economic solvency of the enterprise. Salaries would be raised gradually so as not to disrupt the Arab economy and to allow it to adjust to the conditions prevailing in Israel. . . .*

I should like to add that an invitation was extended to Mr. Rouhi El-Khatib and members of his council to join the Jerusalem Municipal Council. Mr. El-Khatib, for reasons which will become obvious in the course of my statement, refused.

Since then the situation has improved. The public services are operating normally. In all of east Jerusalem, school studies are running smoothly. In all private schools and those of Moslem institutions there has been no change in curriculum. In municipal schools the curriculum current in Israel's Arab schools, which include studies in Arab history and Islam, is followed. The minds of children are no longer poisoned by hatred of their neighbors as had been the case under Jordanian rule. All Moslem institutions, such as the Sharia courts, the Waqf administration, the Red Crescent, charitable organizations and hospitals, are pursuing their activities without hindrance, under the same leadership, with the exception of one person. This applies, of course, to Christian institutions as well.

This is how Bishop Dom José Gonçalves da Costa of Brazil paints the situation in Jerusalem in the *Jornal do Brasil* of September 30, 1967:

For many hours I walked through the streets of Old Jerusalem and watched the faces of the merchants and peddlers; I went into bars and into shops. They all looked lively and very much satisfied with the excellent business they were doing. I felt no signs of anxiety or hate on the part of the Arabs in Jerusalem, Jericho and Bethlehem.

The Government of Israel immediately put the municipal services of of the great City of Jerusalem on a joint basis. There is no doubt that the ridiculous situation of before the war must not recur, where a street dividing two countries passed through a single city, and soldiers armed to

* Official Records of the Security Council, Twenty-second Year, Supplement for July, August and September 1967, document S/8146, paras. 19–21, 29, 67, 92 and 93.

their teeth faced each other from the rooftops, looking at each other with hate. The Mandelbaum Gate, of which little is left now, was a serious obstacle for Christian pilgrims.

The atmosphere of the city was best reflected when the Christian communities, joined by thousands of tourists from abroad, including visitors from the Arab States, recently celebrated the Easter festival. The Moslem community celebrated the holydays of Id el-Fitr and Id el-Adkha in accordance with its own traditions.

On April 27, 1968, the Latin Custos of the Holy Land wrote:

Thanks be to God, pilgrimages to the Christian Shrines are increasing in number from day to day, and pilgrims make their visits as they did a year ago. Only occasionally they are advised, though not prevented by force, to omit the visit to the River Jordan, on account of some danger of shooting in that zone.

All the services (I mean religious services) are going on as usual in the Christian Churches. It would be enough to mention how orderly everything was during the recent celebration of Holy Week and Easter.

As I had the occasion to state on previous occasions, practically none of our Holy Places and churches were damaged or destroyed during the Six Day War. In one or two places minor damage was caused, because the fight went on in the immediate vicinity of the church or monastery. One place which suffered quite a bit was our monastery on Mount Zion.

What I have stated so far are facts that everybody can check. Of course a war is a war; yet in general we must be grateful to Almighty God that the Holy Places were preserved from destruction, and almost in all cases from damage, even small. I suppose that all can see for themselves in what conditions are our churches. And again I should say "Thanks be to God!" that Christians and pilgrims have been able to continue their divine worship in our churches, practically without any break, since last June.

An abusive reference was made here to the Church of the Holy Sepulcher. A reference was made to the burglary of the jeweled crown from the church shortly after the hostilities. Mention, however, was conveniently omitted of the fact that the crown was recovered from the thieves and restored to the church in a ceremony of reverence joined by many. I believe the Koran says: "He shall not prosper who deviseth lies." That applies not only to the distortion concerning the burglary mentioned.

A manifesto on a united Jerusalem by America's leading Christian theologians, published in *The New York Times* on July 12, stated *inter alia:*

During the past twenty years the City of David has experienced an artificial division. This has resulted in a denial of access to their Holy Places for all Jews and for Israeli Arabs of the Moslem faith. It has also severely limited accessibility to Christian shrines for Israeli Christians. This injustice, we must confess, did not elicit significant protests on the part of the religious leaders of the world.

We see no justification in proposals which seek once again to destroy the unity which has been restored to Jerusalem. This unity is the natural condition of the Holy City, and now once again assures the world's religious peoples the freedom of worship at the shrines which remain the spiritual centers of their faith.

This manifesto was signed by theologians representing the entire spectrum of American churches.

The Moslem Kadi of Jaffa, Sheikh Toufiq Assliya, summarized his impressions of united Jerusalem as follows:

We prayed today with our Moslem brethren of Jerusalem in the blessed Al Aqsa Mosque. This is a great day for us to be able to pray at the site for which we were yearning for many years. I pray to the Almighty that He may bestow peace upon our region.

We are convinced that these Holy Places continue to be closely guarded, as they were before. From here we send our blessings to all our Moslem brethren and request of them that they be reassured in the knowledge that the Holy Places are in faithful hands. Let it be known to every Moslem in the world that religious freedom, which we have enjoyed since the establishment of the State of Israel, will continue forever.

These are significant testimonies of non-Jewish leaders. They leave little doubt as to the true situation in Jerusalem.

I should like, however, to emphasize again Israel's policy as elaborated in Mr. Abba Eban's letter to the Secretary General on April 30, 1958:

. . . while I have spoken of Jerusalem's special and unique place in Israel's history, we are deeply aware of the universal interests which are concentrated in the city: the equal protection of the Holy Places and houses of worship; the assurance of free access to them; the daily intermingling of Jerusalem's population in peaceful contact; the removal of the old military barriers; the care of ancient sites; the reverent desire to replace the old squalor and turmoil by a harmonious beauty— all these changes enable Jerusalem to awaken from the nightmare of the past two decades and to move toward a destiny worthy of its lineage. I reaffirm Israel's willingness, in addition to the steps already taken for the immunity of the Holy Places, to work for formal settlements which will give satisfaction to Christian, Moslem and Jewish spiritual concerns. Israel, unlike previous governments in the city, does not wish to exercise exclusive and unilateral control over the Holy Places of other faiths. Accordingly, we are willing, as I stated to you on July 10, 1967, to work out arrangements with those traditionally concerned, which will ensure the universal character of the Christian and Moslem Holy Places and thus enable this ancient and historic metropolis to thrive in peace, unity and spiritual elevation.

What are the basic complaints of the Jordan Government? First of all, it apparently takes exception to Israel's efforts to ensure not only the welfare of the population of the entire city but also its security. There is, for instance, the case of Mr. Rouhi El-Khatib. Mr. El-Khatib was an appointee of the Jordanian Government to the post of mayor of eastern Jerusalem, not an elected mayor. He was a member of the Preparatory Committee of the Palestine Liberation Organization led by the notorious Ahmed Shukairi, the man who last May declared that not a single Jew would remain alive after the Arab attack against Israel. Mr. El-Khatib remains a member of that organization's National Council. As an agent of the Jordanian Government, which on June 5, 1967, rejected Israel's call for peace and launched the attack against Israel and in particular west Jerusalem, Mr. El-Khatib continued to promote tension and public unrest after the establishment of the cease-fire. He maintained contact with the Jordanian Government and acted as an intermediary for the transmission of directives and instructions from Amman and for the transfer and distribution of funds for the purpose of promoting breaches of public order. Realizing that he failed to enjoy public support, he increasingly tried to revert to illicit pressure and threats against local inhabitants. We understand the displeasure of the Jordan Government that such activities have been terminated and Mr. El-Khatib was ordered to cross the cease-fire line.

The same measure had to be taken in respect of three other persons who had been pursuing similar activities. If one recalls the number of demonstrations, the suppression of riots by force, the arrests of hundreds and the banishment of scores of persons from east Jerusalem during Jordanian rule, one realizes how limited the steps taken by Israel are in comparison. In any event, the Jewish as well as the Arab inhabitants of Jerusalem cannot be expected to tolerate within their midst elements which are intent on pursuing their goals of aggression and hostility instead of working for understanding and peace.

Then there are the Jordanian allegations regarding urban development. This applies to three particular projects. The first one is the plan to develop the area of the Jewish Quarter from its western edge to the Western Wall. This is the area destroyed by the Jordanians during their 1948 onslaught on Jerusalem and immediately thereafter and includes the houses in the Maghrabi quarter adjacent to the Wall, a district which the Jordan authorities allowed to deteriorate into a slum.

A delegation of the United Nations Educational, Scientific and Cultural Organization visited this area in 1960. The annual report of the Director General of UNESCO for that year emphasized the danger of leaving the area in such a condition. The report stated *inter alia:* "There should be no deception about the necessity of large-scale future improvements to prevent parts of the Old City becoming ever-increasing slums."

In 1963 the Brown Engineering International submitted a report to the Jordanian authorities stressing the need for urban development.

For example, recommendation No. 5 of the report reads: "Construction of shell public housing units to facilitate the clearance and reconstruction of deteriorated houses in the Old City." Recommendation No. 6 reads: "Reconstruction of destroyed areas along lines similar to the original." Recommendation No. 2 reads: "Removal of temporary structures in the courtyards of the Old City, after a rehousing programme has provided living space for the inhabitants of these structures in public housing units." All—I repeat, all—the inhabitants affected by this project have been provided with alternative housing by the Israel authorities.

A second area is a complex of about 3,345 dunums—or about 800 acres—in and around the Hadassah Medical Center and the Hebrew University compound on Mount Scopus, stretching from there through vacant land westward. Here, in addition to the rehabilitation of the humanitarian institutions on Mount Scopus and the construction of the Truman Center for the Advancement of Peace, new housing construction is planned on empty land for Jews and Arabs. The development of this area is based on a master plan prepared in 1946 by a British engineer, Mr. Kendall, who was engaged for that purpose by the Mandatory authorities well before the Jordanian occupation. Moreover, the Brown Engineering International recommended specifically housing developments in this very area.

The third urban-development project concerns the area of the Jewish village of Neveh Ya'acov in the northern part of east Jerusalem. This village was razed to the ground by the Jordanian Army in 1948.

I reiterate: most of the land in question is Jewish property and public domain. No photomontage charts, no allegations made here away from the records can change this fact. All private claimants would receive compensation. Indeed, this is the fact that necessitated the announcement concerning acquisition of the land and the intent to compensate private owners.

The Jordanian Government is apparently not satisfied with the destruction it has brought upon the city. According to Jordan the destruction, the desecration, the humiliation must not be touched by anyone, it must remain Amman's forever. The Book of Kings in the

Bible states: "Thus saith the Lord: Hast thou killed, and also taken possession?" This is what we ask of Jordan today. Is it not enough that you have shattered, killed and destroyed? Do you also want to take possession? Should our synagogues remain ruined and defiled? Should the tombstones of our forefathers continue to serve as stepping-stones and pavements? Must the Hebrew University and Hadassah Hospital on Mount Scopus remain paralyzed in squalor? Should construction stop in the city? Should slums remain uncleared and gardens not planted? All this only because the lust of war and bloodshed and annihilation still hovers over the region?

Is there any juridical technicality, any private claim that would be allowed anywhere in the world to stand in the way of urban reconstruction and improvement? Why should we allow this to be the case in efforts to heal the wounds inflicted on Jerusalem?

Israel's aim remains peace with its neighbors. Israel shall continue to pursue it steadfastly. It is convinced that this aim can be attained. It is certain that it will bring vital benefits to all nations of the Middle East.

If there is to be progress toward understanding and agreement, active warfare must cease. If the nations of the Middle East are to move toward a peaceful settlement, warfare by terror, warfare by threat and warfare in the international organs must stop. We have faced acrimony in the Security Council, in the General Assembly and in other organs of the United Nations for twenty years. For the good of our peoples we must not continue on this course. Their interest lies on the road to peaceful agreement.

II

The record of Jordan's rule in east Jerusalem (1948–1967) is marked by deliberate desecration of Holy Places; disregard for a signed agreement to provide free access to religious shrines; discrimination by Jordanian authorities not only against Jews but against Christians as well. Following are excerpts from a statement in the Security Council, April 27, 1968, describing Jordan's policies in Jerusalem.

Again we meet in the Security Council, this time at Jordan's initiative. Twenty years after Jordan had launched its war of aggression against Israel in defiance of the United Nations, five months after the Security Council had called for a just and lasting peace in the area, four weeks after the Security Council had decided that violations of the cease-fire cannot be tolerated, Jordan comes before this organ not to declare the end of war, not to embrace the cause of peace, not to renounce warfare by armed attack, raid and sabotage, but to blaspheme and mock and desecrate Jerusalem, the crown of the Jewish people; Jerusalem, the focus of universal spiritual veneration.

What is it that has aroused the displeasure of the Government of Jordan? What is it that Jordan objects to? The Government of Jordan finds it appropriate to come before the Security Council and complain about the celebration of Israel's independence, the reconstruction of synagogues and houses of learning destroyed by Jordanian vandalism in the Jewish Quarter of Jerusalem, the measures taken to restore some semblance of life on the site of Neveh Ya'acov, in the northeastern part of the Jerusalem area, a Jewish village razed to the ground by the Jordanians and turned into an Arab Legion camp. The Jordanian Government is grieved to see the Western Wall of King Solomon's Temple rise again in its tragic glory, freed at last from the slums, the dirt, the profanation which the Jordanians have heaped on it.

To Amman, Israel's independence is an object of vilification; Jerusalem's reconstruction, anathema. Amman would have Israel in mourning rather than in celebration, and Jerusalem in the state of destruction and humiliation in which Jordan has kept the eastern part of the city since its conquest in 1948, rather than in rebirth and restoration.

This is what actually took place wherever the Arab forces succeeded in retaining territory invaded by them. On the West Bank, the Jordanian armies did not leave a single Jewish community intact. All Jewish villages in the areas occupied by Jordan were completely wiped out. Not a single Jew was left alive in the territories under Jordanian control. When, for instance, the village of Kfar Etzion surrendered to the Jordanian Army, after having defended itself to the last round of ammunition, all but four of the 220 inhabitants were mercilessly butchered before the eyes of Jordanian officers. However, the worst fate was reserved for Jerusalem.

The Arab Legion besieged the city and launched an indiscriminate artillery bombardment sparing no residential quarter, disregarding completely the Holy Places. Jerusalem was cut off on all sides. Starvation, pestilence and thirst stalked the streets, and death dug daily new graves. The siege continued for weeks. The toll of death increased. Convoys with food supplies to the unfortunate inhabitants were ambushed. The Arabs did not take prisoners. All men and women were being massacred. Not even medical assistance was respected.

On April 13, 1948, for instance, a convoy of doctors, nurses and medical supplies to the Hadassah Medical Center was ambushed and set afire. Seventy-seven eminent doctors and nurses were killed.

The Jews of Jerusalem looked in desperation toward the United Nations to stop the killing, to put an end to aggression. The Jews of Jerusalem looked expectantly toward the Great Powers to relieve the city's agony. In vain. The aggression continued. The aggressor stayed on in the city. He stayed on for nineteen years.

Is all this forgotten already? The people of Israel have not forgotten.

This is how Abdullah el Tal, the commander of the Jordanian invasion forces, describes the battle in his memoirs:

. . . The operations of calculated destruction were set in motion . . . I knew that the Jewish Quarter was densely populated with Jews who caused their fighters a good deal of interference and difficulty . . . I embarked, therefore, on the shelling of the Quarter with mortars, creating harassment and destruction . . . Only four days after our entry into Jerusalem the Jewish Quarter had become their graveyard. Death and destruction reigned over it . . .

As the dawn of the Friday, May 28, 1948, was about to break, the Jewish Quarter emerged convulsed in a black cloud—a cloud of death and agony.

When the din of battle died down, the invader was able to apply himself more thoroughly to the rape and ravage of the city. In the

Jewish Quarter all but one of the thirty-five Jewish houses of worship
that graced the Old City of Jerusalem were wantonly destroyed. The
synagogues were razed or pillaged and stripped and their interiors
used as henhouses and stables. In the ancient historic Jewish graveyard on the Mount of Olives, tens of thousands of tombstones were
torn up, broken into pieces or used as flagstones, steps and building
materials in Jordanian military installations and civilian constructions,
including latrines. Large areas of the cemetery were leveled and con-
verted into parking places and petrol filling stations.

Again the world stood by in silence. Nobody raised his voice. Where
are the Security Council resolutions about the destruction of Jewry's
Holy Places and religious sites in Jerusalem? Where are the Security
Council resolutions condemning the desecration of the cemetery on
the Mount of Olives? Where are the Security Council interventions
about Jordan's refusal to allow free access to Holy Places and to the
humanitarian institutions on Mount Scopus, in accordance with the
General Armistice Agreement? When had the Security Council called
on the Jordanian invaders stationed on the Old City walls to desist
from keeping Jerusalem's population under constant menace, from
firing indiscriminately, from satisfying the lust for blood in the murder
of children, innocent archaeologists, unsuspecting tourists? What action did the Security Council take last May when Jordan joined the
conspiracy of the Arab States that closed the Strait of Tiran, amassed
huge armies on Israel's borders and proclaimed that the time for
Israel's annihilation had come?

Is all that already forgotten? The people of Israel have not forgotten.

In June 1967, when Jordan faced the choice between peace and
war, it willfully rejected peace and chose war. King Hussein described
it as follows: "On June 5, after the fighting had already started, the
Norwegian General of the United Nations, Odd Bull, handed me a
communication from the Israel side to the effect . . . that if we would
refrain from attacking we would escape the consequences that otherwise would be inevitable. By that time, however, we had no choice."

When the Jordanian Army opened its frontal attack against Israel,
it was again Jerusalem that became the target of the principal on-

slaught. Jerusalem was again under Jordanian shellfire. Jordanian guns placed within the confines of the Holy Places, Jordanian machine guns firing from the roof of the Omar Mosque opened up with a deathly barrage against the city, aiming to kill as many inhabitants as possible and destroy as much of the city's housing as could be attained.

The letter dated April 19, 1968, addressed by the Jordanian representative to the Secretary General, depicting damage to a number of churches on Mount Zion, astonishingly omits the simple but crucial fact that the damage was the result of Jordanian shelling in attacks in 1948 and 1967. The churches and the cemetery remained inaccessible and neglected because Jordanian aggression left the compound in a no-man's land between the Armistice Lines. Of course, truth matters little when the fantasies of hate reign supreme. Nor does the letter tell us how Jordanian fire was directed last June at the world-renowned Dormition Church on Mount Zion, causing grave damage to it.

Today, the invader of 1948, the aggressor of 1967, Jerusalem's destroyer and desecrator, comes to complain that the city is healing the wounds and removing the scars he has inflicted upon it. The reign of terror, profanation and ruin must be perpetuated, he suggests. The devastation of Jerusalem should, he tells us, remain a monument to the outrages of his conquest and rule.

He complains about an Israeli Independence Day parade. He, the aggressor, who for nineteen years had led the parade of peril and violence and demolition in Jerusalem, now turns his wrecking zeal against Israel's twentieth anniversary of regained freedom and sovereignty.

It is not the parade that Jordan opposes but the paraders. It is not the parade Jordan hates but what it stands for—Israel's existence, Israel's liberty, Israel's rout of Arab aggression. Had Jordan shed its destructive policy of belligerency, it would not have tried again, as in the past, to upset Israel's national holiday. Had the Jordanian Government abandoned irresponsible thought and action it would have been spared the illusion that it can dictate to Israel how to celebrate its holiday, a right enjoyed by all nations in the world, a right on which no nation would accept any outside interference.

What is perhaps most remarkable in Jordan's objections to the Israeli Independence Day parade is the claim that it would aggravate the situation in the area. Is not Jordan misjudging the credulity of the world? Does the Jordanian Government really believe that it is possible to accept that the situation is aggravated not by the continuation of war against Israel, not by the refusal to make peace with Israel, not by the persistence in active warfare by armed attack, terror and sabotage, not by official declarations that Israel must be exterminated, but by a one-time parade? Surely there must be a limit to the absurdities that the world would accept from Jordan.

The Jordanian representative has mentioned a demonstration a few days ago in Jerusalem by about fifty women, some of them, like Miss Saidi Nusseibi, sent especially for that purpose from the East Bank by the Jordanian authorities. This reminds me of a story I once heard in the Soviet Union. Not much favorable news appears in the Soviet press about Israel, and a prominent part of such news is reports about the rise in apartment rents in Tel Aviv, strikes of postal workers and demonstrations of all kinds. One Soviet citizen said to another, "How bad the situation must be in Israel, with so many strikes and demonstrations." "You fool," replied the other, "how good the situation is in Israel if people are free to strike and demonstrate there."

Could the Jews imprisoned today in Egyptian concentration camps hold a demonstration? Could the Jews enclosed in the Damascus ghetto, could the Jews of Baghdad, oppressed and discriminated against by new Hitlerite laws, demonstrate? Has the Government represented by the Jordanian delegate left a single Jew alive in its territories who could demonstrate?

Must I recite again the long list of riots and demonstrations that have taken place in the cities of the West Bank and eastern Jerusalem during Jordanian rule? Should I again tell the Council of the thousands of Arab citizens arrested by the Jordanian authorities in actions against demonstrators, of the scores of Arab inhabitants exiled as a result of those riots? Must I remind the Jordanian representative how forces of the Jordanian Army, employing tanks and tear gas, had been used repeatedly to put down such demonstrations?

Let the Jordanian representative come to Jerusalem, as some of his compatriots are in fact doing, to see for himself which Jerusalem is more peaceful, the united city of today or the divided one under Jordanian occupation. Let him come and see for himself where there is more freedom and democracy: in Cairo, in Damascus, in Amman or in Jerusalem.

One of the pretexts for the Jordanian complaint is a concoction of unfounded allegations about housing development in Jerusalem. Most of the land involved in the reconstruction projects is not Arab- but Jewish-owned and public domain. No attempts by the representative of Jordan to distort this basic fact could succeed. The land records happen to be in Jerusalem, not in Amman. No mosque or church, no Holy Place would be affected. It is sufficient to look at the map to realize that all of the land in question situated outside the Jewish Quarter is empty. In the Jewish Quarter itself no home of any Arab inhabitant who has settled there in the last two decades is involved. The undertaking is one of normal urban development, of clearing ruins, restoring houses of worship and reconstructing slum areas. Many of these projects had been worked out not by us, but by the Mandatory Government before the Jordanian occupation of 1948. Had the attitude of the occupying Jordanian authorities toward the city of Jerusalem been different, they would have carried out these projects themselves. An old Latin proverb says, *Facilius est destruere quam construere*—"It is easier to pull down than to build up." Those who for years have wrecked and pulled down, let them at least not interfere with the work of rebuilding and creating.

Today the city of Jerusalem, divided for nineteen years as a result of Jordanian aggression, is united again. The walls, barbed-wired fences and mine fields are no more. The inhabitants of Jerusalem no longer fear bombardment by Jordanian artillery or murderous fire from Jordanian military positions on the ramparts of the Old City. The Holy Places are protected. Discrimination against Christian churches has been terminated. The Holy Sites desecrated by the Jordanians are being restored. The Jewish Quarter, nearly totally demolished by them, is being rebuilt. The city is peaceful and life normal. The Christian communities, joined by thousands of tourists from abroad, including visitors from the Arab States, recently celebrated the Easter festivals. The Moslem community celebrated the festivals of Id el-Fitr and Id el-Adkha in accordance with its own traditions. Close to 250,000 Jewish inhabitants and about 70,000 Arab citizens, this is the national character of Jerusalem; 250,000 Jews and 70,000 Arabs mingle together in ever-growing understanding and communion.

The representative of Jordan arrogates to himself the right to speak on behalf of Arab inhabitants of eastern Jerusalem, Christians and Moslems alike—eastern Jerusalem conquered by Jordan in defiance of the United Nations. I would respectfully suggest that he allow the inhabitants to speak for themselves. In fact, they did speak for themselves when, for instance, the mayor, Council and citizens of Bethlehem petitioned the Israeli Government not to limit itself to the unification of the two parts of Jerusalem, but also to include the town of Bethlehem in the united municipality. The inhabitants of Jerusalem have spoken for themselves in the public pronouncements of their leaders, such as the Custos of the Holy Land, the Greek Orthodox Patriarch, the Armenian Patriarch and others. For the first time in twenty years the world sees that the two peoples, Arabs and Jews, are at least capable of living side by side in peace and constructive endeavor. This is the situation that does not please the Jordanian Government. This is the situation that, in its view, must not continue. This is the situation which the Security Council is called upon to disapprove.

For three thousand years Jerusalem has been the focal point of Jewish history, civilization and religion. Even when the cohorts of Imperial Rome conquered Jerusalem and destroyed the Temple, Jerusalem remained Israel's eternal capital. It is the Bible that says: "If I forget thee, O Jerusalem, let my right hand forget her cunning. Let my tongue cleave to the roof of my mouth; if I remember thee not, set not Jerusalem above my chiefest joy."

For two thousand years, every day, three times a day, Jews all over the world have prayed, "And to Jerusalem, Thy city, return in mercy, and dwell therein as Thou hast spoken; rebuild it soon in our days as an everlasting building, and speedily set up therein the throne of

David. Blessed art Thou, O Lord, who rebuildest Jerusalem." Every day, for two thousand years, three times a day, in all the corners of the world.

Jerusalem is too precious to all of us to wrong it. Jerusalem is too central and too significant a part of the entire Jewish saga, it is too highly venerated by the world's three great religions for the Amman Government to play with it as if it were just another weapon in the campaign of hate and hostility against Israel on which Jordan subsists. Those with an understanding of history, those with a feeling for justice and a respect for equity, will know that the Jordanian complaint is but a malicious attempt to create new tension and misunderstanding.

If Jordan's belligerency, negativism and intransigence continue unchecked, there can be little prospect for peace in the area. Jordan seeks again encouragement to persist in its war against Israel. If Jordan finds such encouragement, it will, of course, draw the appropriate conclusions, and the Middle East will have to brace itself for more hostility and conflict. As on numerous occasions in the past, the present situation calls for a clear, unequivocal summons to disavow belligerency, to terminate warfare, to move onward to peace—the only hope for the nations of the Middle East.

III

Excerpts from a statement in the Security Council, April 27, 1968, on the attitude of heads of the Christian communities in Jerusalem toward Israel's policy in the Holy City.

The Jordanian representative has again set himself up as judge and spokesman of the Secretary General, his emissaries and the Christian communities in Jerusalem. May I suggest again that we allow each to speak for himself. This is what the representative of the Secretary General, Mr. Thalmann, had to say about the situation in Jerusalem in his report:

Prime Minister Levi Eshkol, meeting on June 7 with the spiritual leaders of all communities, declared:

"Since our forces have been in control in the entire city and surroundings, quiet has been restored. You may rest assured that no harm of any kind will be allowed to befall the religious Holy Places. I have asked the Minister of Religious Affairs to contact the religious leaders in the Old City in order to ensure orderly contact between them and our forces, and enable them to pursue their religious activities unhindered."

On June 27 the Knesset adopted a special law for the protection of the Holy Places, and I continue to read from the report by Mr. Thalmann:

These statements and statutory measures were very favorably received. Various religious representatives in fact told the Personal Representative [of the Secretary General] spontaneously that so far the Israel authorities had conformed to the principles which had been laid down and that there was therefore no ground for complaints. They hoped that whatever difficulties still existed or were feared—mostly of a practical and physical nature—would be resolved in a spirit of co-operation.

Although the attitude of representatives of other Christian denominations was rather one of "wait and see," they also described the present situation as satisfactory.

At the beginning of July, the following letter addressed by His Beatitude Theophilos, Patriarch of the Church of Ethiopia, to the Israeli ambassador in Addis Ababa was received in Jerusalem:

The Patriarchate of the Ethiopian Orthodox Church would like to express its appreciation to the Israeli Government for the proper care with which it handled the sanctuaries in the Holy Land in general and the Ethiopian convent in particular. We also extend our thanks to the Israeli authorities for having granted unhindered and free movement to our clergy in Jerusalem during the war and after. We hope that such good care of the Holy Places will continue to enable our people in Jerusalem to perform their religious duties without any difficulty. Please convey this message to your Government.

On July 14 a group of Dutch Catholic and Protestant theologians issued the following statement in Amsterdam:

Catholic and Protestant theologians connected with Het Leerhuis [the Interconfessional Center of Bible Studies] feel themselves called to issue the following statement on Jerusalem, which they hope may offer for Jewish and Islamic theologians an acceptable point of departure for common thinking on the future of Jerusalem.

The Jewish people, the Promised Land and the City of Jerusalem are, through Bible and history, linked with one another in a unique way. To separate by thought or deed the Jewish people from that land or from Jerusalem is tantamount to challenging Jewish identity.

The autonomous existence of the Jewish people in its own country, with Jerusalem as its capital, is felt by the overwhelming majority of the Jewish people throughout the world as a vital condition for its existence. Recognition of the international character of the Holy Places cannot imply any denial of the above-mentioned Biblical and historical links binding the Jewish people with undivided Jerusalem. Neither can such recognition imply distrust with regard to the Jewish people, as if it could not be trusted to have sufficient understanding and respect for the links connecting Christians and Moslems with Jerusalem.

On October 6, the *Catholic Herald* of London published a letter from Les Filles de la Charité de l'Hospice Saint Vincent de Paul of Jerusalem in which a campaign of lies against the Israelis since their victory in the Six-Day War is deplored—and I quote from that letter:

We do not know the source from which those who are hawking such rumors are drawing their inspiration, but they fill us with profound grief. There is no question for us of "taking sides." Our service is at the disposal of all who stand in need of it. This is confirmed by the fact that of the 400 inmates of this Hospice approximately 360 are Arabs of all ages, from babes in arms to the senile.

Some are in good health, others suffering from every conceivable kind of ailment. This, of course, in no way means that we deny a brotherly hand to the Jewish population. Within the charity of Christ we love both Jew and Arab. But we owe it to truth to put on record that our work here has been made especially happy and its path smoothed by the goodwill of the Israeli authorities—in peace and in war alike— smoothed, that is, not only for ourselves but (more important) for the Arabs in our care. . . .

The Jews, like the Christian and Moslem communities, number among themselves a spiritual elite whose moral quality none can mistake and which we, at least, cannot but admire.

Like us, too, they also have their black sheep. But all in all, after an experience extending now over a number of years, we have found amongst them much to appreciate and indeed to applaud. The recent war, moreover, has revealed them to us—both the soldiers and civilians—as deserving of our deepest admiration.

War is war, and the Jews prosecuted theirs with the sole object of preserving their existence, while saving every single human life that they possibly could.

A fortnight ago, on April 12, the Greek Orthodox Patriarch of Jerusalem, Benedictos, made the following declaration: "It is true, and we would like to stress it again, that the Holy Places in general, monasteries and churches, were given full respect and protection by the Israelis before the war, during the war and afterward, and we hope that in the future they will be respected as well and the status quo which exists will be safeguarded."

Finally, the representative of Jordan, both in his letter to which he referred and in his statement, has shown particular solicitude for the Armenian community in Jerusalem to tell us how they fare in united Jerusalem.

On April 8, the Armenian Patriarch of Jerusalem wrote as follows:

I have the honor to refer to Your Excellency's kind visit of today to our Patriarchate and to thank you sincerely for the genuine interest shown by the Israeli authorities to the Holy Places.

In this connection I also present my deep thanks to Your Excellency for your willingness to render us every help in order to restore our Monastery of the Holy Saviour and cemetery, situated on the front line for twenty years.

I am confident that the Israeli authorities have always been animated by a spirit of justice and equity and that the great consideration and respect they have shown for the Holy Places will continue with the same spirit and feeling.

The representative of Jordan referred to the problem of discrimination against Christian communities under Jordanian occupation. May I be allowed to say only this: On the eve of the Six-Day War the slogan in Jordan was, "After Saturday Sunday comes. On Saturday we murder the Jews; the next day, the Christians." That was plainly understood to mean what it said. However relieved the Christian communities may have felt at the liberation of Jerusalem by the Israel defense forces, weeks passed before the story about this slogan was repeated, and then only reluctantly by laymen and clergy to Christian visitors from overseas. Discrimination against Christian communities actually found its way into Jordanian legislation. The Parliament of Jordan enacted a law in 1958 prescribing that all members of the Brotherhood of the Holy Sepulcher should become Jordan nationals. Since its foundation in the fifth century, the members of the Brotherhood have always been Greek; and, if applied, the law would have deprived the bishops and the Patriarch of the Orthodox faith of their Greek citizenship.

Another ordinance, concerning the use of immovable property by moral bodies, was adopted in 1965; it curtailed the development of Christian institutions in Jerusalem by an embargo on their acquisition of further land or property within the bounds of the municipality and its surroundings, whether by purchase, testament, gift or otherwise. The sponsors of that ordinance were apparently Moslems opposed to the building of a church in the neighborhood of Al-Aqsa Mosque. Yet in recent years, wherever possible the Jordanian Government has built mosques cheek by jowl with churches, or, wherever that was not possible, sequestered a room in the premises of a church for Moslem worship and installed a loudspeaker in it.

In October of 1964, the Jordanian Government decreed a stoppage of the work of the Jehovah's Witnesses. That work had been officially permitted by an order of February 21, 1960. The Jehovah's Witnesses were accused of maintaining contacts with Jews, and were consequently persecuted.

In October 1966, the Jordanian Government took other steps discriminating against Christian ecclesiastical institutions and clergy.

For instance, the exemption from customs duty, including that on foodstuffs, formerly granted to churches was withdrawn. Education in Christian schools and institutions was narrowly supervised by the Jordanian authorities, who required that the curricula be sanctioned by them. Christian schools were bidden to close on Fridays. Christian civil servants and army officers suffered, in comparison with their Moslem colleagues, in advancement and often were pensioned off before the age limit in order to make way for the promotion of their Moslem comrades.

If there can be any value to the Security Council's debates and resolutions, it is to the extent that they remain based strictly on fact and law. It is quite clear that the course of history does witness from time to time modifications in international relations. Surely, however, such modifications, especially as they occur between governments rather than between peoples, cannot affect historic fact, the tenets of law, and political analysis.

IV

Statement in the Security Council, April 27, 1968, following the adoption of a resolution which called upon Israel "to refrain from holding the military parade in Jerusalem" on Israel's Independence Day.

The Security Council has adopted a resolution advising Israel not to hold a military parade in Jerusalem. This resolution cannot be accepted by my delegation, because it concerns a question which, under the cease-fire, falls within the purview of Israel's internal jurisdiction. Moreover, there is danger that the resolution might prejudice the efforts now being pursued in the area toward a peaceful and accepted settlement.

I regret very much indeed but I cannot conceal the fact that it is with some bewilderment that I have listened to today's deliberations and read the resolution now adopted. In an adjacent hall the United Nations is considering the grave problems of world peace and the nonproliferation of atomic weapons. The Security Council, entrusted under the Charter with the responsibility for international peace and security, is discussing a forty-five-minute parade. The Middle East is still convulsed in a twenty-year war of Arab aggression. We are examining here the title deeds to parcels of land on which ruined synagogues would be restored.

Israelis are being attacked and suffer casualties on the border while the Council is deliberating how Israel should celebrate its national day. I have listened with attention to the advice given to my Government on what parts and what streets of the areas under Israeli control the Israeli Army should hold its Independence Day march. The advice the Middle East is in need of is of a different nature, the counsel hoped for on a different problem.

For twenty years Israel has been receiving advice of a rather particular character. When Egyptian guns in the Gaza Strip pointed at the very heart of Israel used to attack Israeli territory and Israeli citizens we were advised to stay away from the demarcation line. When Syrian Army positions bombarded the fields of Israeli villages near the border we heard the counsel not to cultivate the fields. When mines began to explode on Israeli roads, killing and maiming Israeli civilians, when commando raids against Israeli villages multiplied, we were told that the footprints of the attackers did not always show clearly on the ground as leading to the border. It is not this kind of advice that the Middle East is looking for. It is not this kind of counsel that is required in order to strengthen the prospects of peace in the area. The counsel the Middle East requires, the advice the world hopes to hear from the Security Council, is how to terminate the twenty-year Arab war of aggression, how to put an end to the active belligerency that the Arab States persist in waging against Israel contrary to the United Nations Charter, in violation of their international obligations. Until such advice is given clearly, unequivocally and effectively, there can be little hope for progress toward a peaceful settlement. Until the Arab States are persuaded to abandon their aggressive designs in Israel, the peoples of the region will continue, unfortunately, to find themselves in a situation of continuous tension and danger.

The celebrations in united Jerusalem will take place. The Jewish people waited for this for two thousand years. People everywhere will rejoice, together with us, in this great hour of Biblical prophetic consummation. Behind the paraders in Jerusalem will march twenty centuries of foreign conquest, exile, oppression, discrimination, genocide and then revival and repulsion of aggression. The twentieth anniversary of Israel's rebirth will be celebrated by the Israeli people and by people of goodwill everywhere. Nothing should or can mar it.

V

Jordan had requested in June 1969 an urgent meeting of the Security Council to protest Israel's enactment of the Legal and Administrative Matters (Regulation) Law, which Jordan alleged was "designed to destroy the character of the city and incorporate the Arab life and institutions into Israeli life."

Following are excerpts from the statement in the Security Council on June 30, 1969.

It is significant that on the very day that the Security Council meets on the Jordanian complaint directed against Jerusalem's life, tranquillity and development, another meeting is taking place in Jerusalem itself. Some sixty internationally outstanding personalities in the humanities, arts and sciences, who have agreed to serve as members of the "Jerusalem Committee" initiated by Jerusalem's mayor, are opening a conference to consider plans and projects for the preservation of the city's historical monuments and religious shrines. Among these are the Reverend T. M. Hesburgh, president of Notre Dame University; Thomas Hoving, director of the Metropolitan Museum of Art in New York; Vittorio Veronese, former Director General of the United Nations Educational, Scientific and Cultural Organization and chairman of the Italian Commission for Human Rights; the Reverend W. Brandful, president of the Christian Council of Ghana; Carlos García, former President of the Philippines; Dr. B. Betancur, chairman of the Writers Association of Colombia; Jorge Amado of Brazil;

Sir Robert Menzies; the sculptors Henry Moore, Jacques Lipchitz and Isamu Noguchi; Mrs. Marietta Tree; John Pope Hennessy, director of the Victoria and Albert Museum, London; Pastor Marc Boegner, past president of the World Council of Churches; Manuel Aguilar, publisher from Madrid; Professor T. Segerstoedt, rector of the University of Uppsala, Sweden; Ignazio Silone; and representatives of religious and cultural institutions from Africa, Asia and Latin America.

If any illustration were required of the difference between Israel's attitude to Jerusalem and that of Jordan it is to be found in the juxtaposition of these two meetings convened on the same day, one here by Jordan and the other in Jerusalem by Israel.

Two years have elapsed since Jerusalem became one again; two years since the city threw off the shackles of war, chased away the invader who had bisected it and had defiled its peace and sacredness and unity for nineteen years. Two years have gone by since the somber walls that tore into the city's heart were brought down, the barbed wire and field mines cleared away. And today Jordan comes before the Security Council to plead the cause of its 1948 invasion, to speak with nostalgia of Jerusalem's past amputation, to put forward the absurd suggestion that the rights of the population's majority be disregarded and violated.

Let there be no confusion. Jordan does not speak even for the Arab minority of Jerusalem. Two decades of occupation of the city's eastern part, achieved by aggression in defiance of the United Nations, cannot bestow that right upon the Government of Jordan. Moreover, that Government can scarcely be regarded as being solicitous of the welfare of the Arab inhabitants of east Jerusalem or the West Bank. The stagnation, the oppression and discrimination which characterized Jordanian rule west of the Jordan River have not been forgotten by the local Arab population.

The pretext for Jordan's call for an emergency meeting is a year-old law which provides for the issuance of licenses and permits for the exercise of commerce and professions. Modern society is largely dependent on the regulation of its life through the process of licensing.

Vehicles must be registered, and their mechanical state checked from time to time; drivers' licenses must be renewed; taxes and rates must be paid. Of even greater importance are such aspects of daily life as, for instance, the need to ensure that only recognized pharmacies handle medical prescriptions and only diplomaed doctors practice medicine. Standards of products and consumer goods and of construction must be assured to meet requirements of quality and safety. It is a simple, fundamental rule in every society that new enterprises and professional workers must receive authorization before they start their occupations. The welfare of the population, Jewish and Arab alike, requires such regulations; and this is the objective of the provisions in question. Most important of all, the regulations which are the subject of the Jordanian complaint provide for the automatic recognition of licenses issued by the Jordanian authorities. They thus simply facilitate the continued and lawful conduct of Arab business and professions in the city. No flight of imagination could portray those regulations as being injurious to Jerusalem's population. The true nature of the Jordanian complaint is best demonstrated by the Jordanian representative's criticism today of a regulation which guarantees the rights of Arab absentee owners of property in Jerusalem. What matters to Jordan is not what Israel does, but that it is Israel that does it, even if the objective is to protect the interests of Arab inhabitants.

The Jordanian representative has allowed fantasy to dominate his description of life in the Jerusalem of today. However, the Security Council and world public opinion are not dependent in this matter on material fabricated in Amman. On any one day there are thousands of foreign visitors in the city, including numerous representatives of foreign governments, international organizations and the press. They would attest to the fact that Jerusalem is basically content and flourishing in its integrity. New commercial and industrial enterprises are springing up all over the city. There is an economic boom, with a shortage of manpower. Joint Jewish-Arab commercial ventures are multiplying. Joint cultural activities are on the increase. Jewish-Arab youth clubs are devoting themselves to creating greater understanding between the two peoples. A combined Arab-Jewish song-and-dance ensemble has already toured Europe. Nearly all Arab workers of east Jerusalem are members of Histadrut, the Israel Federation of Labor, and of its medical-insurance fund. They now enjoy the same social benefits as their Jewish colleagues. There is freedom of movement to and from the Arab States. Thousands of students and others from Arab countries visited Jerusalem last summer. Many thousands have already applied and are expected this year. One can take a taxi or a bus and travel to Amman and beyond. Two Arabic-language dailies are published in the city, one of them outspokenly critical of Israel. There is free access to all the Holy Places without distinction.

On February 3, 1969, the well-known liberal American weekly *The Nation* described daily life in the united city as follows:

Every morning, between 6:30 and 9:00, hundreds of Arab workers from east Jerusalem flow across the old boundaries to their jobs in west Jerusalem. Shops on both sides of town display the most modern Israeli goods. Intra-city bus lines clog the roads. Bus services connect the city with all points in the country, from Haifa to Hebron. And many of the Arab taxis promise even more—a trip to Amman across the Allenby Bridge and from there to Damascus, Baghdad, Beirut, Kuwait.

The city's main problems have little to do with war; much more to do with the fact that, before June 1967, both sides of the then divided city were little more than large villages. Today, the cosmopolitan Jerusalem of pre-1948 is again a reality.

Tension in Jerusalem is beneath a peaceful surface. This is a bi-cultural, bi-national city in which two populations live in 99 per cent peace. A woman can walk alone at night on either side of town. One has the feeling that Jerusalemites, left alone, could solve their own problems.

Incredibly enough, in the war-pocked world of the Middle East, Jerusalem Arabs like to spend long weekends in Amman. They get their passes from the Israeli authorities, travel down to Jericho, cross the Allenby Bridge and then spend a few days shopping in Amman (it's cheaper there) and seeing relatives. I know people who had never before been to Amman who decided they must make the trip. It's easy for Jerusalem Arabs to make the trip east; they must pass a rather innocuous security test, wisely based not on a person's political opinion but on his possible association with terrorist organizations.

The "open border" policy applies to goods as well as to people. A very great trade in agricultural produce and other west bank goods has been crossing the border regularly. The terrorist organizations bitterly oppose this evident accommodation and collusion with the enemy, since it encourages the normalcy of life which they, as good guerrillas, would like to destroy. But to a great many Arabs the trade is essential to life. When Israel shut the border briefly after the (Jerusalem) Mahane Yehuda bombing, in which 12 persons were killed, Arabs throughout the west bank pleaded that trade be restored.

Quiet prevails. One has the feeling that it is possible for Arabs and Jews to live together in the same city—if not in friendship, then at least in tolerance and harmony. Today it is winter in the city, a particularly mild winter with occasional down bursts of fierce rain, but with many bright and warm days. Dramatic clouds form over the hills, sweep and linger, dance over the harsh rock-landscape and disappear.

I believe that peace is a difficult but possible goal, because no one—at least no one in Jerusalem—wants war. The dangers are from outside Jerusalem, from across the borders. It is only from out there that war could come again in Jerusalem.

As far back as a year ago, on June 29, 1968, *The Economist* of London wrote: "With no overt clashes to speak of, mutual adaptation in Jerusalem has reached a point where the city might never have been divided."

Certainly an incident does sometimes occur. Which city in the world is free from it? Indeed, since June 1967, in accordance with law, incidentally in force under Jordan rule as well as in Israel, several houses used as terrorist bases and arms caches were blown up in Jerusalem. Certainly some of Jerusalem's inhabitants may not be entirely happy. Is this an unusual situation in the life of cities? Is this reason for summoning the Security Council to an emergency session?

The representative of Jordan has arrogated to himself the right to speak of the Christian inhabitants of Jerusalem. The records of the debate held in the Security Council in May 1968 contain a long list of public pronouncements by Christian leaders expressing full satisfaction with the situation of Christian communities and their Holy Places. Among these are statements by the Greek Orthodox Patriarch of Jerusalem, the Armenian Patriarch of Jerusalem, the Patriarch of the Church of Ethiopia, Catholic and Protestant theologians and the Latin Custos of the Holy Land.

Today I should like to add a more recent testimony. On December 9, 1968, Dr. G. Douglas Young, president of the Institute of Holy Land Studies, stated:

It is also erroneous to say "Jerusalem has been overwhelmingly Arab from the seventh century until the modern influx . . ." Historically the opposite is true. The Jewish population has been the majority in Jerusalem for many, many years; long before modern times. To unify a Jewish-majority city after 20 years of its being divided by others is surely no cause for antagonism abroad. Our churches damaged by wars since 1948 are being repaired by Israeli compensation funds. The extremely stringent laws protecting holy places and worshipers at them have been consistently and strictly enforced. We feel at peace and at ease in our united city as Christians, with actually less fear of personal assault than in other cities in which we have lived abroad, such is the force of Israeli law and order being maintained. This may be said in spite of the border incidents and occasional Arab terrorist acts.

Two weeks later, Christmas was celebrated in Jerusalem by local Christian inhabitants and thousands of pilgrims and visitors from abroad. Among them was Angelo Cardinal Rossi of São Paulo, who, on his return to Brazil, expressed his gratification with conditions in the city. The traditional Catholic Christmas procession in Jerusalem was led by the Latin Patriarch Alberto Gori. Similarly, the Easter holidays last April were celebrated in a spirit of traditional piety and ceremony.

As for the state of Moslem religious life, it would seem appropriate to rely less on Jordanian Government appointees and more on objective Moslem sources. Thus, Sheikh Ibn Issa, adviser on Moslem Affairs to the President of the Malagasy Republic, stated following a recent visit to the Dome of the Rock in Jerusalem, "One must come to Israel to see for oneself to what great extent peace and tranquillity reign there, and how false is the picture disseminated by Arab propaganda." The president of the All-Moslem Congress of Sierra Leone broadcast the following message after his visit to Al-Aqsa Mosque:

From this Holy Place I declare frankly and with conviction that places holy and consecrated to Islam, the mosques and the chapels are properly guarded and there is no violation of them. The gates of the El-Ghazar Mosque as well as the mosques of all towns and villages are wide open and filled with worshipers who fulfill their religious obligations in complete freedom.

The Kadi, the Moslem religious judge of Jaffa, Sheikh Muhmad Toufiq Assliya, declared on June 29, 1968:

As a Kadi in Jaffa and a native of this country who has in the past fulfilled various religious posts, I would like to put your mind and the minds of the Moslems of your country at rest by assuring you that the Government of Israel is assiduously safeguarding all the holy places in the country without distinction of religion or community . . .

A year has passed since Jerusalem was reunited and I should like to declare that thousands of Moslems from Jerusalem and from other towns in this and the neighboring countries visit these holy places and regularly recite their prayers in them without encountering any interference whatsoever. The Moslem festivals have been celebrated with the usual pomp and ceremony.

Those in charge of the Moslem holy places are Moslem notables and dignitaries who see to it that decorum and cleanliness are maintained there.

The Government of Israel has appointed guards for these places. These ask visitors to conduct themselves in a manner fitting the holy character of the sites. The many Moslems living in Israel have fulfilled one of the five rukn [pillars] of Islam this year by making the pilgrimage to Mecca.

From all the foregoing you will see that the Government of Israel keeps a watchful and solicitous eye over all the Moslem holy places as well as over all the holy places belonging to the other religious communities.

Only lack of understanding of Jewish reverence for Jerusalem and Jewish respect for religion and human rights could create any doubt whatever that the Government of Israel is guided in its policies and actions by its concern for the welfare of the city and its inhabitants and by the determination to give full recognition and protection to the universal interests in it.

During the two years since Jerusalem was restored to life and freed from the nightmare that had enveloped it for nineteen years, the scars of tragic division have been removed, Holy Places, desecrated under Jordanian occupation, have been resanctified, freedom of access and worship have been granted for the first time to adherents of all religions, and coexistence between Arabs and Israel has been proved possible.

For two decades Jerusalem had been a front-line town under the mercy of Arab guns, its peace menaced and violated at the whim of the Jordanian invader, its economy stultified by artificial barriers, its majesty trampled by hate, hostility and fratricide. It was a grim and joyless city, its eternal glory sadly tarnished, its natural splendor mutilated.

Today, the city is free from the chains of division, destruction and desecration. Its people again enjoy the fullness and integrity of their metropolis. They can live and work in peace; at least they can think of cooperation, not of constant hostility and warfare.

The Jordanian Government would have it otherwise. Jordan would rather have a city torn apart and permeated with enmity, stagnation and tragedy as in the nineteen years of its occupation. Jordan is obviously motivated not by concern for Jerusalem's welfare but by continued belligerence against Israel. Perhaps this should not be surprising. Those who would not shrink from inflicting further ordeals on the Holy City and more sorrow on its people have their hands soaked in Jerusalem's blood. They are the ones who turned the city into a battlefield in 1948. It was their artillery that in June 1967 unleashed the merciless bombardment of Jerusalem's residential quarters, causing numerous casualties among the civilian population and deliberately damaging one of the foremost Holy Places, the Church of the Dormition. The Jordanian attitude callously disregards the basic precepts of international law and morality. Jordan occupied the eastern part of the city in a war of aggression. Its occupation had never been recognized by any government, not even by the Arab States, as constituting more than a military presence. The Jordanian attitude is in violation of the rights of the city's population. Jerusalem is inhabited by more than 200,000 Jews, 60,000 Arabs and 5,000 persons of other nationality. It is evident that the great majority of the city's population categorically rejects any Jordanian claims or attempts to intervene in its life. This applies obviously to the Jewish inhabitants. It also applies to the other non-Arab inhabitants. Even as far as the Arab citizens are concerned, as I have already observed, Jordan can hardly claim to represent them merely because it happened to be the occupying Power for nineteen years.

Naturally there are some who still act on behalf of Jordanian interests. There are still some who foster discord and hostility. They are the ones who would object to slum clearing and to the construction of new housing by Israel even if carried out in accordance with Jordanian town-planning projects. They are the ones who would like Jerusalem today to have at least as many demonstrations, incidents and arrests as during Jordanian rule. They are the ones who cannot accept the thought that today's situation is no worse even for the Arab inhabitants and generally much better than before the reunification of the city. These people, however, are not representative of the Arab minority of Jerusalem.

A recently published sociological study, *The Administration of United Jerusalem,* expresses this as follows:

Under the Jordanian regime, about 40 members and ex-members of the Jordanian Parliament lived in and around Jerusalem, together with ten Cabinet Ministers and ex-Ministers, as well as many religious leaders. This group has now lost most of its influence . . . With the blow to its standing, there is also a deterioration in its financial status. On the other hand, the man in the street, on passing from Jordanian to Israeli rule, suddenly feels that he is important, that he is somebody. He sees free competition in every walk of life, and he begins to realize that, if he is talented and hard-working, he may one day reach a social eminence that he never dreamed of under Jordanian rule. He begins to doubt whether his former leaders should be followed blindly in their hostility to Israeli rule.

In any event, the generally accepted principles of human rights and political democracy cannot be suspended in the case of Jerusalem. A small minority, in fact a group of foreign appointees and agents, cannot impose on the majority demands contrary to reason and justice. Jerusalem's unity and integrity will never again be upset by wanton hatred and hostility. Jerusalem will forever be united. Its citizens can look to the future with confidence and calm. Its friends, the world over, can rest assured, Israel will maintain and protect the city's growth, welfare and security; Israel will make certain that Jerusalem, holy to so many, remains a source of light and pride to all religions.

Let us, therefore, turn our thoughts to bringing to Jerusalem bliss, not grief. Let us address ourselves to the wishes of its population, not to the designs of foreign Governments. Let us strive for peace and understanding within its walls, not chaos and discord. Let us repeat after the Prophet:

> Rejoice ye with Jerusalem,
> And be glad with her, all ye that love her;
> Rejoice for joy with her . . .
> That ye may drink deeply with delight on the
> abundance of her glory.

3 Zionism: From the Rivers of Babylon
to Lake Success

*Arab representatives in the United Nations and their avowed supporters
have attempted for many years to misrepresent and distort the true nature
of the Jewish liberation movement—Zionism. The following statement
was made in the Security Council on October 21, 1973, in reply to
a vicious Arab attack on Israel and Zionism, while Israel's defense forces
were successfully repelling Arab aggression in the Sinai and the Golan
Heights.*

Zionism is the love of Zion. Zionism is the Jewish people's liberation
movement, the quest for freedom, for equality with other nations. Yet
in an organization in which liberation movements are hailed and
supported, the Jewish people's struggle to restore its independence
and sovereignty is maligned and slandered in an endless spate of
malice and venom.

In his drive to annihilate the Jewish people, Hitler began by distorting the image of the Jew, by rewriting Jewish history, by fabricat-
ing some of the most odious historic and racial theories. The Arab
Governments, in their campaign to complete Hitler's crimes against
the Jewish people and destroy the Jewish State, have adopted the same
method of falsifying Jewish history, and in particular the meaning of
the Zionist movement and the significance of its ideals.

What is Zionism? When the Jews, exiled from their land in the sixth
century before the Christian era, sat by the rivers of Babylon and
wept, but also prayed and sought ways to go home, that was already

Zionism. When in a mass revolt against their exile they returned and rebuilt the temple and reestablished their State, that was Zionism. When they were the last people in the entire Mediterranean basin to resist the forces of the Roman Empire and to struggle for independence, that was Zionism. When for centuries after the Roman conquest they refused to surrender and rebelled again and again against the invaders, that was Zionism. When, uprooted from their land by the conquerors and dispersed by them all over the world, they continued to dream and to strive to return to Israel, that was Zionism. When, during the long succession of foreign invaders, they tried repeatedly to regain sovereignty at least in part of their homeland, that was Zionism. When they volunteered from Palestine and from all over the world to establish Jewish armies that fought on the side of the Allies in the First World War and helped to end Ottoman subjugation, that was Zionism. When they formed the Jewish Brigade in the Second World War to fight Hitler, while Arab leaders supported him, that was Zionism. When Jews went to gas chambers with the name of Jerusalem on their lips, that was Zionism. When, in the forests of Russia and the Ukraine and other parts of East Europe, Jewish partisans battled the Germans and sang of the land where palms are growing, that was Zionism. When Jews fought British colonialism while the Arabs of Palestine and the neighboring Arab States were being helped by it, that was Zionism. Zionism is one of the world's oldest antiimperialist movements. It aims at securing for the Jewish people the rights possessed by other nations. It harbors malice toward none. It seeks cooperation and understanding with the Arab peoples and with their national movements.

Zionism is as sacred to the Jewish people as the national liberation movements are to the nations of Africa and Asia. Even if the Arab States are locked today in conflict with the Jewish national liberation movement, they must not stoop in their attitude toward it to the fanaticism and barbarism of the Nazis. If there is to be hope for peace in the Middle East, there must be between Israel and the Arab States mutual respect for each other's sacred national values—not distortion and abuse.

Zionism was not born in the Jewish ghettoes of Europe, but on the battlefield against imperialism in ancient Israel. It is not an outmoded nationalistic revival but an unparalleled epic of centuries of resistance to force and bondage. Those who attack it attack the fundamental principles and provisions of the United Nations Charter.

4 I Am My Brother's Keeper

Israel's struggle in the United Nations has not been confined to the vindication of the rights of the people of Israel, but has always included the defense of the human and national rights of oppressed Jewish communities everywhere.

The following statement on the question of Syrian and Soviet Jewry was delivered in the Third Committee of the Twenty-seventh Session of the General Assembly, October 12, 1972.

When the Universal Declaration of Human Rights was adopted by the Third General Assembly on December 12, 1948, at the Palais de Chaillot the memories of World War II were still vivid in man's mind, and it was to prevent a repetition of the inhumanities that had been perpetrated before and during that war that the United Nations enacted a bill of rights for all mankind. The Universal Declaration of Human Rights was humanity's victorious answer to the savage creed of Nazism. The Jewish people had been the main victim of the Nazi blasphemy of racial superiority. Much of the Declaration is written with the blood of the six million Jews and many people of other nationalities annihilated by racist bestiality.

Israel has always supported measures aimed at eliminating racial discrimination and will continue to do so in the future.

The Jewish people, the target of racial discrimination and physical destruction on racial grounds in the past, is still subjected to oppression in certain parts of the world.

One of the gravest situations obtains in Syria.

The plight of the Jewish community in that country has caused worldwide concern. In all parts of the world there has been growing anxiety over the fate of Syria's Jews. Governments, international organizations and public figures have raised their voices against the persecution of these helpless people. Numberless appeals have been addressed to the President and Government of Syria and to Syrian ambassadors in various capitals to end the suffering of Syrian Jews. Media of information, international conferences and mass assemblies have called for their liberation. In France, the United Kingdom and Italy, in Belgium, the Netherlands, Denmark, Norway and Brazil, in Argentina and Sweden, in Finland and Austria, in the Federal Republic of Germany, in Switzerland, the United States, Canada, Australia, Mexico, Uruguay, Chile, Colombia, in Panama, Venezuela and Israel, efforts to save Syrian Jewry have become one of the central elements of the universal struggle against discrimination.

In a statement of November 17, 1971, the International Committee for Jews in Arab Lands, headed by Mr. Alain Poher, President of the French Senate, declared *inter alia*:

The International Conference for the Deliverance of Jews in the Middle East, which is presided over by Mr. Alain Poher assisted by Maître Jacques Mercier and the Reverend Riquet, has just learned from extremely reliable sources that there has recently been a sharp deterioration in the situation of the Syrian Jews.

As long ago as January 27, 1971—the anniversary of the Baghdad hangings—at a press conference held in Paris, two Jews who had managed to flee from Syria were interviewed by press, radio and television and reported on the condition of their fellow Jews still living in Syria, who were being subjected to a veritable campaign of persecution by the Syrian authorities.

Their very detailed statements were also recorded in the minutes of the ad hoc committee of inquiry, presided over by Mr. Rolland, President of the Criminal Chamber of the Cour de Cassation, which gave them a hearing.

The International Conference expresses its concern at this sudden deterioration in the situation of the Jewish minority in Syria. It wishes once again to alert world public opinion and the highest international authorities so as to ensure that the most elementary human rights are respected in that country.

Similar declarations have been published by national Committees for Jews in Arab Lands in such capitals as Rome, Brussels, Oslo, Buenos Aires and in New York. Committees for the rights of man, organizations of jurists, and associations of resistance fighters have also participated in public campaigns in behalf of the defenseless Syrian Jews.

The Jews of Syria live in constant fear for their lives. They are subjected to frequent violence by the authorities and by the Arab population, thrown into jail for trying to escape the inferno, their men brutalized, their womenfolk molested. A number of Jews are still incarcerated. According to the Paris *Tribune juive* of September 15, 1972, four Jewish girls of Aleppo were arrested last August on the charge that they had attempted to escape from Syria. Three of them were sisters, Yvonne, Renée and Henriette Genidi, and the fourth their cousin Renée Genidi.

Moreover, Jews are subject to the following discriminatory and repressive measures:

They carry identity cards which single them out for special treatment. While all identity cards record ethnic or religious affiliation alongside other personal attributes of their bearers, the identity cards of Jews are stamped "Jew" in red letters and have the word "Jew" diagonally inscribed in handwriting across the entire page.

Jews are forbidden to will their property to their descendants.

Jews are restricted to within three miles of their residence. Movement beyond that limit requires a special permit which is rarely granted.

There are night curfews for Jews in Damascus and Qamishliye.

Jews may not be employed in government service or in public corporations.

Civil servants and military personnel are forbidden to patronize Jewish-owned stores.

Except for doctors and pharmacists, Jewish professionals find it difficult to practice their professions.

The overseas mail of Jews is censored and is a cause of frequent interrogations by the authorities.

The few remaining synagogues are under constant surveillance.

The Jewish cemetery of Damascus has been largely destroyed to make room for a highway to the airport. No new land has been allotted for burial purposes. Jews must bury their dead in the remaining portion of the cemetery by covering old tombs and creating a second layer of graves over them.

Many Jewish schools have been closed. Those that are still open are administered by Arab principals, and some of the Jewish teachers have been replaced by Arabs. Recent reports from Syria indicate a continuing aggravation of the situation.

Referring to the plight of Jews in Syria and in other Arab States, the former Secretary General of the United Nations declared in his annual report on the work of the Organization, September 1969, Twenty-fourth Session:

I share the widely held concern for the plight of another, smaller group of helpless persons. Although I have no direct means of knowing exactly the conditions of life of the small Jewish minorities in certain Arab states, it is clear that, in some cases at least, these minorities would be better off elsewhere and that the countries in which they now live would also be better off, given the prevailing circumstances, if the departure of those who would wish to leave could be sanctioned and arranged, since their continued presence is a source of both internal and international tension.

The Israel Government and world public opinion will not rest until the imprisoned Jews are released and Syrian Jewry permitted to reach safety.

Another grave problem exists in the Union of Soviet Socialist Republics.

The Soviet Union is composed of more than one hundred nationalities, ethnic groups and races. According to the Constitution of the

Union of Soviet Socialist Republics and under Soviet law all are equal. Yet in reality one group is not.

The three million Soviet Jews find themselves outside the fold. Unlike other ethnic and racial groups their homeland is not within the confines of the Soviet Union. The Jewish state is not a member of the Union of Soviet Socialist Republics.

Soviet Jews have no national life of their own. Their cultural activities are suppressed. They have no Jewish schools, newspapers, books, radio programs, as other communities do. Their religious institutions have been curbed and deprived of the privileges and facilities enjoyed by others.

The Jews have reacted as any race or people suffering from discrimination would have.

A young Soviet Jew from Moscow, Yaakov Kazakov, wrote in a letter of May 20, 1968, to the Supreme Soviet:

I do not wish to be a citizen of the Union of Soviet Socialist Republics, of a country that refuses to the Jews the right of self-determination.

I do not wish to be a citizen of a country where . . . my people is deprived of its national image and of its cultural treasures, of a country where, under the pretext of a struggle against Zionism, all the cultural life of the Jewish people has been eradicated, where the dissemination of any literature on the history of the Jewish people or on the cultural life of Jews abroad in our times is persecuted.

I do not wish to be a citizen of a country that conducts a policy of genocide toward the Jewish people. If the fascists exterminated us physically you are exterminating Jews as a nation . . .

I do not wish to be a citizen of a country that arms and supports the remaining fascists and the Arab chauvinists who desire to wipe Israel off the face of the earth and to add another two and a half million of killed to the six million who have perished . . .

For Yaakov Kazakov there is only one solution. He writes:

I am a Jew, I was born a Jew, and I want to live out my life as a Jew. With all my respect for the Russian people, I do not consider my people in any way inferior to the Russian, or to any other, people. . . .

I am a Jew, and, as a Jew, I consider the State of Israel my Fatherland, the Fatherland of my people, the only place on earth where there exists an independent Jewish State, and I, like any other Jew, have the indubitable right to live in that state. . . .*

On November 28, 1968, Boris L. Koshubiyevsky of Kiev declared in a letter to the Secretary General of the CPSU Central Committee, Mr. Leonid Brezhnev:

"I am a Jew. I want to live in the Jewish State. This is my right, just as it is the right of a Ukrainian to live in the Ukraine, the right of Russians to live in Russia, the right of a Georgian to live in Georgia.

I want to live in Israel. This is my dream, this is the goal not only of my life but also of the lives of hundred of generations which preceded me, of my ancestors who were expelled from their land.

I want my children to study in a school in the Hebrew language. I want to read Jewish papers, I want to attend a Jewish theater. What's wrong with that? What is my crime? Most of my relatives were shot by the fascists. My father perished and his parents were killed. Were they alive now, they would be standing at my side. Let me go!

I have repeatedly turned with this request to various authorities and have achieved only this: Dismissal from my job, my wife's expulsion from her Institute; and, to crown it all, a criminal charge of slandering Soviet reality. What is this slander? Is it slander that in the multinational Soviet State only the Jewish people cannot educate its children in Jewish schools? Is it slander that there is no Jewish theater in the USSR? Is it slander that in the USSR there are no Jewish papers? . . . I don't want to be involved in the national affairs of a state in which I consider myself an alien. I want to go away from here. I want to live in Israel. My wish does not contradict Soviet law . . .†

This is not only the plea of individuals but of thousands and hundreds of thousands of Jews in the Soviet Union.

In an appeal addressed to the Secretary General of the United Nations in November 1969 the heads of Jewish families in the Georgian Soviet Socialist Republic stated:

* Yaakov Kazakov was permitted to join his people in Israel in 1969.
† Kochubiyevsky, too, succeeded in fulfilling his hopes to live in Israel.

The history of the Jews is the road of sufferings, on which each step is marked with blood. The Jews did not abandon their Fatherland of their own free will—they were expelled.

We are the descendants of those exiles.

It is doubtful whether there can be found another nation that had to defend so long and so stubbornly, with tears and blood, the right before the entire world to its own State . . .

We want you to know what it means to be a Jew: six million Jews were killed in the last World War—this means that each of us has been six million times shot, hanged, asphyxiated in gas chambers; and before this our children were murdered, taken by their feet and their heads crushed against the walls of houses; our mothers, wives and daughters were raped before our eyes.

We want you to know what it means to be a Jew: our hearts are cemeteries . . .

In October 1971 the Jews of Minsk, the capital of the Byelorussian SSR, sent a collective letter to the Soviet leaders with a copy to the Secretary General of the United Nations. They pleaded:

Today we are not requesting anything from you: neither a republic nor schools, nor universities, nor newspapers, nor theaters, nor ministerial positions, nor admittance to the Institute of International Relations, nor for help in finding employment, for protection from drunken or sober anti-Semites. We don't even ask for the erection of monuments at Babi Yar or at other communal graves, where the scattered bones of millions of our brothers lie, since *to ask* for it would mean to profane their memory. We beg only for one thing—

Let us go home! Let us go to the Jewish state—to the country where we are being awaited, where we shall live among our own people.

Recently some Soviet Jews, though their number was small, have been allowed to unite with their families and their people in Israel. People of goodwill throughout the world saw in their emigration a sign of broader tolerance and human understanding on the part of the Soviet Government. Then came a setback. Whilst permitting the emigration of some Jews, the Soviet authorities have placed limitations on the freedom of movement of scores of thousands of them.

In disregard of fundamental human rights, many Jews have been arrested simply for wishing to go to Israel, and have been sentenced to terms of imprisonment. The Soviet information media unceasingly publish calumnies, slanders and incitement against them.

Many of the Jews who register in the emigration offices are dismissed from their employment and thus lose their livelihood.

An open anti-Semitic campaign is being conducted, and in the period 1971–72 alone, dozens of anti-Semitic books have been published in the Soviet Union, in addition to the anti-Jewish campaign conducted in the press and the other official information media.

As part of the attempts to dissuade Jews from submitting applications for exit permits for Israel, the USSR Government decided on August 3, 1972, to impose a special tax on Jews with higher education who wish to go to Israel. Although purporting to be of general application, the decision is directed and used in fact against Jews. The tax effectively deprives thousands of Jews of any possibility and any hope ever to join their families and to realize their national aspirations. A scale has been established for each level of education, sometimes reaching $25,000 and more per person.

I draw the Committee's attention to document A/C3/629 containing an appeal addressed to the Secretary General of the United Nations and to the heads of delegations to the Twenty-seventh Session of the United Nations General Assembly from more than five hundred Soviet Jews from Moscow, Kishinev, Riga, Novosibirsk, Kiev, Odessa, Leningrad, Frunze, Gorki, Chernovtsy, Vilno and Kovno, who call for help in their struggle against the extortionist decree. The say *inter alia:*

During the 2,000 years of living in exile, Jews had frequently met with demands for ransom, in particular from the times of the Middle Ages to the 1930's of the twentieth century. When Jews left a country, they were deprived of all their possessions. In this case we see an unprecedented demand to pay out a sum which is 10 times larger than everything the repatriates possess. Apart from rare exceptions, a Soviet specialist or scientist is not capable of saving such sums even in several decades . . . We ask you to raise the voice of protest against the attempts of the Union of Soviet Socialist Republics to deprive Jews of their lawful right to repatriate to Israel.

The Soviet argument on the brain-drain is irrelevant and inapplicable. The Soviet Union is not one of the needy developing countries, and Israel is not offering Jewish members of the professions who come from the Soviet Union superior financial rewards. Israel is only able to give them a home, where they will feel as Jews who are not being discriminated against because of their being Jews.

In any event those who apply for emigration from the USSR are generally dismissed from their work, and their knowledge is consequently dispensed with by the Soviet authorities.

Likewise irrelevant is the Soviet argument that graduates are obliged, as it were, to repay the cost of their education.

The noted Soviet demographer Urlanis states in an article published on July 26, 1970, in *Literaturnaya Gazeta* that in the conditions obtaining in the Soviet Union, the average university graduate repays by four years' work the State's investment in his training. The majority of the scientists have thus already repaid that investment many times over by their creativity, invention, research and professional work. This decree constitutes not only harassment and oppression of thousands of Jews; it is a serious infringement of intellectual freedom and scientific liberty. It creates a new enslavement, the enslavement of scientists and intellectuals, whose only crime is that they have studied and worked and contributed to the progress of their country, and that today they obey the call of their historic consciousness and wish to pursue their intellectual and social vocation elsewhere.

Scientific personalities and institutions across the world have reacted with astonishment and indignation to this limitation of intellectual freedom.

Thus, René Cassin, president of the International Institute for Human Rights and one of the most revered figures in the international struggle for the rights of man, issued a statement on September 21 condemning the Soviet regulation regarding the imposition of exit fees as a "new procedure calculated to prevent the exercise of a human right expressly set forth in Article B of the Universal Declaration of Human Rights." Professor Cassin compared the Soviet action to the "policies of Hitler" and declared that "they constitute a threat to the stability of all mankind."

Fourteen American Nobel laureates have endorsed the following statement published in *The New York Times* on October 1, 1972:

We are dismayed by reports that exorbitant head taxes are being imposed on Soviet citizens with a higher education who are seeking to exercise the fundamental right to leave their country.

It is painful to contemplate the massive violation of human rights implicit in this policy and its burdensome consequences for the scores of thousands of people who have openly expressed their desire to leave the USSR.

Although the decree affects all Soviet citizens, it is obviously directed primarily against Jews and inflicts a particular hardship on them. Thus, in addition to the policy's violation of intellectual freedom and individual rights—with the consequent loss to scholarship and to humanity—there enters into it also the element of anti-Jewish discrimination.

This is not only a matter of academic and intellectual freedom, or of discrimination against Jews; what is at issue is:

The right to an education.

The right to develop one's intellectual capacity to the fullest.

The right to pursue one's career where one chooses.

The right to leave one's country for reasons of career, family or religion.

To infringe upon these rights is to transform educated persons into indentured servants, and no civilized society has the moral right to do this.

The Soviet decree can only have a depressing effect on the possibility of expansion and enhancement of academic, cultural and scientific exchanges and contact between the peoples of the United States and the Soviet Union.

We, therefore, urge the Soviet authorities to rescind the head tax and to accept fully and without hindrance everyone's right to leave his country.

The statement was signed by Isidor Rabi, Nobel Prize in Physics; Carl F. Cori, Nobel Prize in Medicine; Edwin M. McMillan, Chemistry; Felix Bloch, Physics; Edward M. Purcell, Physics; F. C. Robbins, Medicine; Polykarp Kusch, Physics; Edward L. Tatum, Medicine; Hans A. Bethe, Physics; George Wald, Medicine; Robert W.

Holley, Medicine; Lars Onsager, Chemistry; Julius Axelrod, Medicine; Paul A. Samuelson, Economics.

It is in the interest of all to see greater harmony between East and West in all fields, including that of science. It is precisely because of this that we must raise our voice in protest against such wanton and superfluous obstacles to international coexistence.

World opinion, Governments, international personalities and public organizations could never understand why a Power such as the Soviet Union should have adopted a policy of discrimination and harassment of the remnant of decimated European Jewry. Enlightened mankind can understand even less the considerations that have prompted the Soviet authorities to issue the repressive decree of August 3.

Is it possible that the Soviet Government is seeking to increase its monetary resources by methods reminiscent of the extortionist levies imposed by feudal lords on their serfs? Is it possible that the right to free education guaranteed to all residents of the Soviet Union, including even foreigners, is to become a commodity with a price tag on it? Is it possible that in a society which aspires to socialist ideals, the exercise of fundamental human rights will be subject to repayment in money? Have not the Jews of the Soviet Union repaid amply for everything and anything they might have received through the years from the Soviet State? Has their role in the revolution been forgotten? Has their contribution in all realms of Soviet life, development, defense been lost sight of? Is not Soviet soil permeated with the sweat and blood of generations of Jews who have labored and created and given their lives for the Union of Soviet Socialist Republics? Have they not repaid a thousandfold for whatever the USSR may ever claim to be the indebtedness of individual Jews? Does not the State exist for the good of its citizens? Should not a Government ask itself also what it owes to its citizens? If a debt is to be reimbursed is it not by the Soviet State to its Jewish citizens for all they have given of themselves to Soviet society, for their brain and their brawn, for their blood, for their tears? If now some of them wish to unite with their families and live in the midst of their people as Russians, Ukrainians, Latvians do, are they to be penalized for it? Are they to be like slaves with a price affixed to them? Do not the Soviet leaders see the stigma on their country brought about by the restrictions imposed on Soviet Jews and in particular by the ransom tax? Where are those in the Soviet Government who must have surely discerned that the world can regard such measures only as malicious, purposeless harassment of human beings without any benefit whatever to the Soviet Union itself?

No one who, like myself, has lived in the USSR and come to know the Soviet peoples can feel anything but friendship toward them and wish them well on their course of national progress and achievement. It is in this spirit that the appeal echoed throughout the international community is made to the Soviet Government: For the sake of international understanding and coexistence which you seek, erase the ignominy of anti-Jewish restrictions, let the Jews go, do not bar them from their families and their people.

5 Israel and the House of Israel in America

Excerpts from an address before the Conference of Presidents of Major American Jewish Organizations, New York, May 26, 1975.

A myriad ties link Israel and the United States of America. A myriad bonds join the two nations. Those who glory in the American heritage are inspired by Israel's. Those who take pride in the American War of Independence are captivated by Israel's struggle for liberty and justice. Those who uphold democracy and its interests in the Middle East put their trust in Israel's cause.

However, the most precious of all bonds between the two countries is American Jewry. By its stature and vitality it has made a monumental impact on American life. By its attachment to Jewish values and identification with Jewish destiny it has been and will continue to be a powerful force in Israel's history.

Never before in the Jewish people's centuries-long saga has Jewish independence and sovereignty been buttressed and enriched by a Jewish community abroad as much as it has been by American Jewry.

Israel is a fount of prowess and inspiration to the Jewish community of the United States. The American Jewish community is a pillar of strength in Israel's edifice of statehood. Your future and ours are irrevocably interlocked. You are concerned with our destiny, our development and our security. We have a paramount interest in your well-being, your vigor and your ability to shape the course of events. Today you possess these attributes to the full. However, they must be nurtured and preserved, reinforced and expanded.

This can be achieved only through constant Jewish creativity in America and through uninterrupted participation in the Jewish people's central epos of our times—the struggle for Israel's future. The gravest danger to the attainment of this goal is inaction. A standstill in communal creativeness, a lull in alertness and activity in behalf of Israel would bring regression. A stay in your dynamism as a group would mean weakness. To benumb the power within you is to court paralysis.

A cause lives only as long as it thrusts forward. A cause has strength only when it offers stirring challenges. The masses cannot be stimulated by a call to reticence. The young will not follow the overcautious. There is a fundamental difference between statesmanship and leadership. The art of diplomacy and the art of political guidance and command are worlds apart.

Diplomacy frequently requires caution. Leadership can never permit immobility. There must always be a synthesis between the necessity of continuing movement and the wisdom of prudence.

Israel has always tried to pursue its diplomatic struggle with tactical sensitivity. It could never forgo, however, Jewry's expressions of support and solidarity. These expressions remain crucial at all times and under all circumstances. They always mean added strength. Their strength lies in the public identification with Israel's cause, in backing Israel's position, not necessarily in the criticism of others. An unremitting display of Jewish strength on the side of Israel, a dramatization of Jewish readiness to stand by Israel, a constant reminder of Jewry's unflinching faith in Israel are possible and important. Demonstrations of brotherhood can galvanize without crises. Public opinion in a democracy impresses not only when it emerges in reaction to a blow. Israel's struggle for independence, for peace and for security is a continuing one, and so must be the effort to rally the masses behind it.

Israel is in need of such support more than ever before. We are entering a period in which the power of Arab oil will be offset primarily by the understanding and backing of enlightened public opinion. International relations are dominated by self-interest. Governments usually determine their attitudes and acts not by the merits of an issue but by power considerations. The financial and economic influence of the oil producers has become a factor in state policies. This is, of course, a transitional situation. The search for alternative sources of energy is already on. Such sources are available. It is now only a matter of developing methods that would make their exploitation commercially feasible. If Israel sees its way through the present difficulties, it will find, in a decade or two, that the oil stranglehold will have become a thing of the past. The problem is, therefore, to pull through the vicissitudes and threats confronting us right now. In this endeavor, favorable public opinion is most valuable. In democratic countries it is capable of influencing governmental decisions. In the period immediately ahead it can make the difference between isolation and widespread understanding and friendship.

Such understanding and friendship cannot be created by individual Israeli acts. Israel cannot be guided at every stage of its policy by the criteria of international popularity. There may always be need to adopt positions or take steps which do not find favor with others. Israel's image must, therefore, depend on the overall picture of a state with a just cause, embattled by its neighbors for twenty-seven years; a state for which peace is vital and consequently a supreme goal; a people battling for its basic rights and denying them to no other nation. The fundamentals of the situation—the history of the Jewish people's struggle for national liberty, the inseparability of the Jewish people and its civilization from its ancestral homeland, the truth about Jordan's being a Palestinian Arab state, the uncertainty, till this very day, as to whether the Arab Governments are ready to establish genuine peace with Israel — can and must be restated over and over again. If this picture is projected tenaciously and efficiently the general positive image will not be blurred by vagaries of the moment.

6 Holocaust: I Said unto Thee in Thy Blood Live

Address before a Jewish gathering in New York April 21, 1974, the commemoration of the Warsaw Ghetto Uprising.

Memory is part of the Jewish heritage; remembrance, part of our four-thousand-year-old history.

To remember is to understand the world we live in, to comprehend ourselves, our civilization and our faith. Not to forget is to know who we, the Jewish people, are. It is to make our present more meaningful, our future more fulfilling and secure. To remember is to remain one with our forefathers, one with our children and their children.

Let us, therefore, remember and never forget the inhumanity to which the Jewish people has been subjected through the ages. But let us also remember and never forget our resistance and our redemption. Let the savage crimes of Amalek across the centuries never be obliterated from our memory. But neither should the fact that despite the pain and grief and suffering and cruel bloodshed, our forefathers never gave up, always persevered, always rebuilt and created new life. So shall we always remain unbroken in spirit, resolved to go on and to weather the storms.

Let us thus remember the Holocaust: the barbarism meted out to our people, the merciless bestiality toward innocent children, women and men, the silence of the world. Let us remember the martyrdom of the powerless, the heroism of those who took up arms and fought back. Let us pay tribute to the survivors, those who rose from the ashes and from the ruins to live and to construct anew, and to bear witness to the eternity of the Jewish people.

All of them sanctified the name of the Jewish people. All of them personified Jewish loyalty, Jewish dignity, Jewish idealism. All of them in their death and in their survival, in their martyrdom and in their struggle have inspired the rebirth of the Jewish people.

Let us remember and pay tribute, but also learn. The time to wonder how the Holocaust could have happened is over. The time to ask why it happened is past. Thirty years and more after the tragedy we know why; we know how.

It happened because ours is a world in which cruelty and hatred and brute force are still rampant. It happened because mankind has not freed itself from bloodlust. It happened because the ideals of the Hebrew Prophets, of universal equality, of morality and justice are still foreign to most men even when they pay lip service to them.

It was in such a world that the Jewish people stood alone: weak and defenseless, without a Jewish state to shield their rights, to try and protect them, to offer them refuge and shelter.

The Holocaust came upon us, and so many didn't want to believe that it was possible. It engulfed us, and so many still had illusions, so many were still complacent and confused.

We, the Jewish people, have changed since then. The world has not.

Independent and sovereign at last, the Jewish nation possesses today the principal instrument of survival as a people—the Jewish State. Reborn and free in our historic homeland, the Jewish people is today master of its own destiny. We Jews can and must determine our fate. We have it within our power to shape our future, the future of Jewry as a nation, as individuals. We have it within our power to make it a future of security and achievement, of happiness for the whole Jewish people.

However, to succeed, we must at all times be conscious of the lessons of the Holocaust, the first and foremost of them that the world around us remains essentially the same. It is still a world of violence and bloodshed and war. It is still a world in which starvation, slaughter and subjugation of entire peoples are passed over almost unnoticed.

As for the Jewish State, it is surrounded by neighbors who, imbued with the Nazi design against Jewish existence, have sought for years to destroy our independence and annihilate our people. The Yom Kippur War was a somber reminder of this grim reality. Again, as in the days of the Holocaust, most of the world was ready to stand by and watch the Jewish people bleed.

Let us, therefore, bear in mind the Holocaust's second lesson: illusions are dangerous. There should be no illusion about the menaces still confronting the Jewish people. If the Arab States could, they would have brought about our total destruction. Illusions are perilous, whether they come from within ourselves or from outside.

We hope with all our hearts and souls that we shall have peace for the Jewish people everywhere and for the Jewish State. We shall be untiring in the search for peace. However, when in certain Arab States leaders still say that Israel has no right to exist, when terrorist organizations supported by Arab Governments continue to murder Jewish women and children, when an Egyptian Cabinet Minister declares that Egypt is now pursuing a policy of stages—first to eliminate Israel's alleged aggression of 1967, then of 1956 and then to liquidate Israel's aggression of 1948—when Syria is pursuing its bloody assaults, we must not delude ourselves. We must understand that even as we work for peace, we are still at war for the life and freedom of our people. It is a struggle not of our choice, but unless we face the truth as it is, unless we are ready to cope with reality, grim as it may be, we might find ourselves in situations even more threatening than the Yom Kippur War.

This need not be if we learn the Holocaust's third lesson. This need not be if we remain strong and become even stronger.

Our strength lies in our defense capabilities, for which we owe so much to the United States of America. Our strength lies in you, in the covenant of the Jewish people, in Jewish brotherhood and Jewish solidarity. Our strength lies in the redemption of Soviet Jewry and of Jews in Arab lands, in their liberation, in their union with us.

Above all, our strength lies in our faith and our determination. There is always room for introspection and new thought. There is no room for weakness, for hesitation, for uncertainty. This too is one of the lessons of the Holocaust. Those who sow doubt and dissention and controversy have no place in our midst. We are still in the throes of a crucial struggle for life, for the preservation of our heritage, for the ideals and values for which the heroes of the Warsaw Ghetto fought and the martyrs of the Holocaust laid down their lives. In this struggle there is only one way to be—strong and united. Our destiny is one. We must all be one.

We can be. We can be strong and united. And if we are, we shall make the Jewish people secure and the State of Israel forever a source of pride and glory to us all.

II Israel and Ishmael

1 The No's of Arab Leadership

Three months after the Six-Day War, Arab heads of state gathered in Khartoum for a summit conference to plan future strategy in their continuous struggle against Israel. On September 1, 1967, the summit adopted its notorious resolution which was based on three no's: "no peace with Israel, no recognition of Israel, no negotiations with Israel." These three no's served as principal guidelines for Arab political warfare against Israel in the United Nations for many years before the Khartoum summit and for years after the summit and cast their shadow on the Middle East situation and on debates in the various organs of the United Nations.

Following are excerpts from statements delivered in the course of the diplomatic warfare waged against Israel by Arab delegations and their automatic supporters.

I

Excerpts from the first statement in the United Nations Security Council convened at Jordan's request to discuss Israel's action against terror bases in Jordan, March 21, 1968.

I come to address the Security Council for the first time, and I should like to take this opportunity to express to you, Mr. President, and to all the members of the Council my profound respect. I arrived from Israel only several weeks ago. I come from a land still in the throes of a twenty-year-old war. I come from a people longing desperately for peace. For thousands of years my people have prayed daily for peace. Today, even more than ever, we know how priceless it is.

In the war against the forces of darkness in which these United Nations were born, the people of Israel, unlike most of its neighbors, fought in the ranks of those who rose to defend freedom and democracy. During that war a third of the Jewish people was mercilessly annihilated in an orgy of genocide. When the war ended for the world, it continued for us. When all began to heal their wounds, to rebuild the ruins of their homes and to return to their fields and factories, we were confronted with further strife. First it was the struggle for national freedom. No sooner had we succeeded in gaining our independence than another ordeal of battle was forced upon us when the Arab States launched their war of aggression against Israel's existence.

This war still continues by the will of the Arab States. Despite United Nations decisions calling for permanent peace, despite armistice agreements which were to lead to a final peaceful settlement, in defiance of Charter obligations, in violation of a Security Council resolution prohibiting the exercise of belligerency, the Arab Governments went on and on with their warfare against Israel. It was waged through terror and sabotage, blockade and boycott. It was waged with persistence and malice. It ebbed at times, only to be resumed and pushed forward again in all its odious purposefulness. The publicly proclaimed aim remained unchanged: the total destruction of Israel.

The last concerted attempt by the Arab States to achieve their goal of ruin and death was made last June. Fifteen hundred tanks, hundreds of planes and hundreds of thousands of troops were massed on our borders ready for the kill. We can still hear reverberating in our ears the slogans broadcast in those days over the radio from the Arab capitals: "Kill, kill, kill the Jews. Butcher the Jews."

Then came the signal. The Strait of Tiran was blocked. Israeli villages in the Gaza area were shelled. And on the morning of June 5 full-scale operations began. We repulsed the enemy, we thwarted their plan to raze an independent State, a member of the United Nations, and to put its population to the sword.

The Security Council established a cease-fire, and Israel pleaded again to be granted that elementary right not begrudged to other nations: the right to peace and security. Ten months have passed since then.

In a rare demonstration of unanimity the Security Council on November 22, 1967, adopted Resolution 242 (1967), which called for a just and lasting peace in the Middle East. Nevertheless, it is still war that our neighbors are offering us. Peace is still being rejected openly and unabashedly. The cease-fire is ignored; armed attacks, sabotage raids and murder continue. The guns have not been silenced, and that is why we are here today. The eyes of the world are upon the Middle East. People everywhere are anxiously awaiting a sign that the Arab Governments are at last ready for peace. So far they have waited in vain. It is still belligerency that guides Arab thinking. It is still war that dominates their action. Today the representative of Jordan confirmed this again, and in all defiance proclaimed: the war is not over.

II

A debate on the "situation in the Middle East" was initiated by Egypt, whose Foreign Minister demanded inter alia that the Assembly take "adequate measures" against Israel.

Following are excerpts from an address before the Twenty-seventh Session of the General Assembly, November 29. 1972, in reply to Egypt's demands.

The millennial Jewish history is the saga of the few struggling to survive and defend their rights against the onslaught of the many. This has been true in all epochs. The avalanche of attacks directed in every debate in this Organization against the Jewish people, against Jewish civilization and Jewish statehood, the spate of resolutions unmindful of Israel's position reflect the numerical disadvantage we have lived with since time immemorial. They have little in common with the merits of the issues, with the realities of the situation, or with Israel's right and determination to continue to defend its legitimate interests. The result has been that these debates and resolutions not only have failed to contribute to the solution of the conflict, but by their inequity and partisan hostility have in effect created impediments to a settlement.

The acrimonious exchanges of rhetoric and the resolutions reflecting them could not have brought nearer a settlement of the conflict, for they lacked that basic element in the search for concord—consultation with and concurrence of the parties directly concerned.

In fact, the Arab Governments appear to have always looked upon debates in United Nations organs as a substitute for and an escape from the need for negotiation. Thus, we have gone through session after session, with resolutions becoming more and more pronounced in their partiality and adding ever new obstacles to understanding between Israel and the Arab States. Such an approach would not have helped in the consideration and solution of any problem, least of all one as complex as the Middle East situation.

At the root of it all lies the attempt by Arab States to deny the Jewish people its fundamental right to self-determination, freedom and renewed sovereignty in its ancient homeland. This negation of Jewish rights has found expression in the Arab invasion of Israel in 1948, in the Arab refusal to make peace with Israel, in the pursuance of terror warfare against Israel since the early 1950s, in the war acts of 1967 designed in the words of Egypt's President Nasser "to strike the death blow at Israel" which led to the June hostilities. This attitude is today reflected in the Arab Governments' identification with the campaign of wanton murder and barbaric atrocities directed against Israelis and Jews everywhere and carried out by organizations which have proclaimed their goal to be the Jewish State's destruction and the annihilation of its people.

The Arab leaders do not conceal their attitude. "Israel is a foreign limb which has been forced onto the body of the Arab nation and this body rejects it," declared President Sadat on February 17, 1972. "Nor do we have the right to compel the Palestinian people to accept the Security Council resolution," he added, "because the land is their land, both the areas occupied in 1948 and the remainder of Palestine occupied in 1967."

"There are only two specific Arab goals at this stage," explained President Sadat's confidant Hassanin Heykal in *Al Ahram*. "(1) elimination of the consequences of the 1967 aggression through Israel's withdrawal from all the lands it occupied that year; and (2) elimination of the consequences of the 1948 aggression through the eradication of Israel."

Nothing that has been said by Arab representatives in the course of the Twenty-seventh session of the General Assembly has altered the ominous implications of this Arab attitude. On the contrary, Israel, whose history, civilization, language, people are inseparable from the region, has been called here by Arab Foreign Ministers and representatives "an alien creation" and a "usurper State." Zionism—the Jewish people's love for its historic homeland, the Jewish people's national liberation movement—has been calumnied and abused. Even the Foreign Minister of Tunisia, referring to the murder of Israeli athletes at the Olympic Games in Munich and expressing only regret that "the wrong arena was chosen," declared that at that international gathering "the flag of Israel flew instead of the one that should have been there—the Palestinian flag." Today we heard the Foreign Minister of Egypt refer to Israel as part of an Arab country.

Is it possible to disregard such facts and such statements of policy? Is it possible to consider any aspect of the Middle East situation without bearing in mind these grim realities? What can be the import of a tactical position adopted by an Arab Government at a particular stage of the Middle East developments, as compared with the significance of the shattering truth that the Arab States continue to consider Israel as an anomalous entity and that Arab Governments are backing terrorist organizations whose avowed objective is to eliminate Israel and uproot its people? This is what Egypt's Foreign Minister described today as "Egypt stands by law." What credence can be attached even to those rare professions of good faith and of desire for peace as long as Arab Governments have not definitely abandoned their passion for Israel's perdition?

All elements in the Middle East situation are overshadowed by this dark specter. All difficulties, all differences, all threats are dwarfed by it. When voices are heard in the Arab world proclaiming that the use of force is the only way to deal with the conflict and that battle is inevitable, we in Israel feel that we know what sinister thoughts lurk behind them. We feel that the battle aspired to is one that would wrest from the people of Israel its freedom and sovereignty. We have reason to believe that when the Egyptian Government calls for a return to the vulnerable 1967 military lines it intends to leave the door open to the possibility of continuing hostility toward Israel from more advantageous positions.

Thus, President Sadat declared on May 1, 1972, "In our coming battle I will not be satisfied to liberate the land." We know what the Arab Governments have in mind when they unleash the terror squads against innocent Jewish men, women and children in Israel and abroad. We still remember the Egyptian Prime Minister's declaration of praise for the Lod massacre. We have not forgotten his refusal to cooperate with the West German Government to prevent the Munich killings.

Indeed, by resorting to and by openly supporting these Nazi-like outrages of indiscriminate slaughter, Egypt and other Arab States have created a worldwide danger which requires the adoption of preventive and punitive measures on a national, international and regional scale. If there is an aspect of the Middle East situation that necessitates immediate action by the United Nations it is Arab terrorism. The international community cannot stand by and watch the Arab Governments go on spreading this plague. Effective steps must be taken before it plunges mankind into barbarism. There is no room in the family of nations for Governments which continue to back savage murder of innocent human beings, as carried out by the Arab terror organizations.

Israel has been subjected to the Arab assault for twenty-five years. Today it is clear that it is not over. It is clear that the Arab Governments are still after our blood, our life. That is the primary issue. Life is the supreme value: its preservation is the ultimate obligation. Some may wish to examine the Middle East situation as a matter of documents and resolutions or of lines drawn across tracts of rock and sand. For us it is a question whether we and our children could be free from the threat against our lives. The preservation and security of the life of a State and of its citizens is not merely a central preoccupation. It is also the preeminent law. It is enshrined in the basic principles of national and international conduct. It is the essence of the Charter of the United Nations. It takes precedence over all other precepts. Three imperatives guide us in this debate: Israel's sovereignty, independence and security. Nothing shall impair or replace them.

How wanton appear in these circumstances the plaints of Arab Governments and the aspersions cast by them on Israel's position.

First of all there is their innate unhappiness with Israel's success in prevailing against foreign rule and then against Arab aggression and emerging to freedom and sovereignty. The entire enlightened world understood and welcomed the triumph of the Jewish people's age-long struggle to overcome the consequences of conquest, dispersion, oppression and discrimination and to restore its independence. The Jewish epos has inspired all who believe in the equality of peoples and in the rights of man. If a nation uprooted and living for centuries in bondage in distant lands could have preserved its national identity and its spiritual heritage, resisted the most horrifying and sanguinary racial persecutions and gathered again in its native land to regain its freedom and to rebuild its sovereignty, there was hope for all peoples, even the small and the weak and the downtrodden. There is no justification for shutting one's eyes to it all. There is no justification for Arab Governments to begrudge the Jewish people the very rights of self-determination and liberty in the land of its fathers that the Arab nation has attained in eighteen sovereign Arab States, including the Palestinian State of Jordan. When Israel's peace boundary is established it will be up to the Palestinian Arabs east of it to determine themselves, as an internal Arab matter, the structural and constitutional framework of their sovereignty.

Another cause for complaint by the Arab Governments is their repeated failures in the war they themselves launched against Israel, in defiance of the United Nations, in 1948, and which they have pursued ever since. Contrary to the Charter, in violation of their international obligations, they have claimed for themselves the right to wage war on Israel for more than two decades but have denied Israel the right to resist and to repel them. Whenever Israel repulsed their attacks, whenever the Israeli defense forces thwarted their aggression, whenever the Arab armies recoiled from one military line to another, the Arab Governments raised the cry of Israeli expansionism and aggression. If the war blockade instituted by President Nasser in 1967 were now strangling Israel, if the Egyptian armies, whose leaders had driven out the

United Nations Emergency Force to open the way for attack against us, were now sitting in the Negev, in southern Israel, Egypt would not be speaking today of expansionism or of the alleged sanctity of the old demarcation lines. Had Arab terror warfare proved successful, Arab Governments and their spokesmen would have had little reason to refer to Israeli actions against it. The Arab Governments are the fathers of the twenty-five-year war to which they have subjected Israel. They are the fathers of the consequences of this war.

This is true also of the fact that Israel remains on the lines established in accordance with the Security Council cease-fire resolutions and is responsible for territories within those lines. To refer to the Israeli presence on these lines and in those areas while ignoring that Israel arrived there in the course of a war of Arab making is to pervert fundamental truth. Whatever the vicissitudes of the situation, Israeli policy has been and is to ensure normal, peaceful life in these areas and the welfare and security of their inhabitants. The success of this policy is a matter of general knowledge. It has been affirmed by all objective observers. It has been attested by the 200,000 citizens of Arab States who have visited Israeli-administered areas in recent months and the hundreds of thousands who preceded them. It expresses itself in the considerable rise in the standard of living of the inhabitants, including Palestinian refugees; in full employment; in impressive increases in agricultural and industrial production; in educational and cultural development; in freedom of movement, expression, commerce with neighboring Arab countries. Israel's concern for the well-being of the population has been impugned and even derided by certain Arab Governments. It appears that they would rather see stagnation and misery prevail. They would rather not have free elections to local Arab authorities. They would prefer disorder, tension and violence to play havoc with life. They have done all in their power to instigate that. They would do all in their power to prevent the process of coexistence and cooperation between Jews and Arabs from taking root in these areas. They would seize upon any difficulty or mishap, they would misrepresent any fact, they would push through any one-sided resolution in an attempt to blur reality. It cannot be blurred—

and especially not by the kind of distortions we have heard today from the Foreign Minister of Egypt. The best evidence of the true situation is the tranquillity which marks it and the rejection by the local Arab population of terrorist elements and of hate propaganda.

This dramatic change, this historic transformation in relations between Arabs and Israelis in these territories, has been the most significant development in the last few years. Indeed, it has become evident that, just like the Jews, the Palestinian Arabs do not want war. It has become clear that they do not want violence and bloodshed, that the Black September and Al Fatah do not represent them, that the bellicose statements of Arab Governments and their representatives do not reflect their views or their aspirations. This change which has taken place in the Israel-held territories is the most hopeful sign that peaceful coexistence in the region is possible. It must be guarded and nurtured as one of the foundations of peace.

It has become obvious that, when given the opportunity, Arabs desire to live in peace with Israelis, to work and build and create in tranquillity side by side with them. Could not such an opportunity be given to all the Arab peoples, to the peoples of the Arab States and of Israel, to live together in the region in harmony and brotherhood? The key is in the hands of the Arab Governments.

The main obstacle to peace is still the Arab Governments' fundamental attitude toward Israel, in flagrant violation of the Charter, their apparent longing for Israel's downfall, their resort to and identification with means, even such as savage terrorism, that envisage Israel's ultimate destruction and the indiscriminate slaughter of its people. Yet it would take only one decision to change it all. A single decision would be sufficient to accept the justice of Israel's rebirth. It would take only one decision to stop inculcating the Arab peoples with fanatical hatred and bloodthirstiness toward Israel and begin teaching them that Jews and Arabs are brothers, that they are of the same family, of similar language, of related civilizations, and, above all, that they must end their feuds and live together and in peace. It would take only a decision by the Arab Governments to put an end to the criminal activities of the terror organizations initiated by these Governments, operating from bases and headquarters in Arab States, assisted by them militarily, financially and politically. The question is, will the Arab Governments take such a decision? The question is, when will such a decision be taken?

Another obstacle to peace is the Arab Governments' view that there might be no need to work out an agreement between them and Israel, with Israel; that it might be possible to impose on Israel a solution in accordance with Arab terms. Thus far the Arab States, and in particular Egypt, have adamantly followed this course. Egypt tried to force its terms on Israel by the war of attrition in 1969 and 1970. It has attempted to dictate its terms through the Great Powers and through international organs. It has failed time and again. However, it has not drawn the appropriate conclusions from those failures. Egypt still seems to be under the illusion that pressure can be exerted to bring about Israel's surrender to the Egyptian *Diktat*. Yet it is obvious that pressure and imposition are hardly the way to reach a settlement with Israel. A people defending its life knows how and is ready to withstand pressure. A people subjected to war, bloodshed and terrorist outrages for twenty-five years has seen the worst and cannot be swayed by duress. A people struggling to ensure that at least its children will not live under the constant threat of bloodshed and will not have to go on fighting wars to preserve their liberty cannot be moved by force or coercion.

The goal of the United Nations in the Middle East conflict is to promote agreement between the parties on a just and lasting peace. It is to assist in bringing about an accepted settlement. This is the very foundation of the United Nations position in this conflict. The quest for an accepted agreement cannot proceed parallel to the application of constraint. The two are diametrically opposed methods. The exertion of outside pressure is the road to collision, not agreement. The Egyptian Government must choose between the two. It cannot have both at the same time. The experience of the last few years leaves no doubt as to which is the open road and which the blind alley, which leads to an understanding and which to increased confrontation. One thing is evident. If the choice falls to pressure and coercion, the basis for United Nations efforts toward agreement will be undermined.

III

In the years 1970 to 1973 the main goal of Egyptian diplomacy was to compel Israel to commit itself to a total withdrawal from occupied territories without negotiations. Accordingly, Egypt initiated a special session of the Security Council, attended by the Egyptian and many Arab Foreign Ministers, in an effort to induce Israel to make a prior commitment on withdrawal. A draft resolution to this effect was vetoed at the end of the debate by the United States. The following statement was made in the course of the session to repel a coordinated overall Arab diplomatic offensive (July 20, 1973).

Disappointment and anxiety were widespread when Egypt asked two months ago for a Security Council debate on the Middle East situation. It was clear that the cause of peace could not be served by public polemic and sterile recrimination. In all parts of the world conflicts were being settled and international differences resolved by dialogue and agreement. Confrontation was being replaced by negotiation, inveterate hostility supplanted by understanding and cooperation. There was hope, indeed expectation, that constructive diplomacy would not stop at the gates of the Middle East and that Israel and the Arab States as well would find some way to initiate a process of negotiation. Instead, Egypt chose again the course of collision.

In his speech of July 16, President Sadat made it clear that Egypt did not go to the Security Council for a peaceful solution of the conflict. "There is no peaceful solution," he added, revealing Egypt's true attitude.

Yet Israel will remain undeterred in its search for peace. It will not abandon hope that Arab Governments will eventually realize that peace is better than continuation of the conflict, that if seriously pursued peace is attainable, and that all the peoples of the Middle East, including the Arab nation, are yearning for it. Despite Egypt's persistent refusal to enter into a meaningful dialogue on peace, Israel will try again and again to persuade it that such a dialogue would be beneficial and essential in bringing about a peaceful settlement.

Two conceptions of the Middle East situation are vying with each other in the present Security Council debate. One conception draws inspiration from the age-long saga of the Jewish people, uprooted from its homeland by foreign conquerors, struggling through the centuries to preserve its civilization, faith and national identity and to restore its freedom and sovereignty. The other originates in a refusal to recognize this saga and in a denial of the Jewish people's rights to liberty, self-determination and equality with other nations. Israel, and with it enlightened world opinion, holds that the Jewish people's rebirth in its ancient homeland and the reestablishment of the sole Jewish State has been an epos of supreme justice. The Arab Governments continue to view it as a wrong against the Arab nation, although that nation has attained its rights in eighteen sovereign states, including the Palestinian Arab State of Jordan.

On the one hand, there is the drama of the Jewish people, beleaguered and embattled for a quarter century, its very right to independence and sovereignty under constant assault. On the other, there is the demand to penalize Israel for having withstood this relentless onslaught on its life, for having repelled the aggressor and driven back the forces which seek its destruction.

Egypt and other Arab States, having persistently tried to bring about Israel's downfall, now wish the world would ignore the origin, nature and duration of their war against the Jewish State. They would have all disregard the chain of Egyptian acts of war in 1967 that led to the outbreak of hostilities in June of that year: the imposition of a war blockade, the expulsion of the United Nations Emergency Force, the conclusion of military pacts with other Arab States for coordinating the attack against Israel, the massing of huge armies along the frontiers for an all-out onslaught against Israel, the bombardment of Israeli villages, President Nasser's proclamation of the final battle to annihilate Israel. To them the only development in recent years worthy of attention is Israel's success in frustrating Arab designs on its existence, resulting in the deployment of Israeli forces on the present cease-fire lines established by the Security Council. Juxtaposed to this is the realization that such a selective and distorted view of the Middle East situation must inevitably impede the solution of the conflict. It is the realization that efforts to attain a peaceful settlement between Israel and the Arab States cannot succeed if they are based on the one-sided contention that the main problem is Israeli withdrawal, while in fact the Israeli presence on the cease-fire lines is a mere by-product of the protracted war of aggression pursued by the Arab States since 1948, a war those States have refused till this day to terminate fully and definitively.

Israel's position is that after all the years of violence and bloodshed there appears to be a possibility of attaining genuine peace in the region and establishing secure and recognized boundaries where only truce, armistice or cease-fire lines have existed until now. The Arab Governments demand the restoration of the old military lines, the very lines which had been a principal cause of the insecurity, chaos and belligerency of the past.

Israel calls on the Arab States to start building peace together by talking peace with each other. The Egyptian and other Arab Governments counter with the demand that the Arab views and terms be imposed on Israel from the outside in total disregard for Israel's rights and vital interests. They have tried to achieve that objective by a variety of means, including resort to force and pressure by third Powers, individually and collectively. It seems that the Arab leaders' deliberate insensibility to the history and struggle of the Jewish people has led them to repeated mistakes in the assessment of Israel's attitude and mood. A people which has been ready and able to resist oppression and cruelty, force and inhumanity for thousands of years in order to preserve its heritage and to defend its rights will not yield to its assailants now that it stands on the threshold of ensuring for itself, at long last, the right to live in peace and security.

Such a people can be reasoned with. It can be convinced by thoughtful and understanding deliberation. It cannot, however, be pressured. When the Arab States come to accept this fundamental truth they will turn away from confrontation aiming at forcing their will upon Israel, and then there will be agreement in the Middle East.

In the United Nations, Egypt and other Arab States still deceive themselves, at times, that by marshaling their automatic majority to pass one-sided resolutions they could sway Israel from defending its basic rights and legitimate positions.

The Arab States forget that in its millennial struggle to remain alive, the Jewish people has come to learn that the strength and merit of its heritage and the justice of its cause cannot be weakened by the fact that its opponents are numerous. The Arab States also forget that in the United Nations, even at this Security Council table, there are Governments which thought little of General Assembly resolutions, some adopted by more than a hundred votes, or of Security Council resolutions which had gained thirteen or fourteen votes and were vetoed, and even of resolutions inequitable and prejudicial to their national interests.

The only resolution that has played any significant role in the Middle East conflict since 1967 is Security Council Resolution 242 (1967). This has been so because it was adopted unanimously following consultation and understanding with the parties. One thing is self-evident: resolutions not based on the parties' consent cannot contribute to the attainment of agreement between them.

This is sometimes recognized in Egypt as well. Thus, a detailed analysis of the first stage of the present debate published in *Al Ahram* on June 13, 1973, referred to such United Nations resolutions as "rusty medals." *Al Ahram* cited Egypt's Foreign Minister as having said, "Can you imagine the representative of Egypt to the United Nations walking through the *couloirs,* his chest covered with these rusty medals? He will make people laugh."

The partisan political views expressed in such resolutions which do not serve the cause of peace in the Middle East cannot affect Israel's position founded on the precepts of international law and the Charter of the United Nations. It is not surprising that in these circumstances Egypt should seek to mask the real meaning of its demands by invoking principles of international law and of the United Nations Charter. It is surprising, however, that Egypt should assume that the misinterpretation and distortion of these principles would go undiscerned even when the Egyptian Foreign Minister calls to his aid the statements of the Soviet representative who misused his office of president to put forward one-sided and warped interpretations without prior consultation with members of the Security Council.

Thus, the Egyptian Minister of Foreign Affairs has singled out the concept of nonadmissibility of acquisition of territory by war which appears in the preamble of Resolution 242 (1967). That entire resolution is a series of principles on the application of which the parties are to reach agreement. It is, of course, up to the parties, not up to others, to agree between themselves how those principles should be applied in practice.

The most important of the principles appear, as usual, in the operative part of the resolution and not in its preamble. In any event, whatever their relative significance, and even if all the principles in the preamble and in the operative part alike were to be considered of equal importance, it is clear that they cannot be tampered with by selectively singling out one or another for special emphasis. To do that would destroy Resolution 242 (1967) and its carefully constructed balance. Yet that is precisely what Egypt demands: to single out one of the many points in the resolution, thus consciously undermining the resolution as a whole. Egypt goes even beyond that and, when citing the concept of inadmissibility of acquisition of territory by war, deliberately omits the second part of that concept. Indeed, the relevant paragraph of the preamble to Resolution 242 (1967) states: "Emphasizing the inadmissibility of the acquisition of territory by war and the need to work for a just and lasting peace in which every State in the area can live in security . . ." To have any meaning whatever in the Middle East context, the first part of this provision can be read and must be interpreted only in conjunction with its second part that calls for peace, the central element of which would have to be security. This is further elaborated in the operative paragraph of the resolution envisaging the establishment of secure and recognized boundaries between Israel and the Arab States.

A similar distortion and misinterpretation is resorted to by Egypt when it invokes the concept of territorial integrity. This is also one of the points in Resolution 242 (1967). However, as already indicated, it must be considered together with the others. To separate it from the other principles would subvert and destroy Resolution 242 (1967).

Moreover, the full text of the resolution's provision which refers to territorial integrity calls for the application of the following principle: "Termination of all claims or states of belligerency and respect for and acknowledgment of the sovereignty, territorial integrity and political independence of every State in the area and their right to live in peace within secure and recognized boundaries free from threats or acts of force . . ."

It is clear from this text that the establishment of secure and recognized boundaries is a prerequisite for the acknowledgment of territorial integrity. The idea of territorial integrity does not stand in exclusive solitude. It is part of a broader principle. In the Middle East contest it is a purely theoretical idea unless and until secure and recognized boundaries between Israel and the Arab States are, for the first time, determined by agreement between the parties. In examining the Middle East question we are dealing with a concrete situation and with the need, specifically enunciated by the Security Council, to agree on the application of a number of principles to that situation through a peace agreement. Such agreement will not be reached by maiming and amputating those principles or by singling out some while relegating others to secondary positions.

It is to be observed that even in General Assembly resolutions unrelated to any specific problem or situation and enumerating general principles in the abstract, the notions which Egypt seeks to single out are only a part of elaborate, complex and balanced formulations.

Egypt's demands are contrary not merely to Resolution 242 (1967) but also to the provisions of the United Nations Charter. The Charter stipulates: "All Members shall refrain in their international relations from the threat or use of force against the territorial integrity or political independence of any State, or in any other manner inconsistent with the Purposes of the United Nations." For twenty-five years Egypt and other Arab States have resorted to threats and to the use of force against Israel and its independence. For twenty-five years they have remained in a state of war with Israel in defiance of the United Nations Charter. Egypt cannot invoke against Israel the provision that Egypt itself has consistently violated and continues to violate in relation to the Jewish State. Nothing prevents Israel from responding to the Arab war by a war of self-defense and succeeding in its response.

Article 51 of the Charter declares unequivocally: "Nothing in the present Charter shall impair the inherent right of individual or collective self-defense if an armed attack occurs . . ." Israel's recourse to arms in self-defense has been in accordance with the Charter and not in contravention of it. Furthermore, no principle or provision of the Charter precludes border changes, especially following the use of force in self-defense and especially where no secure and recognized international boundaries had existed between the victim of aggression and the states that have been waging war against it for two and a half decades in violation of the Charter.

The argument that the 1967 line between Israel and Egypt should be considered a State boundary, despite the specific provision to the contrary contained in the Israeli-Egyptian Armistice Agreement, is groundless. The Egyptian claim that the 1967 line was not final on the Israeli side but was a definitive boundary on its Egyptian side is a concept devoid of any foundation and even of logic. A line has no width; it has the same meaning and validity for both parties which it separates. If the 1967 line established for Egypt in relation to Israel is, as stressed by the Foreign Minister of Egypt, a mere separation of military forces, it could only be a military, temporary line of identical nature for Israel in relation to Egypt. Thus the Egyptian thesis regarding the 1967 line as transmitted to Israel, *inter alia,* in the Jarring memorandum of February 8, 1971, is a travesty of international law. To give it support is to demolish Resolution 242 (1967), which deliberately left the question of secure and recognized boundaries to be determined by agreement between the parties.

It is immaterial by what semantic stratagem Egypt tries in 1973 to impose its *Diktat* that the old vulnerable and provisional lines be restored and that Israel withdraw to those lines, a *Diktat* repeatedly rejected by the General Assembly and the Security Council in 1967. Whether Egypt formulates this demand in specific terms, or by reference to the Jarring memorandum which suggested that Israel should accept the Egyptian position, or by reference to resolutions supporting it, or whether it does that by professing to invoke general principles, the effect would be the same. The central problem on which the parties are to reach agreement, the question of secure and recognized boundaries, would be excluded from the process of agreement. The essence of the peacemaking efforts, attainment of agreement between the parties, would be shattered and replaced by the notion of imposition from the outside. Resolution 242 (1967), the only generally acceptable basis for United Nations action, would be wrecked. To the complexity of the Middle East conflict would be added a jurisprudential void and complete chaos. If there is a flicker of hope that the parties could be brought to reason together and to try to accommodate each other, it must not be stamped out by shortsighted partisanship. A situation in which there is still some opening, no matter how modest and even disappointing, is, after all, preferable to a stark wall with all the openings hermetically closed. It would be unfortunate indeed if the Security Council itself became instrumental in creating such a situation.

Another attempt endangering Resolution 242 (1967) is Egypt's demand regarding the alleged issue of the rights of Palestinians. Egypt would replace the resolution's call for a just settlement of the refugee problem by a provision on Palestinian rights. In view of the opposition to such a change that would inevitably sound the death knell of Resolution 242 (1967), Egypt has on occasions spoken of the possibility of using phraseology that would not mention those rights specifically and would conceal Egypt's true objectives by invoking the general principle of self-determination.

To satisfy the Egyptian demand regarding the principle of self-determination would mean introducing a new element into the framework of Resolution 242 (1967) in the full knowledge that this would completely upset it. This particular Egyptian claim has, however, two additional ominous implications. The Security Council is not a technical drafting committee dealing with abstract formulations. In a debate on the Middle East situation the principle of self-determination or inalienable rights must be viewed in the light of the realities of that situation. The earlier part of the debate established that behind Egypt's references to self-determination and to Palestinian rights lurks a design to dismember Jordan.

This has been confirmed in the meantime, both by the governmental Egyptian media of information and by the Arab terrorist organizations. Approval of the Egyptian demand would therefore, in the present political realities of the region, constitute, in fact, approval of the dismemberment of the Palestinian Arab State of Jordan. This is doubtless the interpretation that has been given and would be given again in the region to such a step by the Security Council.

Moreover, the Foreign Minister of Egypt has made it clear that the new additional Palestinian entity should be created by recognizing the 1947 partition lines as Israel's boundaries. Support of the Egyptian demand regarding self-determination would thus be tantamount, in the Middle East context, to an invitation to Egypt to carry out its notorious two-stage plan: first to bring about Israel's withdrawal to the 1967 lines, and then to pursue the struggle for Israel's truncation and ultimate liquidation.

It is to be recalled that the Palestinian terror groups which claim to speak on behalf of Palestinian rights, and which are actively supported by Egypt, openly proclaim the destruction of Israel as their objective. This is being reiterated daily with the full knowledge and consent of the Egyptian Government on Radio Cairo.

It has been clear from the very beginning of the Middle East debate that, as President Sadat declared last Monday, Egypt did not initiate the Security Council deliberations to advance a political solution. The first part of the debate already made it evident that Egypt was thinking in terms of continued confrontation with Israel, rather than agreement with it. Egypt was merely seeking the Security Council's support in this confrontation. Thus it called for approval of views and demands rejected by the Council in 1967 because they would have made agreement between the parties impossible.

The discussion, adjourned on June 14, revealed the Egyptian designs and the baselessness of Egypt's argumentation. It showed how, in the last six years, Egypt rejected one suggestion after another made by Israel and by the Secretary General's Special Representative to advance the peacemaking efforts. The discussion brought out that the Security Council in its Resolution 242 (1967) had purposely left the secure and recognized boundaries undefined so that the parties could agree on them between themselves.

The discussion further clarified that all, including the Arab delegations, as acknowledged by the Minister of State of the United Arab Emirates, and their supporters, as confirmed by the Indian representative on the Council in 1967, understood that Resolution 242 (1967) envisaged changes in the 1967 lines and that no distinction was made in this respect between the line separating Israel from Egypt and the lines between Israel and the other Arab States. It was clear from the discussion that Egypt's demands, if granted, would undermine Resolution 242 (1967) and that some of them, such as the claim regarding the so-called Palestinian rights or that Israel's recognized borders should be the partition lines of 1947, would play havoc with the situation in the Middle East.

It is regrettable, therefore, that Egypt has not modified its attitude and that it pursues the same course in the resumed debate. The grave implications of this course were highlighted by Egypt's Foreign Minister when, according to the governmental Egyptian News Agency, he declared in Paris on July 17, just before his departure for the United Nations, that a Security Council resolution in support of Egypt's demands would give Egypt "a declaration enabling us to resort to any means in order to end the occupation." The significance of that statement is obvious. Egypt's aim in the Security Council is a resolution that could be used to justify Egypt's continued confrontation with Israel, including renewed resort to force. This was confirmed today by the Minister of Foreign Affairs of Egypt.

This is not a course which could lead to agreement and peace; this is not a position which could create conditions propitious for any constructive effort within the United Nations framework. This is not an attitude that could pave the way for a visit to the region by the Secretary General. In fact, it brings the United Nations close to a point at which it might find itself unable to play any role in the search for peace in the Middle East.

The first stage of the present debate and developments since its adjournment have actually pointed the way for effective peacemaking. As the discussion in the Security Council progressed, it became increasingly apparent that the one method that could bring about agreement between the parties was that of negotiation. The truth of this conclusion was so obvious that the Arab Governments could no longer ignore or reject it unceremoniously, as in the past. The Egyptian Foreign Minister himself found it necessary to declare that his Government accepted the idea of talks with Israel. He accompanied that statement with the allegation that Israel prevented the initiation of such negotiations by insisting on prior conditions. That allegation, however, is no more credible today than when it was first made, in the light of the known fact that Israel is calling for negotiations without any preconditions, and in view of the assurances reiterated in statements before the Council that Israel does not ask Egypt to accept in advance any of the Israeli positions. In the meantime, the President of Tunisia and other international personalities have spoken publicly of the need for Arab negotiations with Israel.

In these circumstances, no pretext, no argument or allegation can justify Egypt's refusal to enter into a genuine dialogue with Israel. If there is now general recognition that negotiations between the parties to the conflict are essential and inevitable, there can be no reason whatever for delaying them.

The first round in the Middle East debate was suspended on the eve of an historic event that underlined the importance of contact and talks between nations. The American-Soviet summit meeting in Washington has dramatically demonstrated the effectiveness of the process of negotiations. None of the summit's significant results could have been envisaged and achieved without the serious exchanges of view which had taken place between the two Powers. Could anyone imagine the understandings reached and the agreements concluded in Washington resulting from a public debate in the Security Council? Would anyone suggest that the Vietnam agreement, the epoch-making improvement of relations between the United States and China, the progress on the German problem, would have been possible if not for the patient, constructive "quiet diplomacy" that had been put into motion? There can be no excuse for not applying this proven method also in the Middle East.

The twenty-five-year Arab war against Israel is a story of fundamental errors of judgment and missed opportunities by Arab leaders. The time has come to free the situation from the entrapment in futile slogans and sterile prejudices. The sufferers in this situation are the peoples of the Middle East. For them there can be no plausible explanation why, with Israel's continuously expressed readiness to negotiate peace, the Egyptian Government has remained adamant in its refusal. The peoples of the Middle East, including the people of Egypt, are not interested in the nuances of the Security Council debate and its resolutions. They know one thing: in all parts of the world, representatives of hostile Governments meet face to face and try to settle their differences. Only in the Middle East do they remain immersed in the mire of fruitless rhetoric, semantic quibbling and doctrinaire postures in vain attempts to justify the absence of a constructive effort to reach understanding and harmony. How can one explain to the people the tortuous arguments and endless polemics in the Council chamber? How can one explain to them the refusal to meet with Israel and discuss any matter seriously and fruitfully with a view to making progress toward peace? How can insistence on prior conditions and prior commitments outweigh the need to test at least the possibility of making such progress?

Few are the capitals of the world that Egypt's leaders have not visited in the last six years to discuss the Middle East situation. They have tried various ways and means and traveled everywhere except to the one obvious destination—peace talks with Israel. The time has come to take this road. The peoples of the Middle East are sure to give their blessing to such a step.

2 Arab Terror Warfare

I

The Security Council was convened in March 1969 at Jordan's request to discuss an Israeli action against terror bases in the As-Salt area. Between the end of January 1969 and March of the same year, there was a marked upsurge in terror warfare from Jordanian territory against Israel. More than two hundred sabotage raids and attacks by firing across the cease-fire line were recorded.

Following are excerpts from a statement in the Security Council, March 27, 1969.

Arab warfare by terror has been employed continuously in Arab aggression against Israel. Months before Israel's independence and its invasion by the regular armies of seven Arab States, paramilitary units and other irregular forces were sent across the border to attack Jewish villages, throw bombs at Jewish buses, murder Jewish civilians. The most notorious of these forces were those from Syria under the command of the Nazi agent Fawzi el Kawukji, and those from Jordan under the Husseinis, whose leader Haj Amin el Husseini spent the Second World War years, together with Kawukji, in Berlin as adviser to Hitler and Eichmann. Husseini was considered by the Allies a war criminal.

There was no mistaking the spiritual parentage of these paramilitary terror forces. These Nazi sympathizers and collaborators were bent on completing the Nazi "final solution"—the annihilation of the

Jewish people. This objective became clearer when Arab regular forces joined in the aggression and the Secretary General of the Arab League announced on May 15, 1948, that this would be "a war of extermination which will be spoken of like the Mongolian massacres."

Thwarted in their invasion, the Arab States signed armistice agreements with Israel, but after a short interval they resumed their aggression by means of terror acts. There was nothing new in their methods. Again, Israeli farmers were killed in outlying village houses; civilian buses were ambushed and their passengers shot in cold blood; grenades were thrown into classrooms and small children at study were killed. In the Arab capitals, the perpetrators of these acts were called *fedayeen,* as they are today, and, as today, they were hailed as heroes. The Arab press gleefully reported their exploits; the Arab radio stations broadcast war communiqués about their attacks.

Then, as today, the Arab Governments played a two-faced game.

While organizing, directing and inspiring terror warfare and glorifying it at home, the Arab Governments tried to disclaim responsibility for it abroad. These were Palestinian refugees acting on their own, they argued in the United Nations with tongue in cheek. Even those who were ready to ignore the obvious and the direct involvement of the Arab Governments, and the use of their territory for launching attacks against Israel, found it impossible to explain how individuals could acquire land mines, machine guns and grenades and how their exploits could be carried out without professional military training and direction.

The fact is that the United Nations has never accepted the contention of the Arab Governments that they bear no responsibility for warfare by terror.

As early as 1948, the Security Council established the principle that Governments are responsible for acts of violence committed by individuals, groups of individuals and irregular forces. In its Resolution 56 (1948) of August 19, 1948, adopted after a discussion on this very point, the Security Council spelled out the meaning of cease-fire. It decided that

(a) Each party is responsible for the actions of both regular and irregular forces operating under its authority or in territory under its control;

(b) Each party has the obligation to use all means at its disposal to prevent action violating the truce by individuals or groups who are subject to its authority and/or who are in territory under its control.

These provisions are basic United Nations doctrine on Arab terror warfare. This was forcefully brought to the attention of the Security Council by the United States representative at the Council meeting of March 24, 1968. He said:

We oppose acts of terrorism, which are in violation of the cease-fire resolution of the Council, and we are not blind to the additional problems they create.

We have long believed, as I also stated to the Council on March 21, that the rule which should guide all the parties in these situations was first and wisely expressed many years ago in the Security Council Resolution 56 (1948) of August 19, 1948 . . .

We deem these principles to be applicable to the cease-fire resolutions of June 1967 . . .

As years went by it became more and more difficult for the Arab States to conceal their responsibility for the terror warfare. Starting in 1955, Egypt began to publish official communiqués about terror operations, and since then the other Arab States have been doing the same, or placing their Government-controlled public information media at the disposal of the terror organizations. Jordan was no exception.

When in 1956 Israeli forces seized and published the archives of the *fedayeen* headquarters in Khan Yunis, in the Gaza area, there was no further doubt not only of the legal responsibility of Egypt and other Arab States, including Jordan, for the continuation of terror warfare from territory under their control, but also of their direct responsibility in fact. Documents which came into the possession of Israel in the hostilities of 1967, and again at Karame a year ago, give further proof of the direct responsibility of the different Arab Governments, including the Jordanian Government, for the terror-warfare activities from their different territories.

From the experience that has been gained since 1956, it has been clear to all that terror warfare is waged when the Arab Governments decide to wage it, and it stops when they so decide. Egypt took such a decision to wage terror warfare in the early fifties. Terror warfare from its territory stopped only in 1956 after Israel had destroyed the *fedayeen* bases in Gaza and Sinai. Terror warfare continued intermittently from Jordanian territory so long as the Jordanian authorities took no action against it. The world witnessed a dangerous upsurge in terror warfare when a new regime in Syria in the mid-sixties decided to resort to this method of aggression to increase tension on the border. The usual disclaimers of responsibility were heard. As before, the terrorists were glamorized as freedom fighters in a so-called "people's war." Again, the Security Council rejected these arguments. It tried to call on Syria to put an end to this campaign of aggression, but it was thwarted by the veto. The formal outcome of a vote, whether as a result of the veto or of the other voting disabilities which Israel faces in the Council, cannot, however, derogate from the validity of international principles that are part of United Nations doctrine. Terror attacks are violations of the cease-fire. Governments from whose territory these attacks are launched are responsible, regardless of the extent of their direct involvement in the terrorist operations. This is true even more of Governments directly engaged in sponsoring, organizing and assisting such warfare. And this is what the Arab Governments have in fact been doing since June 1967.

Their armies thrown back by Israel, the Arab States have turned again to the tried method of warfare by terror. A decision to this effect was taken at the Khartoum Conference of the heads of Arab States in September 1967. This decision was confirmed in other official meetings, including the meeting of the Arab Foreign Ministers in Cairo in September 1968. This all-Arab decision was reiterated by the Undersecretary General of the Arab League, Said Naofal, on February 24, 1969.

In previous Security Council debates and in official letters to the President of the Security Council I have described the active participation of the Arab Governments in terror warfare. This has also been extensively reported by the world press and by other public-information media. Jordan, Egypt and Syria have set up training camps for terror units. Instruction is given by officers of the regular Jordanian, Egyptian and Syrian armies. Training bases exist also in Algeria. Officers and soldiers of the regular armed forces of Jordan, United Arab Republic and Syria are assigned for commando training and transferred to the terror organizations. Moreover, recruitment of terrorists is conducted openly in headquarters in Amman, Cairo, Beirut, Baghdad and Damascus. Financial resources and arms are supplied directly by the Arab Governments. The governmental radio stations in Arab States have established special broadcasts.

The slogans under which these organizations operate and their avowed objectives are the same as they were ten and twenty years ago: Kill all Jews, destroy Israel.

Yassir Arafat, the Al Fatah leader and head of the council of all terror organizations, stated in an interview with the Middle East News Agency: "Al Fatah started its activities in 1956 and its armed struggle in 1965. Its aim—the liquidation of Zionist, i.e. Israeli, existence."

Such is the organization openly sponsored and supported by the Arab Governments. President Nasser in a speech before the Egyptian National Assembly on January 20, 1969, proclaimed, "The UAR places all its resources at the disposal of these organizations." King Hussein welcomed Arafat on his return to Jordan and announced his Government's full support.

Today, as in the past, the most gruesome aspect of warfare by terror is that it is directed for the greater part against civilians. Bombs exploded in crowded stations and markets, grenades thrown into crowds of worshipers, explosive charges placed in school buses, button-shaped mines and other booby traps scattered in schoolyards, cowardly attacks on civil aircraft with passengers and crew aboard— these are the characteristic exploits of the terrorists. To compare thugs who murder indiscriminately innocent men, women and children to resistance fighters is blasphemy of the name of resistance. The resistance fighters of Europe have expressed their utter repugnance for the Arab terrorists.

In a resolution adopted at the plenary session in Brussels in April 1968, in which delegations of World War II resistance fighters from Austria, Belgium, Cyprus, Denmark, France, Israel, Italy, Luxembourg, Netherlands, Norway, the United Kingdom and the United States took part, the International Union of Resistance and Deportees' Organizations declared:

No one can compare the spirit of resistance to terrorist activities and odious and blind crimes intended to provoke fear and insecurity, to give rise to violence, when all possibilities are openly offered for an open discussion, or try to compare to the resistance against Nazism the fanatics surrounded by former Nazi criminals who merely prolong the Hitler genocide and thereby offer an insult which is felt deeply not only by the citizens of Israel who courageously fight for their right to life but by all those who resisted and who remain true to themselves.

This total rejection by the anti-Nazi resistance fighters is particularly understandable when one bears in mind that Arab terror warfare against the Jewish people of Israel has been in reality permeated by Nazi doctrine, organized by Nazi war criminals like Haj Amin el Husseini, and is directly assisted by Nazi German instructors. The following facts are ominous. Among those who have been training the terror units are Erich Atlen, alias Ali Bella, onetime head of the Jewish Department of the Gestapo in Nazi-occupied Galicia; Willy Berner, alias Ben Kashir, an SS veteran from the Mauthausen concentration camp; and Colonel Baumann, alias Ali ben Khader, one of the exterminators of the Warsaw Ghetto. Hitler's *Mein Kampf,* translated into Arabic and printed and distributed by the Egyptian and Syrian Governments, is standard reading for the members of all the terror organizations.

Lieutenant General Burns, the Canadian head of the United Nations Truce Supervision Organization, by no means uncritical of Israeli policy, wrote in his book *Between Arab and Israeli:* ". . . I felt what Egyptians were doing in sending these men, whom they dignified with the name of fedayeen, or commandos, into another country with the mission to attack men, women and children indiscriminately, was a war crime. It was essentially of the same character . . . as the offences for which the Nazi leaders had been tried in Nuremberg, to cite the most recent example."

The venerable René Cassin, Nobel Peace Prize winner of 1968, has again raised his voice against the sophistry inherent in the Arab position. On February 10, 1969, he wrote in *Ici Paris:*

Since 1967, injustice, I note with sorrow, has continued under various forms, consisting on the one hand in causing the Security Council to adopt decisions which are contrary to international law, and on the other in devising these decisions in a manner that deprives Israel of the juridical benefits which it could legitimately expect.

Israel remains bound to respect the "cease-fire," but its adversaries are never condemned when, having violated it, they incur reprisals. Even more than that, they are acting through irregular forces, in this case the Palestinians, who are equated, for the sake of argument, with our resistance fighters.

Do they seek in New York the triumph of the doctrine of the destruction of a State admitted in 1948 as a Member of the United Nations?

I, on my part, desire a just peace and am far from ignoring the interests of the Moslem populations of Palestine. However, are not the greatest enemies of these poor people those who make of them, as of the Jewish individuals themselves, the instruments of a policy of aggression, in utter disregard of the real interests of the refugees and those in occupied territories?

Indeed, whether juridically or morally, Arab warfare by terror is a loathsome, criminal policy. It violates the cease-fire; it undermines the peacemaking efforts; it is directed against Israelis and harms the Arabs; its victims are innocent civilians. It is inspired by unmitigated Nazi-like hatred toward the remnants of a people victimized by the Nazis in history's most horrifying genocide.

Whatever one may think or say about Arab terror against Israel, in whatever form this warfare is wrapped up by the Arab Governments for presentation to the United Nations, its real test for Israel is one, and one only: Is it or is it not directed against Israeli lives? Does it or does it not aim at the murder of innocent Israeli men, women and children?

Whatever pretexts the Arab Governments offer for continuing terror warfare and refusing to suppress it, Israel, like any other State, cannot acquiesce to the organized, premeditated murder of its citizens. If the Arab Governments are unwilling to stop it, Israel itself must take all necessary measures to put an end to it. Enough Jews have been barbarously murdered in this century; Jewish mothers have wept enough for their dead. This must stop; this cannot go on, and we shall not allow it to go on.

The United Nations has called on the parties to the Middle East conflict to terminate the fighting, to reach agreement, to talk—not to kill. It is high time that the Arab Governments abandoned their sanguinary designs and ceased warfare by terror and started to talk peace. Surely they must realize by now that terror and sabotage and the killing and maiming of civilians will not weaken Israel's determination to attain a just and lasting peace. It has not weakened Israel during the last twenty years; it will not make Israel falter now. Peace and security are the fundamental rights of all nations. The Arab Governments must understand and accept that Israel too has this right to real peace and real security.

II

The Security Council was convened in June 1972 at Lebanon's request following a clash on the Israeli–Lebanese cease-fire line between an Israeli patrol and a Syrian military convoy. Five Syrian officers connected with terror operations against Israel were taken prisoner. The following statement was made in the Security Council on June 23, 1972.

Arab terror warfare is the outgrowth neither of the 1967 hostilities nor of the Palestine refugee problem. This heinous method has been used against the Jewish people's struggle for liberty in its ancient homeland for more than fifty years, long before the Six-Day War, long before there were any Palestinian refugees. We still remember the indiscriminate killing of Jews, the destruction of entire Jewish villages, the massacre of Jewish communities by Arab terror gangs in the 1920s and 1930s. Terror against the civilian Jewish population was first unleashed on a large scale by the notorious Haj Amin el Husseini, who later spent the World War years in Berlin as an adviser to Hitler and Eichmann on the extermination of Jews and who was declared by the Allied Powers to be a war criminal.

When in 1948 the Arab States launched their war of total destruction against the nascent Jewish State, terror warfare became part of their arsenal. In the last twenty-four years, whenever the Arab regular armies have suffered defeat or felt hesitant about engaging in full-scale hostilities, they have resorted to terror carried out by special organizations established for that purpose.

Thus, to claim, as the Lebanese Government sometimes does, that terror operations from Lebanon are a function of the presence in that country of Palestinian refugees is to play on gullibility or ignorance. For almost two decades the Israel–Lebanese frontier served as an example of tranquillity and coexistence, while Palestinian refugees have lived in Lebanon since 1948. During that period Israeli and Lebanese farmers cultivated their land side by side. Israeli and Lebanese shepherds peacefully watched over their flocks in adjacent meadows. On the Israeli side a highway runs along the entire border only a few meters from Lebanese territory. A parallel road follows the length of the boundary on the Lebanese side. Visitors crowded into the beautiful countryside. Travelers waved to each other across the line. That remained the situation after 1967 as well, until the Arab Governments and the terror organizations sponsored by them decided that Lebanese territory would be the most appropriate base for continuing their aggression against Israel. The Syrian cease-fire line remained relatively calm because the Syrian authorities, fully in control of the terror organizations on Syrian soil, preferred that they operate from neighboring Lebanon. The Jordan River line quieted down when the Jordanian Government curtailed the terror organizations. The Lebanese Government, however, allowed the terror groups to turn Lebanon into their base of operations and to establish their headquarters in Beirut. From there their tentacles reach abroad.

The extent of terror warfare waged at any particular time from an Arab country has no correlation whatever to the presence or absence of Palestinians in that country or to their numbers. The Arab terror organizations, established, financed and equipped by Arab Governments and frequently commanded by officers seconded from regular Arab armies, operate whenever and wherever the Arab Governments allow them to operate. That is precisely what the Lebanese Government is doing today.

References to Arab terror warfare as Palestinian resistance are consequently utter distortions. Associations of freedom fighters in various parts of the world which represent the true struggle of peoples and their interests have categorically rejected all claims of Arab terror groups to the status and name of a resistance movement. The tranquillity, progress and development obtaining in Israeli-held territories, in which the Arab inhabitants can express freely their attitude toward coexistence with Israel, are evidence of how unrepresentative Arab terror organizations are of the Arab people and of their true interests. This has also been illustrated by the demonstrations held recently in a number of Lebanese localities against the presence of terror squads.

Arab terror has been from its very inception a method of warfare against the life of the Jewish people, against the independence of the Jewish State. It is a method born of blind hatred, steeped in cowardice, reflecting the failure of the Arab States to attain the objective of their war against Israel—the demolition of the State and the ravage of its people. This despicable mode of warfare, directed primarily against the civilian population, is a product of the fanaticism and bloodlust characteristic of Arab hostility toward Israel, which culminated in the heinous massacre at Lod Airport on May 30, 1972.

On that day three gunmen, who had arrived at Lod on a regular Air France flight en route from Paris and Rome, entered the passenger terminal, took out of their luggage automatic rifles and grenades and opened fire and hurled the grenades indiscriminately at the crowd at the airport. Twenty-five persons were killed and seventy-eight wounded. Among the dead were sixteen American Christian pilgrims from Puerto Rico, five of them women.

Two of the assailants were killed. The third, who was caught alive, testified that he and his accomplices were Japanese nationals recruited by an Arab terror organization known as the Popular Front, trained by it in a camp in the vicinity of Beirut and dispatched on their dastardly mission from Beirut. Immediately after the massacre, it was the Beirut headquarters of the Popular Front that announced its responsibility for the slaughter.

The Lod massacre took place shortly after Arab terrorists, again operating from Lebanon, had seized on May 8 a Sabena aircraft and prepared to blow it up with one hundred passengers aboard but were foiled by Israeli forces.

The entire world was aghast. Expressions of shock and condemnation of the Lod outrage came from Governments, organizations, public figures and media of information.

The Secretary General of the United Nations issued a statement that he was "shocked at this ruthless and irresponsible act of violence against innocent people in an international airport."

Pope Paul called the massacre at Lod "a senseless and atrocious crime."

Governments of Security Council members expressed their abhorrence.

The vile nature of Arab terror warfare against the Israeli people's existence was clearer than ever before. There seemed to be general recognition that such criminal ways could not be tolerated.

In the Arab States, however, there was macabre jubilation.

"The self-sacrifice in Lydda is a testimony of the greatness of those young men, which is parallel to the great justice of the Palestinian cause," announced a broadcast from Cairo on May 31. "The operation was effective," boasted the radio, "and without flaws, full of courage and placed the enemy in a state of fright and complete paralysis."

And the reactions in Syria were similar.

Egypt's Prime Minister, Aziz Sidky, gave the massacre the official

Arab blessing. On June 1 he declared, "I want to say that what happened at Lod proves that we can, with Allah's help, achieve victory in our battle with Israel. This is the only reaction I have on this matter." Then he proceeded to elaborate:

I want to speak about what the *fedayeen* wrought at Lod Airport. I want to refer to this subject from one aspect, which is the implication of the fact that three men with three submachine guns could succeed in accomplishing what occurred at Lod Airport. This action reveals the truth about Israel. Where is the talent, the genius, the organization and the supreme capability which are unequaled in the whole world?

When such are the reactions to premeditated carnage of innocent people; when such views are coupled with the indoctrination carried on for years that the State of Israel and its people should be annihilated, it is not surprising that the thirst for blood should remain unquenched and that vows be made to continue such crimes in the future.

Israel hoped that the international outcry, in the wake of the Lod massacre, against Arab terror attacks would restore the Arab Governments to reason. The Secretary General and various Governments tried to impress upon the Arab States, and especially upon Lebanon and Egypt, the need to terminate the terror operations. In letter after letter to the President of the Security Council, Israel called on the Governments of Lebanon and Egypt to put an end to the murderous operations of the terror organizations.

The Arab reaction was one of callousness and frivolity. In disregard for established and generally known facts and in brazen contempt for its obligations, the Lebanese Government simply disclaimed responsibility for the dastardly attacks initiated, planned and perpetrated from its territory. Yet it is a matter of common knowledge that Lebanon is today the main base for terror operations against Israel. Some five thousand terrorists are on Lebanese soil: some in the southern region, some in "Fatahland" and some in the east, close to the Syrian border. The terror squads are not confined to these areas; Lebanon as a whole is becoming to an increasing degree a stronghold of the terrorist organizations, and a base for their operations against Israel. Their political, propaganda, intelligence, welfare and medical centers are located in Beirut. Members of the organizations recruit, train and arm refugees, and dispatch gangs into Israel, unhindered by the Lebanese Government.

The image of a peace-loving little country which Lebanon is trying to project here is nothing but a cover for the hostile activities which the terror organizations are permitted to carry on in Lebanon with a view to sowing murder and destruction in Israel. The Lebanese Government is not a passive bystander; the support it has extended to the terror organizations has been active and tangible.

Thus, on November 3, 1969, an agreement of cooperation was formally concluded in Cairo between the Government of Lebanon and the terror organizations. General Emil Bustani, commander in chief of the Lebanese Army, signed on behalf of his Government. The notorious Yassir Arafat, who had said, "Peace for us means Israel's destruction and nothing else," signed for the terror organizations. That accord, supplemented by the additional agreements of February 1970, April 1970 and May 1970, constitutes the basis on which the terror squads continue to operate freely on Lebanese territory and from it.

There is no way in which the Lebanese Government could evade responsibility for those attacks. Like any Government in the world, the Lebanese Government must be held responsible for what is going on inside Lebanon. It is the Lebanese Government that is responsible for the agreement of cooperation with the terror organizations. Who, if not the Government of Lebanon, is accountable for harboring the headquarters of those organizations in Beirut and for permitting them to use Lebanese territory as a base for attacks on Israel? Who, if not the Lebanese Government, has allowed the high-ranking Syrian officers to plan and prepare operations hostile to Israel on Lebanese soil?

It is sheer arrogance and mockery to declare, as Lebanese spokesmen have, that Lebanon is not required to safeguard Israel's security. It has never been suggested that Lebanon should play such a role. However, it is the duty of the Lebanese Government to ensure that its territory is not used as a springboard for aggression against a neighboring State. That is a fundamental obligation under international law and the Charter of the United Nations. When Lebanon repudiates that obligation it leaves Israel no alternative but to act in self-defense. Lebanon cannot at one and the same time refuse to abide by its obligations in respect of international peace and security and expect that Israel, the victim of Lebanon's lawlessness, take no measures to protect itself and its citizens. That is precisely what Israel was compelled to do.

Israel's position is well known and well founded. The Jewish people has a right to freedom and independence, to peace and security, like any other nation. The Jewish people has struggled to restore this right in its homeland since the legions of the Roman Empire deprived it of its sovereignty. Israel will defend this right with all its strength and all its soul and all its heart. The sooner the Arab States recognize and respect this right and abandon their designs on the life of Israel and of its people, the sooner there will be peace in the Middle East.

Lebanon's resort to the Security Council falls into the familiar pattern of Lebanese duplicity. As long as it is Israel that is subjected to armed attacks, as long as Israelis are being murdered and maimed, the tenets of the United Nations Charter and the obligations under international law do not exist for Lebanon. The Lebanese Government calmly presides over a campaign of terror and slaughter and destruction pursued from its territory against the State of Israel and the people of Israel. It cynically disclaims responsibility. It arrogantly asserts that murder assaults perpetrated from its territory on Israeli citizens are of no concern to it. It refuses to stop these assaults and to suppress the terror organizations which carry them out. However, when Israel, as a last resort, acts on its own to defend itself and its people, the Lebanese Government suddenly finds use for law and the Charter of the United Nations. Having ignored, repudiated and trampled them, the Lebanese Government invokes international principles—not in order to repent and mend its ways but to justify its lawlessness and to encourage the continuation of warfare against Israel. In apparent ridicule of reason and justice, Lebanon calls for action against Israel; the criminal cries "thief." At a time when there is a growing feeling in the world that steps must be taken against countries supporting and abetting such terror operations as air piracy, at a time when voices are heard saying that the Security Council should have provided for firm measures against States which back or give refuge to those who attack innocent civilians, Lebanon has the audacity to suggest punishment of action against such criminals.

In fact it is the inability of the United Nations, throughout the years, to deal equitably and effectively with Arab aggression pursued against Israel since 1948 that has been one of the most serious international failings. For years Israel has called on the Security Council to take action to try to stop Arab armed attacks against Israel and its people. The Security Council has remained silent. Whether because of the veto or because of its composition, the Council has been unable to condemn even the murder in cold blood of innocent Israeli citizens, perpetrated in attacks from neighboring Arab States. The fact that Israeli prisoners of war have languished for years in Syrian and Egyptian captivity and that the Arab Governments have refused to agree to an exchange of prisoners with Israel has gone unnoticed.

If one examines Security Council resolutions it appears as if Jewish blood, Jewish suffering and Jewish grief are of no concern to it. It is only when Israel, as a last resort, strikes back in self-defense, to repel and avert attacks, to protect the lives of its citizens, that the Council seems to awaken to action. This is a double standard which is contrary to the fundamental principles of the Charter. This is a double standard which neither the Government of Israel nor any other Government of good faith can accept. Whether this will be corrected remains up to the Security Council. For its part, Israel will continue to seek and hope for peace with its neighbors, but it will also remain steadfast in its defense against all aggression, terror and violence directed against it.

III

Statement delivered August 13, 1973, in the Security Council, convened at Lebanon's request following an abortive attempt by Israel to capture George Habash, leader of the Marxist "Popular Front for the Liberation of Palestine" (PFLP). Habash, whose group had claimed responsibility for

numerous acts of terror, including murder, sabotage and hijacking, was
thought to be on a Lebanese aircraft diverted to Israel. He had confirmed,
later on, that it was his intention to board that particular plane and had
changed his plans only at the last minute.

In Beirut and Damascus, in Cairo, Baghdad and Tripoli, Arab Governments are sheltering and assisting murder gangs openly engaged in the indiscriminate killing of innocent civilians at international airports, in air piracy by hijacking and blowing up passenger aircraft, in the slaughter of athletes, diplomats and other defenseless persons. These savage atrocities are being perpetrated for the avowed purpose of destroying a member State of the United Nations and depriving its people of the right to self-determination and independence. There is not a single precept of law and morality that these bloodthirsty murderers of guiltless men, women and children are not violating. There is not a single principle of international law and of the Charter of the United Nations that is not torn asunder by the Arab Governments which harbor, protect and connive with the terror organizations.

Yet these selfsame Governments object when Israel refuses to acquiesce in the persistent attacks on its life and on the lives of its citizens and takes measures to defend itself and to eradicate the scourge of barbaric terrorism. The organizers of the Lod massacre are still on the loose. The surviving murderers of the Israeli athletes in Munich have been released to the Arab States, where they were given a hero's welcome. The leaders of Al Fatah and its organ Black September, the Popular Front and similar organizations are still in their headquarters in Arab capitals, traveling freely from one conference to another, mapping out the slaughter of innocents. Lenanon and Iraq and Egypt feel, however, that Israel must do nothing about it. Israel categorically rejects such counsel. Those who have turned the world into a dangerous jungle cannot complain that the man-killing beasts in it are being pursued, or that the pursuit is conducted not necessarily in white silken gloves.

On the one hand, there is thus heinous premeditated murder; on the other, there is an effort to prevent murder. On the one hand, there is merciless random killing for the sake of killing; on the other, there is an attempt to seize killers but to avoid hurting the innocent. Enlightened world opinion will not fail to notice that the Security Council was convened to discuss a two-hour detention of an airplane for the purpose of weeding out international murderers, while silence had been imposed on the Council regarding the carnage in Athens, Khartoum, Munich and Lod.

The Arab terrorists, operating with the permission, support and complicity of Arab Governments, stand accused of waging a persistent campaign of worldwide bloodshed directed against helpless civilians in utter mockery of the sovereignty of States and of fundamental human rights. Juxtaposed to this is the Arab charge that in the pursuit of such terrorists Israel had entered into Lebanese airspace and diverted a Lebanese airplane. Surely the sanctity of human life comes before the sanctity of air—all the more so when a State allows its territory and its airspace to be used for the promotion of terror warfare against a neighboring country.

Only if international concepts are completely warped and principles of humanity callously disregarded can exception be taken to the struggle against international terrorism and air piracy waged by Israel. This struggle is directed against criminals who endanger the very fabric of international relations. If others are affected, it is only an incidental occurrence that cannot override the necessity and legitimacy of the struggle. No formalistic argumentation can justify interference with efforts to put an end to premeditated, indiscriminate murder. Only if we agree to live in a world of inverted values can international terrorism and air piracy, as carried on by the Arab murder organizations, be allowed to invoke some legal notions derived from entirely different circumstances and to seek protection behind them. The murderers of children on school buses, the dispatchers of letter bombs through the mails, the barbarians who kill men, women and children at airports and in civil aircraft have no right to refuge in town or village, on the ground or in the air. Mankind is confronted today with a situation similar to the days when pirates roamed the seven seas attacking ships, killing, maiming and taking hostages. As it was then in the case of the seas, striking today at air pirates and terrorists—enemies of mankind—is imperative and justified at all times and everywhere.

Measures by individual States against terrorism have become even more urgent and indispensable as a result of the sabotage by Arab States of all international action. The attempt at last year's General Assembly session to take concrete steps for the suppression of terrorism was torpedoed by Arab delegations and their supporters. They did the same in the Ad Hoc Committee on Terrorism, which, in a session lasting four weeks, devoted only two days to the examination of measures against terrorist attacks and ended its discussions in dismal failure and utter helplessness. The absence of effective international action against terrorism is dramatically illustrated, for instance, by the fact that seventy of the 110 Arab terror agents apprehended in various countries, including members of this Council, have been freed without trial or punishment and allowed to rejoin their murder organizations in Arab States. These developments have undoubtedly encouraged the terror groups to pursue their nefarious crimes.

Israel, still warding off Arab warfare launched against it twenty-five years ago, cannot forgo its right to self-defense and the duty to protect its citizens, merely because Arab Governments have thwarted international measures against terrorism. Neither can Israel forgo military defense action against terrorism, said to be improper in normal international conditions, while Arab States are actively carrying on with their belligerency and permit Arab attacks against Israel to be organized and initiated from their territories. The Government of Israel has always observed, and will continue to observe, the cease-fire on the basis of reciprocity. By permitting the use of their territories as bases for armed attacks against Israel, by harboring the headquarters and training camps of the terror organizations, by allowing leaders of the murder squads to dwell in and move freely in and out of their cities, Arab Governments are guilty of flagrant violations of the cease-fire. By making it possible for murderers such as Yassir Arafat and George Habash to operate from Beirut, to fly abroad without hindrance and then to return to Beirut, the Lebanese authorities show no regard for Israel's rights under the cease-fire and, therefore, cannot complain that Israel does not respect their rights.

As for Iraq, which has joined Lebanon's complaint, it has not even accepted the 1967 cease-fire. In fact, following the 1948 Arab invasion of Israel, in which it had participated, Iraq refused to conclude an armistice and has continued ever since to negate Israel's right to independence, repeatedly rejecting all thought of peace with Israel. Iraq, through its representative, declared again today that independent Israel, a member of the United Nations, is "occupied Palestine." Simultaneously, Iraq has been a principal supporter of terror warfare against Israel, with George Habash and his Popular Front as the objects of special Iraqi attention and assistance. The Iraqi position on terrorist activities has been expressed as follows in the Government-controlled daily *Al Noor:* "Seizing Israeli planes and their destruction, kidnapping Israelis and people serving the Israelis, bombing Israeli institutions and paralyzing Israel's information media—this strengthens the resistance movement, and its influence is no less effective than that of military operations."

In its attitude toward Israel, Iraq has thus completely repudiated international law and the Charter of the United Nations. It is farcical for Iraq to base any of its arguments on principles of law or provisions of the Charter. Nothing could throw more light on the situation confronting Israel than Iraq's aligning itself with Lebanon's complaint to reiterate in the Security Council the view that Israel has no right to exist. May I suggest that members of the Council ponder over this aspect of the problem before pronouncing themselves on Israel's struggle to vindicate its right to live.

Egypt too has joined the chorus. It is never a surprise when Egypt rushes to the defense of Arab terrorism and the Arab terrorist organizations. Without Egypt, there would have been no terror warfare in the Middle East. Without Egypt there would have been no massacres at Lod, at Munich and at Athens. After the 1948 defeat of the invasion of Israel by Arab States, headed by Egypt, it was the Egyptian Government that organized the first murder squads and sent them out on their missions of death against Israeli schoolchildren in their classrooms, against Israeli women asleep at night in their houses, against Israeli men at work in the fields. While Beirut has become in recent years the principal operational headquarters of Arab international terrorism, Cairo is undoubtedly its political capital. This was expressed as follows in a statement by President Sadat on April 6, 1972, at a conference in Cairo of all the terrorist groups.

We have come together once again at one of your assemblies which you generally hold in Cairo, your meeting place and your home. I do not believe that this is a matter of chance; no, I do not see it even as a deliberate choice, but as something natural, a matter of course. For you and for us, there is nothing before us but to fight.

The assistance given to the terrorist groups was summed up by President Sadat in an interview published in a Lebanese newspaper, *Al Bayrak,* on January 8, 1973. To the question "To what extent do you assist the fedayeen?," Egypt's President replied, "Our assistance is unlimited."

We still remember how on June 1, 1972, the Prime Minister of Egypt publicly praised the massacre at Lod. We still remember how the Egyptian Government refused the request of the Government of the Federal Republic of Germany to try to avert the slaughter of Israeli sportsmen at the Munich Olympic Games.

We all know that should the Egyptian Government so desire, the terror organizations would cease to exist. As long as they continue their criminal operations, Egypt will be held responsible for their bloody atrocities.

By now, little credence is given to the hackneyed pretexts in Lebanon's or Egypt's vain attempts to justify support for Arab terrorism against Israel. By now all know and remember that the objective of the Habashes and Arafats is not to bring about Israeli withdrawal from the cease-fire lines, but to eliminate Israel as a sovereign State and to annihilate its people. All are aware that Arab terrorism, aimed against the Jewish people's right to self-determination, began fifty years ago, and not in 1967. Those who are acquainted with the true situation in Israeli-held territories and the attitude of their inhabitants need no convincing that the paid killers operating from Lebanon or other Arab States are not representative of the Arab population of those territories or of Palestinian Arabs in Arab States. Indeed, the allegation that terrorism is the product of the Palestinian-refugee problem cannot stand up to any serious examination. It is a fact that for two decades the presence of large numbers of refugees in Lebanon had not given rise to any terrorist operations on or from Lebanese soil and that such operations began only when Jordan suppressed the terror organizations and it was consequently decided to move their centers and their bases to Lebanon. The whitewashing of the terrorist groups and their notorious leaders ill behooves the representative of a Government which only recently described them as "an army of occupation" and even had to fight off their attacks in various parts of the country, including the UNRWA refugee camps. The Lebanese authorities' failure to curb this terrorist army of occupation does not change the latter's character, nor the fact that it constitutes a threat against which Israel is entitled to act.

This is illustrated to the full by the activities of the Popular Front and its leader, George Habash, who was thought to be on the Lebanese aircraft diverted to Israel. As a matter of fact, Habash himself has confirmed, in the meantime, that it was his intention to board that particular plane and that he changed his plans only in the last minute.

The following are some of the attacks carried out by him and his organization.

(1) July 23, 1968: An El Al airliner en route from Rome to Israel was hijacked and taken to Algiers. The hijackers were immediately released by the Algerian Government, but the Israeli passengers were held as hostages. Under pressure of world opinion, the ten Israeli women and children passengers were released on July 27, but the twelve men were detained for five weeks, until August 31.

(2) December 26, 1968: An El Al plane was attacked at Athens Airport. One Israeli passenger was killed and a stewardess wounded. Two of the Arab terrorists were detained by the Greek authorities.

(3) February 18, 1969: A terror squad of the Popular Front

opened fire on an El Al plane about to take off from Zurich, killing one member of the crew. The assailants were arrested, tried by a Swiss court and sentenced to terms of imprisonment.

(4) August 29, 1969: A TWA airliner en route from Rome to Tel Aviv was hijacked to Damascus by three Popular Front members. After passengers had disembarked there, an explosive charge was set off, causing serious damage to the plane. Two Israeli civilians traveling on the plane were imprisoned by the Syrian authorities for ninety-eight days.

(5) December 17, 1969: Two British citizens, hired by agents of the Popular Front, were arrested in the act of attempting to blow up an El Al plane at London Airport. Convicted by a court in London they were sentenced to ten years' imprisonment. The Egyptian military attaché, who was involved in the case, left London.

(6) December 21, 1969: Two Lebanese citizens, agents of the Popular Front, were arrested in Athens and charged with conspiring to hijack a TWA airliner.

(7) February 21, 1970: Members of the Popular Front placed a bomb in a Swissair plane en route from Zurich to Tel Aviv, causing its explosion in midair. Forty-seven passengers and crew lost their lives.

(8) September 6, 1970: Three aircraft of Pan American, TWA and Swissair respectively were hijacked by terrorists of the George Habash group. The Pan American plane was taken to Cairo, after a stopover in Beirut. The Arab hijackers placed explosive charges on the plane. On arrival in Cairo the passengers were allowed to disembark and the aircraft was blown up. The TWA and Swissair planes were diverted to Zerqa, Jordan. The hijackers held several hundred passengers as hostages and demanded the release of all Arab terrorists detained in the United Kingdom, Switzerland and Germany. On the same day terrorists of the Popular Front tried to seize an El Al plane in flight from Amsterdam to New York, but were overpowered by members of the crew. One hijacker was killed in the struggle, and the other was handed over to the British authorities when the plane made an emergency landing in London.

(9) September 9, 1970: A BOAC airliner on its way from Bahrain to London was hijacked by a squad of the Popular Front and forced to land in Jordan, its passengers joining the others at Zerqa, already there, as hostages. In exchange for the release of these passengers, all the Arab hijackers detained in the United Kingdom, Switzerland and Germany were set free. The BOAC, TWA and Swissair planes were blown up by the terrorists.

(10) February 22, 1972: A Lufthansa airplane was seized by Arab hijackers and forced to land at Aden in the People's Democratic Republic of Yemen. Negotiations for the payment of ransom to the Popular Front were then conducted in Lebanon, and a sum of five million dollars was paid to the terror organization for the release of the plane. It was widely reported at the time that the sum of a million dollars had been retained by the Government of the Democratic Republic of Yemen.

(11) May 30, 1972: Three Japanese mercenaries trained in Lebanon by the Popular Front arrived at Lod Airport on an Air France flight from Rome. With submachine guns and hand grenades extracted from their luggage in the passenger terminal, they murdered twenty-four passengers and wounded seventy-eight. Two of the attackers were killed, and a third was captured, tried and sentenced to imprisonment in Israel.

(12) December 1972: A terror squad of the Popular Front left Lebanon with instructions to reach Haifa by ship with a view to perpetrating terrorist attacks or, if unsuccessful, committing suicide. The squad was discovered in Greece and its members were returned to Beirut.

George Habash's views could be summarized by the following excerpts from his statements which appeared in the Popular Front's organ *Al Hadaf*, on Radio Baghdad, in *Life* Magazine and in the German weekly *Stern:*

The objective is to put an end to Israel's existence.

It is our right to hit the enemy anywhere.

To kill a Jew far from the battlefield has more of an effect than killing a hundred of them in battle; it attracts more attention.

Of course we do not want peace. Peace would mean the end of our hopes. . . . We will continue in the future to sabotage every peace effort. . . . If that is the only way to destroy Israel, Zionism and Arab reaction, then we want a third world war.

There is no question why Israel tried on August 10 to apprehend an archcriminal like Habash, responsible for so many savage atrocities.

The real question is: Why is Habash still free? Why is it that he and others like him are permitted by the Lebanese Government—in violation of international law and the Charter of the United Nations —to continue to plot and perpetrate the killing of innocent men, women and children? Why is Beirut still the planning center and staging base for terrorist operations such as the Lod and Athens massacres? Why is the 1969 Cairo agreement between the Lebanese Government and the terrorist organizations which granted the murder groups freedom of operation within the country and turned the Lebanese Government into their partner still in force? Why do Arab Governments continue to support and subsidize Habash's Popular Front and other terrorist organizations such as Black September/Al Fatah? Why do certain non-Arab Governments consort with the Habashes and the Arafats? Those are some of the questions that confront the Security Council and other United Nations organs if they are to act effecively against international terrorism.

However, it is clear that the objective of the Arab convocation of the Council is precisely the very opposite. It is evident that, having prevented United Nations action against terrorism, the Arab States— led this time by Lebanon—seek to exploit once more the sheer weight of their numbers in order to demand action against the victims of Arab terrorism. Nothing could be more ridiculous and dangerous than focusing on Israel's act of self-defense against the continuous onslaught of terrorism and letting off scot free the barbaric murderers of Athens, Lod and Munich and the Arab Governments which are backing them. That is what has happened in Security Council debates on several occasions in the past.

Israel warned at the time that surrender to the Arab designs in the Council would encourage the terrorist organizations in their campaign of murder. That is in fact what has taken place. The terrorist attacks have increased and their bestiality has intensified.

The failure of United Nations organs to take effective steps against the plague of terrorism sweeping across the world is grave enough. This failure must not be compounded by Security Council action that would give further satisfaction and encouragement to the carriers of this plague.

It is Israel's fervent hope that the international community will overcome the obstacles put in its way and curb international terrorism. Israel on its part stands ready to cooperate with all international efforts to stamp out terrorism, and in particular to ensure the safety and security of international air travel. Are the Arab States also ready to pledge themselves to this objective? Are they prepared to undertake to act against the hijacking of aircraft by Arab terrorists, to act against the blowing up of planes in the air and on the ground, to act against sanguinary attacks on innocent passengers at air terminals? Will Lebanon and Iraq and Egypt give such pledges right here and now? It is on them and on other Arab Governments that the security of international travel and communications will depend. If they decide to abide by their international obligations, if they terminate terrorist operations, there will obviously be no need for defensive action against terrorism as on August 10.

In the meantime what is to be done? The international community has thus far been unable to take measures against the Arab campaign of murder and atrocity. Is Israel to watch passively as the terrorists strike again and again, shedding innocent blood? Are rules of international conduct to be twisted in such a way as to protect murderers and brand their victims? Is the supreme right of self-defense enshrined in the Charter to be adulterated by the distorted concepts used by those who claim that the killing of Israelis by the Habashes and the Arafats is understandable and legitimate, but that Israel's striking back at its assailants is not?

Even in everyday life a citizen who calls for the assistance of the authorities against an assailant and fails to obtain help is entitled to act on his own in self-defense and to effect what is known as a "citizen's arrest"—and this although it may involve crossing into a neighbor's courtyard where the criminal has found refuge. This is Israel's sole objective: to stop the orgy of bloodshed by Arab terror groups.

Israel will continue to hope that the United Nations will live up to its responsibilities and strive toward the same objective. However, self-preservation, self-defense, the protection of its people are obligations which a Government must be prepared to fulfill even if it has to act on its own. The Government of Israel will fulfill them.

Israel's strongest aspiration is to attain peace with its Arab neighbors. The terrorist organizations are openly fighting against peace in the most despicable manner—by indiscriminate murder of the innocent and defenseless. Those who really want peace in the Middle East will work together with Israel to put an end to this campaign of morbid bloodlust.

IV

On September 5, 1972, eleven members of Israel's Olympic team were murdered by a terror squad of Al Fatah/ Black September in Munich. Following the massacre, the Secretary General of the United Nations requested the General Assembly to discuss the question of international terrorism and the measures to prevent it. The item was transferred from the Assembly plenary to the Sixth Committee (the Judiciary Committee) and was buried there as a result of Arab pressure.

The following statement was delivered in the Sixth Committee on November 16, 1972.

When the Secretary General of the United Nations requested the Twenty-seventh Session of the General Assembly to discuss measures for the prevention of terrorism and other forms of violence which endanger or take innocent human lives or jeopardize fundamental freedoms, he declared:

The world has been plagued, on an increasing scale, by acts of terrorism which have taken the lives not only of national leaders and diplomatic envoys, but also other human beings whose only offense lay in their race, religion or national origin, and even innocent bystanders. These acts of violence have created throughout the world a climate of fear from which no one is immune.

The Secretary General considers that the current trend toward terrorism and senseless violence is so alarming and has such grave implications that it should be considered by the General Assembly, with the hope that agreed measures can be found which will help to reverse this trend and prevent such tragedies in the future.

It is clear what acts of terrorism are currently plaguing the world. It is clear what recent tragedies have alarmed and shocked the international community. It is clear what crimes of senseless violence the United Nations are called upon to prevent. Munich and Lod are still fresh in everyone's memory. So is the blowing up of civil aircraft in midair. The letter bombs continue to be distributed through the mails.

To the enlightened world the criminality of such acts is obvious. No philosophical or sociological studies are needed to establish it. They are assaults on elementary principles of civilized behavior. They have been condemned by Governments and by public opinion in Africa and Asia, in the Americas and in Europe. What is required at this stage is a concerted effort to stamp out these atrocities before they plunge mankind into barbarism.

International terrorism is manifesting itself in various forms in different parts of the world. The United Nations must remain alert to all these manifestations. One cannot, however, shut one's eyes to the fact that the most vicious and persistent terror crimes are those originating with terrorist organizations in the Middle East.

If as stated by the Secretary General there have been victims of terrorism "whose only offense lay in their race, religion or national origin," these are the citizens of Israel and Jews in general. Israel cannot therefore approach the problem of international terrorism with academic equanimity. Jewish blood is being shed again in brutal outrages in the Middle East, in Europe and elsewhere. For Israel this is not a time for serenity or silence. All too frequently through the ages Jews have been subjected to terrorism and bestiality while the world stood by in silence or weighed the propriety of action till it was too late.

It is not our intention to engage in polemics, but it is our duty to raise our voice in the United Nations debate on international terrorism against the vicious campaign of indiscriminate murder directed against the Jewish people.

The generally felt shock and indignation at this campaign is due in large measure to its particularly sinister features.

First, the atrocities to which Jews in Israel and abroad have been subjected are conceived, initiated, organized and perpetrated as assaults on innocent civilians. The ambushing of school buses, the detonation of explosive charges in supermarkets crowded with women shoppers, the murder of athletes at Munich are all acts purposely directed at defenseless civilians.

Secondly, these crimes are planned and executed in a manner in which the killing is indiscriminate. It does not matter to the assailants who the victims are. The blowing up of civil aircraft in flight, the slaughter of passengers who happen to be at an air terminal are not concerned with the identity of the casualties. The aim is murder for murder's sake.

In fact, in the words of a leader of one of the terror organizations interviewed some time ago by the London *Daily Mail,* it is immaterial who the dead are "so long as they are Jews." This is one of the most revolting aspects of the terrorist campaign. In a way reminiscent of the Nazi atrocities against the Jews of Europe, Jewish people in various parts of the globe have been earmarked for physical destruction. In Israel, every Jew, whether man, woman or child, is considered a target for murder, but the plague has spread to other regions. Already in 1970 Arab terrorists set fire to a Jewish home for the aged in Germany, killing seven of its innocent elderly inhabitants. Recently booby-trapped letters have been sent to a Jewish home for the aged in Frankfurt. A Jewish welfare organization in Rome has received similar letters. So did Jewish women in New York active in an organization devoted to medical assistance. Jewish businessmen in the United Kingdom have been showered with the deadly envelopes.

Non-Jews have frequently fallen victim to these assaults. At times the terrorist groups direct their murderous attacks even against Arabs.

These characteristics of the campaign of atrocities conducted against Israel and the Jewish people: the fact that it is directed by premeditation against guiltless civilians, the fact that it aims at indiscriminate murder for murder's sake and the fact that it regards Jews everywhere as targets for physical destruction, are sufficient to make it a heinous onslaught on humanity requiring effective countermeasures.

The barbarism of this onslaught is further deepened by its openly declared objective—to destroy a State member of the United Nations and to wrest from the Jewish people its rights to self-determination, freedom and independence. This is the banner under which Jewish blood is spilled. It is in the name of this savage goal that men, women and children are being slaughtered.

Mankind is confronted here with a design to murder individual members of a people in the hope that this would eventually bring about the annihilation of the people as a whole. It is a design to take the life of individual Jews so as to deprive the entire Jewish people of the rights enjoyed by other nations.

Yet the Arab Governments have unleashed a campaign to shatter the Jewish people's national existence and destroy its sovereign State restored in part of the ancient Jewish homeland. There is no objective that could be more despicable. Violence has rarely been put in the service of so criminal a cause. Not since the days of Hitler have Jews been the target of a campaign of premeditated slaughter. Not since Hitler have Governments praised the planned indiscriminate murder of Jews. Not since the Nazi SS and their Einsatz Commandos have organizations acting with governmental blessing gloated over the blood of innocent Jews, men, women and children, shed in bestial atrocities. Arab terrorism is doing that again. Arab terrorist organizations are again engaged in such outrages. Again there are Governments, the Arab Governments, that stand behind crimes which draw inspiration from the genocide of the Jewish people by the Hitlerite hordes.

The historic and ideological affinity between the Nazi atrocities and Arab terrorism is well known.

Only ignorance, gullibility or willful malevolence will accept the propaganda distortion that Arab terrorism is a result of the 1967 hostilities. In fact this reprehensible mode of bloodshed had its beginnings half a century earlier.

The spiritual father and organizer of Arab terrorism is the notorious Haj Amin el Husseini, the former Mufti of Jerusalem, who initiated in the 1920s a campaign of violence and terror against the Jews of Palestine. On April 4 of that year Husseini launched an attack on the Jews of the Old City of Jerusalem, massacring, burning and pillaging during four days. The following year forty-seven Jews were killed in terrorist attacks. Then came other assaults such as the massacre of the Jewish communities of Hebron and Safad in 1929 in which 133 defenseless Jewish men, women and children were slaughtered and 339 wounded. The campaign of terror and murder continued under the same leadership during the 1930s. Throughout this period Husseini maintained close contact with the Hitler regime. When World War II broke out he went to Berlin, where he acted as Hitler's and Eichmann's adviser in the extermination of European Jewry. The Allies declared him a war criminal. After the war he was arrested, but escaped and made his way back to the Middle East. This is the man who initiated Arab terrorism and conducted it for twenty years. This is the man who, though a war criminal on the Allied Powers' wanted list, is free today in the Arab States to pursue his nefarious activities and to continue the incitement to shed Jewish blood.

This is the true face of Arab terrorism. Since Israel's independence in 1948, terror warfare has been used during those periods in the continuing Arab war against Israel when attack by regular Arab military forces appeared too hazardous. This is what happened in the 1950s and in the 1960s. This is what is taking place today.

Just as the Hitlerite Mufti Haj Amin el Husseini, in a frenzy of anti-Jewish fanaticism not shared by the majority of the Arab people, organized in the 1920s the first terrorist gangs to murder innocent civilians, so have the Arab Governments established or encouraged terror squads to carry on their onslaught on the Jewish State when their attempt to stifle its independence failed in 1948. The first murder

f confusion, misrepresentation of concepts and terms,
ation of United Nations helplessness on this grave prob-
as a call to responsible Governments to redouble their
inst terrorism and to strike even harder at its initiators,
d supporters.

overnments must understand that the scourge of terror,
r and atrocities will be rooted out as the Nazi scourge
ades ago. The only question is whether the United Na-
a role in this or remain on the sidelines.

ollow with attention the course of the debate and draw
onclusions in respect of the measures it is duty-bound to
errorism. So, undoubtedly, will other responsible Gov-

squads were organized by the Egyptian Government in Gaza and
Sinai. They were named *fedayeen,* and their flag appropriately enough
was the old SS emblem—the skull and bones on a black background.
In the early 1950s they launched a campaign of incursions into Israel,
blowing up houses with their inhabitants asleep, throwing grenades
into classrooms, ambushing civilian buses on highways.

These crimes were brought to an end in 1956 when Israel destroyed
the *fedayeen* bases in Sinai and Gaza. Terror warfare moved, however,
to Israel's eastern and northern frontiers. El Fatah was established in
the late 1950s and began its armed attacks in 1965 on the initiative of
the Syrian Government.

Indeed, the 1960s were years of growing armed forays by terrorist
gangs from Jordan and particularly from Syria directed against Israeli
civilians in towns and villages, on the roads and in the field. This campaign of cruel violence and murder against the people of Israel was
one of the factors that contributed to the outbreak of the 1967 hostilities.

Again defeated in their design "to strike," in the words of President
Nasser, "the death blow at Israel's existence," the Arab States turned
once more to terror warfare. Frustrated in their effort to undermine
the Jewish people's determination to defend its inalienable rights,
taken aback by the refusal of the Arab inhabitants of Israeli-administered areas to cooperate with them, the terror organizations began
to have recourse to increasingly barbaric methods, trying in this manner to earn at least international attention. They have. Savage outrages
became their trademark. The world suddenly realized that no one, nowhere was safe from the atrocities of Arab terrorists. Their crimes
became a plague that is threatening to destroy the fabric of international life.

The initiators and perpetrators of this campaign of terror have been
trying to conceal its true nature behind a screen of borrowed slogans
and misappropriated ideals. The objective of destroying the sole Jewish
sovereignty is explained away as "purification" of the land and a struggle against aggression. An unabashed effort to wrest the right of self-
determination from the Jewish people of Israel is presented as a war

of liberation in the name of self-determination. The indiscriminate and cowardly murder of innocent Jewish civilians is hailed as heroism. Gangs unrepresentative of the Arab population and composed of paid assassins, foreign mercenaries and military personnel from regular Arab armies are depicted as champions of lofty ideals and humane values.

The Nazi roots of Haj Amin el Husseini, the counsels of the Nazi propaganda advisers employed by Egypt and Syria, are bearing fruit. The Nazis too killed Jews saying that they were purifying the land. They too shed Jewish blood under the pretext that they were liberating Germany and then Europe from the Jews. The Nazis too awarded the laurels of heroism to the slaughterers of Jewish women and children.

No semantic contortions can remove the stigma of savage bloodshed from the Arab terrorist organizations and the Arab Governments which are backing them.

In view of these facts it is not surprising that the Arab delegations should have fought against the discussion of international terrorism by the United Nations. It is not surprising that the Arab delegations should now be trying to sabotage the debate on measures against terrorism. They have already done so on the question of the prevention and punishment of crimes against diplomatic agents and other internationally protected persons. By distortion and confusion of the meaning of international terrorism, by pressing for delay and inaction, they are doing their utmost to bring this discussion to naught despite the worldwide desire to put an end to atrocities such as the Lod massacre and the Munich killings.

There can be no silence about this sabotage. The mask of academic phraseology under which it is being carried on must be torn off. Compromise with this sabotage would mean compromise with the continuation of terrorism. The international community must beware of procedures and terminology that could be used as excuses for the pursuance of outrages such as Lod and Munich and the hijacking or detonation of civil aircraft. The response to those who seek to undermine international action against terrorism is not accommodation with them. It is that international terrorism may be working in their favor today but might be turned against them in the future.

The key to combating int Governments taken individual

Thus it is a matter of genera no Arab terrorism were it not tary, financial and political, gi the latter were to stop supporti the world would be saved from by international terrorism. It is Governments to abide by their i all activities and eliminate withi and hideouts of organizations en Arab States must be made to rea remain the source of a plague spr

In addition to Governments fro murder is being conducted, action affected by this campaign. Some ready initiated measures against in doubtedly be borne in mind is that particular State encourages and bre all States. International terrorism c and West, between socialist and cap

Israel will support all effective scourge. In its view the General As condemn international terrorism; (b) giving any assistance, shelter or pro acts; (c) call on all States to extradite to trial; (d) convene a conference wl tional convention for submission to th General Assembly; (e) call on all state conventions on the prevention and pu rorism.

The Arab sabotage effort may, of c outcome of the present debate. Howev action against international terrorism. In effectiveness of the discussion here emp ments to take action by themselves and

Every display and every indic lem will serve own efforts ag perpetrators a

The Arab wanton murd was a few de tions will play

Israel will appropriate c take against ernments.

3 The PLO: An Antiliberation Movement

I

On October 14, 1974, the United Nations General Assembly adopted a resolution which invited the "Palestine Liberation Organization" (PLO) "to participate in the deliberations of the General Assembly on the question of Palestine." The following statement was delivered in the General Assembly before the adoption of the resolution.

The declared purpose of the United Nations is "to save [mankind] from the scourge of war," but today it is being asked to extend its facilities to those who live by war and violence waged against the fundamental precepts of the United Nations Charter. For years the United Nations has tried to combat international terrorism. Now it is called upon to welcome those who have turned the premeditated murder of innocent children, women and men into a profession.

The so-called Palestine Liberation Organization (PLO) did not emerge from within the Palestinian community. It was the first summit meeting of Arab Governments held in Cairo in January 1964 that decided to establish an organization under the cover of which terror warfare would be pursued and intensified against Israel. They named it the PLO and assigned its leadership to the infamous Ahmed Shukairi. Under the umbrella of that organization were brought all the existing terrorist groups, such as Al Fatah, established by the Intelligence Branch of the Syrian Army in the late 1950s, and the other terror organizations formed since then. Though one group has recently withdrawn from the Executive Council of the PLO, none has left the organization as such.

There was no pretense at the time of its establishment that the PLO was in any way representative of Palestinians. There is no room for such pretense today. The organization has never been anything other than a mere instrument of those who have been conducting a campaign of savage atrocities aimed explicitly at the destruction of Israel. It represents only itself—namely, the approximately ten thousand murderers trained and paid for the slaughter of innocent human beings. To equate them with the Palestinian community is to do a grave injustice to the latter.

Surely if peace is to be attained in the Middle East, the Palestinians must not be identified with those who wage war against peace and revel in barbaric bloodshed.

The covenant of the PLO, adopted in May 1964, as amended in 1968, stipulates *inter alia:*

Article 19: . . . the establishment of Israel is fundamentally null and void . . .

Article 20: The claim of a historical or spiritual tie between Jews and Palestine does not tally with historical realities . . . The Jews are not one people with an independent personality.

Article 22: . . . the liberation of Palestine will liquidate the Zionist imperialist presence in Palestine.

Article 9: Armed struggle is the only way to liberate Palestine and is therefore a strategy and not tactics.

Also, according to the covenant, only Jews who lived in Palestine in 1917—I repeat, in 1917—would be allowed to remain.

The official PLO information publications and the statements of its leaders are even more explicit. For example, the Al Fatah manual No. 8, entitled "The Liberation of the Occupied Lands and the Struggle Against Direct Imperialism," declares:

Liberation action is not only the removal of an armed imperialist base, but—more important—the destruction of a society. [Our] armed violence will be expressed in many ways. In addition to the destruction of the military force of the Zionist occupying State, it will also be turned toward the destruction of the means of life of the Zionist society in all its forms— industrial, agricultural and financial. The armed violence must seek to destroy the military, political, economic, financial and ideological institutions of the Zionist occupying State, so as to prevent all possibility of the growth of a new Zionist society.

The aim of the Palestinian liberation war is not only to inflict a military defeat but also to destroy the Zionist character of the occupied land, whether it is human or social.

In recent years this objective has sometimes been presented, for obvious propaganda reasons, under the guise of the slogan of a "democratic de-Zionized Palestine" in which Moslems, Christians and Jews would live, allegedly, in harmony and peace.

Appearing on French television on May 31, 1974, Yassir Arafat, head of the PLO and its largest component grouping Al Fatah/Black September, explained that the establishment of the so-called "democratic State in which Moslems, Christians and Jews will coexist" is merely "a civilized slogan."

In fact, there are such supposedly democratic Arab States—for instance Yemen and Algeria—from which the entire Jewish populations were fortunate to escape to Israel. Another example is Syria, and the entire world knows full well the plight in which its ancient Jewish community finds itself today and has been throughout the centuries.

The joint communiqué issued on June 15, 1974, by Yassir Arafat and President Qaddafi, following Arafat's visit to Libya, stated: "The Libyan revolution . . . supports the Palestine revolution . . . until all the Palestinian soil is liberated and the Arab struggle achieves its aim of establishing Arabism and freedom in Palestine."

In a speech he made in Tripoli two days earlier, on June 13, 1974, Arafat announced: "We shall drench with our blood every inch of our land. As this Arab land [Libya] has been freed from American defilement, so our Palestine land is being freed from Zionist defilement."

The objective is therefore clear, under whatever propaganda slogan it appears.

Zuhier Muhsin, a member of the PLO Executive and head of its military department, said on September 26, 1974, "Israel will not remain, in any of its parts, not even in Tel Aviv."

Arafat himself declared recently in Cairo, "Our progress will stop only in Tel Aviv, when we will create our Palestinian Democratic State."

Speaking on December 7, 1973, at the Beirut Arab University, Naif Hawatmeh, another PLO leader, who is sometimes presented as, supposedly, especially moderate, stated that he "supports the liquidation of the State of Israel and the uprooting of the Zionist entity."

On April 23, 1974, Ahmed Jibril, leader of another PLO murder group, proclaimed at a rally in Kuwait: "The struggle between us and Israel is one of existence. It is either we or they. We will not allow American or Soviet Jews to remain in Palestine. We will scatter anew the Jews who came from Arab lands."

At its most recent meeting, held in Cairo on June 8, 1974, the PLO Executive Council confirmed these objectives and decided that the establishment of the PLO's authority in every area wrested from Israel would be only a step toward the elimination of the Jewish State.

The propaganda speeches and conversations in these halls, which for tactical purposes sometimes try to mask these facts, cannot conceal the truth.

These, then, are the goals of the PLO: to liquidate the Jewish State; to destroy, uproot and scatter its people; to deprive them of their independence, sovereignty, self-determination and equality with other nations. The annals of the United Nations know of no objective more sinister and more flagrantly opposed to the principles and purposes of the Charter.

This is a fundamental difference between the PLO and national liberation movements. The PLO is an antiliberation organization. It seeks to deprive the Jewish people of its liberty. Liberation movements strive to free subject peoples from the yoke of colonialism. The PLO, however, ignores the existence of an independent Palestinian State of Jordan and rejects the premise that if there are Palestinian needs which have not yet been fully satisfied, they could be dealt with in negotiations between Israel and that Palestinian Arab State. Israel, on its part, holds, as stated in the General Assembly on October 3, 1974, by Foreign Minister Yigal Allon, that the question of Palestinian identity can and should be resolved in the context of the settlement of the dispute with its neighbor to the east.

In the pursuit of its objectives, the PLO employs the most despicable of methods witnessed by mankind in recent decades—the deliberate murder of guiltless civilians. This is not the accidental loss of civilian lives that occurs in warfare against military targets, but willful, cold-blooded, carefully prepared, bestial assaults on innocent and defenseless children, women and men.

This is the type of atrocity that General Burns, the former Chief of Staff of the United Nations Truce Supervision Organization, condemned as "a war crime" and as "essentially of the same character . . . as the offences for which the Nazi leaders had been tried in Nuremberg."

This is the kind of savage outrage which the venerable René Cassin, a Nobel Prize winner and the international community's greatest authority on human rights, described as follows: "Arab warfare by terror is a loathsome, criminal policy. It violates the cease-fire. It undermines the peacemaking efforts. It is directed against the Israelis and harms the Arabs. Its victims are innocent civilians. It is inspired by unmitigated Nazilike hatred toward the remnants of a people victimized by the Nazis in history's most horrifying genocide."

It is the perpetrators of these crimes that the United Nations is asked to honor. The international community has tried for years to put an end to this scourge of savagery. Now it is called upon to bow to it in utter humiliation.

Still fresh in the minds and hearts of all civilized men is the sacred memory of the children massacred on ambushed school buses, of athletes slaughtered at the Olympic Games, of high-school pupils murdered on an outing, of diplomats killed in embassies, of civil aircraft hijacked and blown up in the air and on the ground, of passengers at air terminals mercilessly butchered. It is the criminals responsible for such abominable crimes that the General Assembly is about to invite into its midst. Yassir Arafat, who heads the PLO, continues to serve also as head of the Al Fatah/Black September murder grouping. This is the gang which has officially and publicly claimed responsibility for such outrages as the killing of the Israeli sportsmen in Munich, the massacre of Israeli children and women in Nahariya and the slaughter of American and Belgian diplomats in Khartoum. Yassir Arafat personally commanded, by radio from Beirut, the entire Khartoum operation.

It was after the Munich killings that the Secretary General of the United Nations asked the General Assembly to decide on effective measures against terrorism.

Now Arafat and his henchmen are to be greeted by the United Nations. Could there be a disgrace more appalling for the international community? Could there be a stigma more degrading for the United Nations than to become a forum open to the bearers of barbarism? Throughout the years there have been some General Assembly resolutions which proved useless or unhelpful. Rarely has there been one more ignominious and ludicrous than the draft resolution which alleges that the representatives of a people are not its elected representatives, not its internationally recognized Government which speaks for the vast majority of the Palestinians in the world, but a bunch of international criminals pursued by the police of tens of countries.

The Governments supporting it demonstrate an unparalleled disregard for international law and morality. Those who are against it can be proud at not having abandoned the ideals for the achievement and protection of which the United Nations was founded. The stand adopted by these Governments creates a chance, though admittedly not a considerable one, to limit the pernicious consequences of the draft resolution. What are these consequences?

First, the draft resolution makes a mockery of the United Nations and of its Charter.

Secondly, the draft resolution would be a source of encouragement to international terrorism. Many a Government represented in this chamber faces severe tests in coping with acts of terror perpetrated by local or foreign terrorist groups. These groups will undoubtedly read the draft resolution as a sign of acquiescence and permissiveness on the part of the United Nations and of the Governments which will make the adoption of the draft resolution possible. This, of course, applies equally to the PLO itself, which has subjected numerous countries outside the Middle East to its criminal and sanguinary operations.

Thirdly, the draft resolution threatens the diplomatic process toward a solution of the Middle East conflict. It creates an obstacle on the road to agreement between Israel and the Arab States. The latter and their supporters will have only themselves to blame for the consequences of this development.

Fourthly, by promoting the draft resolution, Arab Governments—and this includes the parties to the current peacemaking endeavors—have raised grave doubts regarding their ultimate intentions toward Israel. This will not remain unnoticed by Israel.

Fifthly, Governments which permit the adoption of the draft resolution clearly demonstrate that the tenets of the Charter and fundamental principles of international law and morality are of no import to them. It is evident that they thereby divest themselves of the right to speak in the name of these tenets and principles, at least with regard to the situation in the Middle East. Their views on these matters will be treated accordingly.

These are thus the connotations and foreseeable repercussions of the draft resolution. None of them is positive. All of them are damaging.

It is equally important to indicate what the draft resolution will not bring about.

It will obviously not bring about any change in Israel's position toward the PLO. Votes and resolutions in the United Nations do not modify the nature of the PLO. It has been and it remains an association of murder squads unrepresentative of Palestinians.

The draft resolution will not affect Israel's defense against the atrocities that are being perpetrated by the PLO. The Government of Israel will protect its citizens from the nefarious crimes of the PLO. It will continue to take all the necessary measures to put an end to these crimes. It will continue to strike at the PLO terrorists and at their bases.

The draft resolution will not weaken Israel's resolve to pursue agreement and peace with the Arab States and will strengthen the understanding of Israel's need for secure boundaries.

Israel regrets the negative repercussions of the draft resolution, but Israel itself will remain steadfast in its positions and policies. In accordance with the United Nations Charter, the draft resolution is arbitrary, illegal and not binding, and Israel will regard it as such. Israel will go on searching for peace with the Arab States, while strengthening itself to ward off their aggression, should it be renewed. Israel will continue to build and develop the land and to invigorate its society. It will not permit the barbarism of the PLO to disturb these endeavors. As to the question of how the draft resolution would affect the United Nations and its international standing, as well as Governments which make possible the passage of the draft resolution, that is another matter. As the Bible says: "Can a man take fire in his bosom and his clothes not burn?"

II

On November 13, 1974, Yassir Arafat, leader of the PLO, delivered his address before the United Nations General Assembly in which he stated that his "dream" was "one democratic state where Christian, Jew and Moslem live in justice, equality and fraternity." The following statement was made in the General Assembly after Arafat's address in order to expose Arafat's real "dream"—the destruction of the State of Israel.

I come before the General Assembly on behalf of a nation which has struggled through twenty centuries for its liberty and equality and for the restoration of its independence. I rise to speak in the name of a people which, having at long last regained its freedom and sovereignty in its national homeland, remains embattled, beleaguered by those who deny to it the rights of all nations. One third of the entire

Jewish people was annihilated in the Second World War, which gave birth to the United Nations. A million Jewish soldiers in the Allied armies and in partisan ranks helped make the United Nations a reality. Representatives of the Jewish people were among those who drafted the Charter of the United Nations.

Yet today Arab States most of which knew not the struggle that made the world safe for the United Nations, Arab States some of whose leaders collaborated with the forces of darkness in their fight against the United Nations, are in the vanguard of a fanatical assault on the Jewish people, an assault that tramples to dust the ideals of the United Nations.

On October 14, 1974, the General Assembly turned its back on the United Nations Charter, on law and humanity, and virtually capitulated to a murder organization which aims at the destruction of a State member of the United Nations. On October 14 the United Nations hung out a sign reading: "Murderers of children are welcome here."

Today these murderers have come to the General Assembly, certain that it would do their bidding. Today this rostrum was defiled by their chieftain, who proclaimed that the shedding of Jewish blood would end only when the murderers' demands had been accepted and their objectives achieved.

On October 14 the United Nations and Governments which made the invitation to the Palestine Liberation Organization (PLO) possible became the object of worldwide criticism. Editorials and caricatures in the press and demonstrations on all continents expressed revulsion at the spectacle of the United Nations tearing asunder its own principles and precepts and paying homage to bloodshed and bestiality.

Today bloodshed and bestiality have come here to collect the spoils of the United Nations surrender. This surrender must be absolute, they told the world this morning. The victim of bloodshed and bestiality should not even defend himself.

The United Nations is entrusted with the responsibility to guide mankind away from war, away from violence and oppression, toward peace, toward international understanding and the vindication of the rights of peoples and individuals. What remains of that responsibility now that the United Nations has prostrated itself before the PLO, which stands for premeditated, deliberate murder of innocent civilians, denies to the Jewish people its right to live, and seeks to destroy the Jewish State by armed force?

Throughout the years, the United Nations has dealt with the problems of many peoples in many parts of the world. On no people, however, has it lavished greater attention than on the Arab inhabitants of Palestine.

Is it because the problems of others have been solved?

Has the Kurdish people, subjected to a continuing war of annihilation by the Iraqi Government, ever had its plight discussed and its rights upheld by the United Nations? Has this organization tried to avert the massacre of half a million non-Moslem Africans in south Sudan? Have the fundamental human and political rights of the hundreds of millions who live under totalitarian regimes been ensured by the United Nations?

Is it because the needs of others are less pressing and less deserving than the needs of the Palestinians?

Are the Arabs of Palestine suffering starvation as are, according to United Nations statistics, almost 500 million people in Asia, Africa and Latin America? Has the United Nations left the Palestinian refugees without assistance as it has tens of millions of refugees all over the world, including Jewish refugees in Israel from Arab lands? Are the Palestinian refugees the only ones who cannot be reintegrated as others have been? Have the Palestinian Arabs no State of their own? What is Jordan if not a Palestinian Arab State?

The real reason for the special consideration accorded to questions concerning the Arabs of Palestine has been one and one only—the continuous exploitation of these questions as a weapon of Arab belligerency against Israel. As King Hussein said of the Arab leaders, "They have used the Palestine people for selfish political purposes." This is also the real motivation of the present debate.

In fact, no nation has enjoyed greater fulfillment of its political rights, no nation has been endowed with territory, sovereignty and independence more abundantly, than the Arabs.

Of common language, culture, religion and origin, the Arab nation stormed out of its birthland in the seventh century and conquered one people after another until its rule encompassed the entire Arab peninsula, the Fertile Crescent and North Africa.

Everywhere in these areas ancient cultures were replaced by the Arab civilization. Everywhere the vanquished were, with a few exceptions, assimilated into the Arab nation. There was, however, one people which refused to disappear and to shed its national identity. Whether in the land of Israel or in regions such as present-day Yemen, Iraq, Syria, Egypt and Morocco, the Jewish people maintained its national personality and preserved its own culture and faith.

Now, as a result of centuries of acquisition of territory by war, the Arab nation is represented in the United Nations by twenty sovereign States. Among them is also the Palestinian Arab State of Jordan.

Geographically and ethnically Jordan is Palestine. Historically both the West and East Banks of the Jordan River are parts of the land of Israel or Palestine. Both were parts of Palestine under the British Mandate until Jordan and then Israel became independent. The population of Jordan is composed of two elements—the sedentary population and nomads. Both are, of course, Palestinian. The nomad Bedouin constitute a minority of Jordan's population. Moreover, the majority of the sedentary inhabitants, even on the East Bank, are of Palestinian West Bank origin. Without the Palestinians, Jordan is a State without a people.

That is why when, on April 29, 1950, King Abdullah inaugurated the commemorative session of the Jordanian Parliament, he declared, "I open the session of the Parliament with both banks of the Jordan united by the will of one people, one homeland and one hope."

On August 23, 1959, the Prime Minister of Jordan stated, "We are the Government of Palestine, the army of Palestine and the refugees of Palestine."

Indeed, the vast majority of Palestinian refugees never left Palestine, but moved, as a result of the 1948 and 1967 wars, from one part of the country to another. At the same time, an approximately equal number of Jewish refugees fled from Arab countries to Israel.

It is, therefore, false to allege that the Palestinian people has been deprived of a State of its own or that it has been uprooted from its national homeland. Most Palestinians continue to live in Palestine. Most Palestinians continue to live in a Palestinian State. The vast majority of Palestinian Arabs are citizens of that Palestinian State.

"Jordan is Palestine and Palestine is Jordan," declared on December 9, 1970, the late Dr. Kadri Toukan, a prominent West Bank leader and former Foreign Minister of Jordan.

Mr. Anwar Nusseibi, another Palestinian West Bank personality and a former Jordanian Defense Minister, stated on October 23, 1970: "The Jordanians are also Palestinians. This is one State. This is one people. The name is not important. The families living in Salt, Irbid and Karak maintain not only family and matrimonial ties with the families in Nablus and Hebron. They are one people."

This is recognized even by the PLO covenant, and the Rabat resolutions do not alter this reality.

Even if the appellation "Palestinian" were confined to the West Bank, there is today, as already indicated, an overwhelming preponderance of Palestinians of West Bank descent in the population of the East Bank, as well as in the Jordanian Government. For instance, Queen Alia, Prime Minister Rifa'i, more than half of the Cabinet ministers and of the members of Parliament, the Speaker of the Parliament, the mayor of Amman all hail from the West Bank.

Certain Palestinians might be unhappy with their system of government, with the constitutional structure of their State or with its leadership. This, however, can in no way substantiate a claim that the Palestinian Arabs have been shorn of their rights as a people. Like all other branches of the Arab nation, the Palestinians too possess the political entity within which they exercise their national, political and cultural rights. To the extent that some of their needs have not been fully satisfied, to the extent that some aspects of their national identity require solutions, they could be dealt with in the context of negotiations between Israel and its eastern neighbor, the Palestinian State of Jordan.

In these circumstances it is obvious that the initiators of the discussion of the so-called question of Palestine are concerned primarily not with the realization of the rights of the Palestinians, but with the annulment of the rights of the Jewish people. Israel's destruction and the denial to the people of Israel of its rights to self-determination and independence are the officially enunciated objectives of the PLO at whose behest the Arab Governments have asked for this debate. By doing so, by initiating the invitation extended to the PLO and by the decisions adopted at the recent Rabat Conference, the Arab Governments have reaffirmed their association with the umbrella organization of the Arab murder squads. This is not surprising. The PLO did not emerge from within the Palestinian community. It is not representative of the Palestinian community. It is a creation of the Arab Governments themselves. It was established at the first summit meeting of the heads of Arab States in Cairo in 1964 as an instrument for waging terror warfare against Israel. Its covenant stipulates: "The establishment of Israel is fundamentally null and void. The claim of historical or spiritual ties between Jews and Palestine does not tally with historical realities. The Jews are not one people with an independent personality." In the pursuit of its objectives the PLO employs the barbaric method of deliberate murder of guiltless civilians. This is not the accidental loss of civilian lives that occurs in warfare against military targets, but willful, cold-blooded, carefully prepared, bestial assaults on innocent and defenseless children, women and men in towns and villages, in schools and marketplaces, at airports, in the air and on the ground. No wonder that associations of anti-Nazi freedom fighters have repeatedly condemned the PLO atrocities as crimes reminiscent of Nazi savagery.

Support for the PLO's murderous ideology and sinister objectives is expressed in the United Nations in various terms. References are frequently made to "the root problem" of the Palestinian question, a euphemism for Israel's statehood. On occasion speakers lash out unabashedly against Israel's independence, slander it as colonialism, call for its replacement by a second Palestinian Arab State, in addition to Jordan. At times, the terms employed are more general, such as restoration of the inalienable rights of the Palestinian people, self-determination, and so on. Since the June 8, 1974, Cairo meeting of the PLO and the Rabat Summit Conference the talk is of establishing

PLO authority in territories wrested from Israel, making it clear that this would be only a first step toward Israel's elimination.

Indeed, whatever the phraseology, its true meaning remains obvious.

In a press conference held at United Nations Headquarters, after the General Assembly vote on October 14, 1974, the PLO representative declared: "Our short-term goal, which has been approved by our congress, is to establish in any and every part liberated in Palestine a national authority provided that in no way should that compromise our right to the whole of Palestine."

The official organ of the Syrian Government, *El Baath,* wrote on October 17, 1974, about the October 14 resolution to invite the PLO: "The United Nations resolution constitutes a victory of the principle of armed struggle which began in the war of liberation on October 6. This is so because the world does not respect anything but the language of revolutionary violence which is the only language to be used at this time."

Yassir Arafat made this view even more specific. In an interview published on October 21, 1974, in the Cairo daily *Rose el-Yussuf* he declared: "I do not see the possibility of a peace settlement in the Middle East, but a fifth war."

On October 28 the Arab Governments and the PLO decided at Rabat that the immediate goal should be the establishment of a PLO base to the east of Israel. The ultimate objective remained the same— the destruction of Israel and its replacement by an Arab State.

At a press conference in Rabat on October 30, Yassir Arafat had no qualms about confirming that this was the meaning of the decision adopted two days earlier. He said that the establishment of PLO authority in areas that might be evacuated by Israel would be "the first stage toward the creation of a democratic State where Jews, Christians and Moslems could coexist." And this he reiterated in interviews published in *The New York Times* on November 9, in *Time* Magazine of November 11, and in other recent pronouncements, including this morning's statement. Still fresh in the minds of all are Arafat's own explanations that such terminology is used only because it is more "civilized," and that behind it looms, as always, the design to deprive the Jewish people of its independence, to liquidate the Jewish State and to establish on its ruins another Arab State in which Jews would again live as a minority as they do today, persecuted and tortured in Syria, and as they did in the past in countries such as Iraq, Yemen or Algeria, suffering all the pain and sorrow of oppression.

This is the supposedly moderate objective of the PLO's leader, the man who continues to serve as commander of Al Fatah/Black September, the gangster who received five million dollars from President Qaddafi of Libya as a prize for the slaughter of Israeli sportsmen at the Olympic Games in Munich, the criminal who personally directed the murder of diplomats in Khartoum.

Some of his henchmen disagree with his "civilized" terminology. They would like him to be more outspoken, more blunt, as he was when he told the Italian weekly *L'Europa:* "Our goal is the destruction of Israel . . . Peace for us means Israel's destruction, nothing else."

Arafat, today, prefers the Nazi method. The Nazis killed millions of Jews in death camps, the gates of which bore the sign "Work Brings Freedom." Arafat kills Jewish children and seeks to strangle the Jewish State under the slogan of creating a "democratic Palestine." Neither kings nor presidents, neither artifices of speech nor the plaudits of accomplices or of the misguided, can conceal this sinister fact.

The speakers who opened today's debate have confirmed its real purpose—to undermine Israel's rights, to question the inalienable right of the Jewish people to its homeland, to strengthen and encourage the PLO in its activities directed against the life of Israel and of its people, to establish a PLO springboard from which the murder organization can continue its efforts to destroy the Jewish State. This is what justice means to the PLO. This is what the PLO's olive branch is.

Jewish history is the saga of a people which has remained one with its land through millennia of independence and foreign conquest, of uprooting and dispersion, of struggle to rebuild its statehood and of final restoration of national liberty. Unparalleled national tragedies, centuries of suppression, repeated massacres through the ages culminating in the genocide of six million by the Nazis, have never weakened the Jewish people's attachment to its land and its resolve to live in it in freedom and independence. Since the dawn of history thousands of years ago and until the creation of Jordan in a part of Palestine, no people, other than the Jewish people, ever established or even thought of establishing a State of its own in the land of Israel. No people, except for the Jewish people, ever looked upon the land of Israel as a separate entity. To the Jewish nation, however, this land has been the very essence of its existence.

Even when defeated by the Roman Empire and carried off to bondage in foreign countries, the Jews of the Diaspora continued to live in spirit in their homeland. They prayed for rain when rain was needed in the land of Israel. They celebrated the harvest when it was harvest time in Israel. They retained the customs of the land, its traditional holydays and its ancient language. Above all, they never ceased to struggle against the consequences of foreign imperialist subjugation. They never stopped striving to regain their independence and sovereignty. In the land of Israel itself, though decimated by successive conquerors, the Jewish community clung to the soil of its forefathers, determined that the day should come when it would be free again.

If in world history there is a classic example of a struggle for national liberty, it is the struggle of the Jewish people, pursued for almost two thousand years in resistance to imperialism and colonialism, exile and dispersion, racial discrimination and physical annihilation. To vilify this age-long struggle, Zionism, to question the Jewish people's equality with other nations, to deny the Jewish people's right to self-determination and independence in its homeland is willful blasphemy. It is a sacrilege of the most revered concepts of the equality of peoples and of national liberation. It is Nazi-like abuse of the kind that has been heaped upon the Jewish people through the ages by bigots, racists and anti-Semites. How sad that such anti-Jewish prejudices should be rampant in the United Nations.

The Jewish people, however, has defended its rights, fought and bled for centuries, outlived empires and survived holocausts not to be swayed from its course by a gang of murderers who thrive on Jewish blood or by the whims of regimes which claim to seek justice for Palestinian Arabs, but openly deny it to Jews.

The choice before the General Assembly is clear. On the one hand there is the Charter of the United Nations; on the other there is the PLO, whose sinister objectives, defined in its covenant, and savage outrages are a desecration of the Charter.

On the one hand there is Israel's readiness and desire to reach a peaceful settlement with the Palestinian Arab State of Jordan in which the Palestinian national identity would find full expression. On the other hand there is the PLO's denial of Israel's right to independence and of the Jewish people's right to self-determination.

The choice is between understanding and continued conflict in the Middle East, between suppression of terror and its encouragement, between satisfying the needs of Palestinians through the peacemaking process already under way and undermining that process by trying to introduce into it a murder organization which aims at the elimination of one of the negotiating parties.

The question is: Should there be peace between Israel and its eastern neighbor or should an attempt be made to establish a Palestine Liberation Organization base to the east of Israel from which the terrorist campaign against the Jewish State's existence could be pursued?

On October 14 the General Assembly opted for the PLO, it opted for terrorism, it opted for savagery. Can there be any hope that it might now undo the harm it has already done, by that action, to the cause of peace in the Middle East and to humanity in general? Israel has also made its choice.

The United Nations, whose duty it is to combat terrorism and barbarity, may agree to consort with them. Israel will not.

The murderers of athletes in the Olympic Games of Munich, the butchers of children in Ma'alot, the assassins of diplomats in Khartoum do not belong in the international community. They have no place in international diplomatic efforts. Israel shall see to it that they have no place in them.

Israel will pursue the PLO murderers until justice is meted out to them. It will continue to take action against their organization and against their bases until a definitive end is put to their atrocities. The blood of Jewish children will not be shed with impunity.

Israel will not permit the establishment of PLO authority in any part of Palestine. The PLO will not be forced on the Palestinian Arabs. It will not be tolerated by the Jews of Israel.

Israel will continue to strive for peace with the Arab States. Peace would bring a new era of development, social progress and happiness for all the States and all the peoples of the Middle East.

In its decision of July 21, 1974, the Government of Israel declared that it would work toward negotiating a peace agreement with Jordan and that in the Jordanian-Palestinian Arab State east of Israel the specific identity of the Jordanians and Palestinians will find expression in peace and good-neighborliness with Israel. This remains Israel's policy.

However, if the peacemaking process becomes paralyzed as a result of the Rabat and General Assembly resolutions, Israel will find a way, by the exercise of its sovereignty, to ensure its political and security interests, while also doing justice to the Arab population living in the administered areas.

No resolution of the General Assembly can mask the murderous nature of the PLO. No resolution can wash the hands of Yassir Arafat and his henchmen clean of the blood of their innocent victims. No resolution can confer respect on a band of cutthroats. No resolution can establish the authority of an organization which has no authority, which does not represent anyone except the few thousand agents of death it employs, which has no foothold in any part of the territories it seeks to dominate. The PLO will remain what it is and where it is— outside the law and outside Palestine.

A resolution that would respond to the PLO demands would, however, encourage the extremists in the Arab world who reject a peaceful settlement with Israel and call for continued war against it.

I repeat, Israel remains ready to take, together with the Arab States, the road of peace. Should they, however, espouse continued hostility and aggression, the Arab States will find Israel equally ready. The Jewish people's independence will be safeguarded with the same determination, with the same perseverance, with the same firmness with which it has been restored after an age-long struggle and defended since. The Jewish people's hymn, Israel's national anthem, says:

Two thousand years we cherished the hope
To live in freedom in the Land
Of Zion and Jerusalem.

To those in this Assembly who challenge or ignore our rights we reply:
In freedom the people of Israel shall live now and forever.

III

By an act of the President of the General Assembly, the Algerian Foreign Minister, Israel's delegation was prevented from active participation in the debate on the "Question of Palestine." The following address was made at the conclusion of the debate on November 22, 1974.

Inscribed at the portals to the United Nations, the Prophet Isaiah's admonition reads: "Nation shall not lift up sword against nation." Today, the General Assembly is helping lift up a sword against the very nation which brought that message to the world.

These are sad days for the United Nations. These are days of degradation and disgrace, of surrender and humiliation for the international community.

They began when the General Assembly, having decided after the massacre of Israeli athletes at the Olympic Games to consider measures to combat terrorism, capitulated to the murder organization responsible for the massacre. They continued when Yassir Arafat, responsible for that massacre and for many others, appeared on this rostrum with a gun in his holster, was received in a spectacle which made a mockery of the Charter, and defiantly reaffirmed that the Palestine Liberation Organization's objective is the destruction of a member State. Then came the President's unprecedented initiative of muzzling freedom of speech. Thereafter, the debate turned into a monotonous monologue of falsehood and distortion, of hostility and fanaticism, interrupted only on rare occasions by a voice of reason.

One Palestine Liberation Organization supporter after another denied the Jewish people's right to life and independence, negated its national identity and its history. One after another disparaged the people of Israel by trying to present it as a stranger in its own homeland.

Even Islam's holy book, the Koran itself, states, with reference to the Jewish people, "Enter, O my people, the Holy Land which God hath assigned for you." However, nothing seems sacred to the Palestine Liberation Organization murderers and their followers. They derided the truth as mendacity, right as wrong. To them, savagery is praiseworthy, defense against atrocities condemnable. Terror against civilians is acceptable, but a State's protection of its citizens is terrorism. The murder of Jewish children and the destruction of the Jewish State is called liberation. Zionism, the Jewish people's national liberation movement, is calumnied as evil. Verily, the debate often appeared like a Sodom and Gomorrah of ideals and values.

Even while it was proceeding, Israeli civilians were being murdered in Beit Shean by PLO agents.

It was not always like that.

On January 3, 1919, an agreement was signed by Emir Feisal, head of the Arab national liberation movement and of the Arab nation's revolt against Ottoman rule, and by Dr. Chaim Weizmann, representing the Zionist movement. The agreement provided for "all necessary measures to encourage and stimulate immigration of Jews into Palestine."

In a letter written on March 3, 1919, to Mr. Felix Frankfurter, a prominent American Zionist and later a United States Supreme Court Justice, Emir Feisal declared: "We Arabs, especially the educated among us, look with deepest sympathy on the Zionist movement . . . We will wish the Jews a hearty welcome home . . . We are working together for a reformed and revised Near East, and our two movements complement one another. The Jewish movement is national and not imperialist."

Whose views are to be accepted—those of the leader of the Arab national political revival, or those of the assassins of children? In whom will Arab history take pride—in the statesman who led the Arab nation to liberty, or in the murderer of Munich and Ma'alot, of

Khartoum and Beit Shean? By whose attitude will relations between Jews and Arabs be guided? Will it be by the wisdom of Emir Feisal or by the bloodlust of Yassir Arafat? Will it be cooperation and creativity or warfare and destruction?

Of all the peoples represented in the United Nations, the Jewish nation is one of the most ancient. Its struggle for survival, for self-determination and independence is probably the oldest and most tenacious in history.

It is a strife not of fifty or a hundred years, as is that of most nations represented here, but of two millennia. The Jewish people was unable to carry on this struggle solely in its own homeland as others could. It had to wage it in all the lands among which it was dispersed after having been conquered by the Roman Empire.

It did not resist the oppression and domination of one Power, as most newly independent nations have, but fought back the despotism and discrimination and racism of many.

The Jewish struggle—Zionism—was an inspiration to numerous other peoples. The late President Nasser of Egypt himself found it appropriate to include in his book *The Philosophy of the Revolution* the following passage:

A few months ago, I read some articles written about me by an Israeli officer named Yeruham Cohen, which appeared in the *Jewish Observer*. In these articles the Jewish officer relates how he met me during the armistice negotiations.

"The subject which Gamal Abdul Nasser always talked about with me," he [Cohen] wrote, "was the struggle of Israel against the English, and how we organized the underground resistance movement against them in Palestine, and how we were able to muster world public opinion behind us in our struggle against them."

It is not an accident of history that Israel's independence in 1948 was a landmark following on which one nation after another in Africa and Asia achieved freedom and sovereignty.

Yet these facts have been willfully ignored or distorted by the PLO supporters. To them a murder organization dedicated to slaughter and to the destruction of a people's independence constitutes the embodiment of liberty.

Liberation should inspire and elevate. It should restore human rights and human dignity. It should bring happiness and creation. It should be rebirth and life. Thus it is with individuals and thus it is with nations.

The names of Washington, Garibaldi, Gandhi, Senghor, Kaunda or the Maquis and other partisans of the Second World War are enshrined in the history and the glory of national liberation struggles. Only arrogant effrontery can mention Arafat and the PLO in the same category. Neither by its objectives nor by its methods can the PLO be classified as a liberation movement.

Almost every national struggle has known the use of force. No liberation movement, however, has used force indiscriminately; none has deliberately directed acts of violence against innocent civilians; none has engaged exclusively in premeditated murder of guiltless children, women and men.

Almost all liberation struggles have at one stage or another resorted to arms. However, the targets have generally been of a military nature. Sometimes there might be incidental civilian casualties. Sometimes an individual civilian might have been purposely assassinated, but this occurred usually when the person was a political figure engaged in the suppression of the liberation movement.

Arafat and the PLO, on the other hand, have concentrated entirely on murder for murder's sake. Their targets have never been military targets. They have always planned and carried out attacks on civilians only. They have always chosen the most savage method and the most innocent and defenseless target. Massacres of schoolchildren have been their specialty, the hijacking and blowing up of civil airliners their favorite. The killing of helpless persons in their homes, of defenseless passengers at air terminals, of sportsmen in Olympic Games, of diplomats at embassy receptions has become synonymous with the names of Arafat and PLO.

Only PLO thugs could stoop to drinking in public the blood of Jordan's Prime Minister Wasfi at-Tal after killing him on a Cairo street. Only a PLO leader could have said to a correspondent, "It does not matter whether they kill women or children, as long as they kill Jews." Only Arafat's agents could slaughter children by shooting them one by one in the head, as in Ma'alot. Only one other movement ever practiced such savagery—the Nazis. The PLO murderers are their heirs in method and in objective.

Every national liberation movement strives to free its own people from the colonial yoke. No liberation movement aims at subjugating another people and depriving it of its national rights. The PLO's avowed goal is, however, to destroy the Jewish State and to wrest from the Jewish people its liberty and its independence. Again, only the Nazis denied to the Jewish people the rights of all nations. Only the Nazis refused to recognize that the Jewish people was equal with others. Arafat and the PLO hold the same view. The only right that the PLO is prepared to grant Jews is to live as an oppressed minority in one more Arab State.

This very morning, the *Wall Street Journal* carried an interview with Farouk Qaddumi, head of the PLO's political department and chief of its delegation here, which reads as follows:

As a practical first stage, the PLO was prepared to establish a "National Authority" over any "liberated territory," specifically the West Bank and Gaza. As a second stage, said Mr. Qaddumi, "we would have to see to it that refugees would return to their homes and to their property according to a scheduled time." And in the third and final stage, he said, "we will decide how we can establish our democratic, secular State."

"We would get the support of the Soviet Union and China," he added.

Israel has no intention of being replaced by the Nazis of the Middle East. The Jewish people will not be swallowed up by PLO barbarity.

The Arab nation has attained its rights in twenty independent States. There are a Yemen and a Democratic Yemen. There are a Qatar and a Bahrain, an Oman and Kuwait and the Emirates—all of them of the same tongue, culture, religion and history. And they dare to challenge the rights of Israel with its distinctive civilization and history—Israel, the only Jewish State, the State of the oldest nation in the region.

The orgy of hatred and abuse now reaching its climax must raise grave questions about the future destiny of our Organization. By trampling in the dust its own Charter, by submitting itself to violence and savagery, by hailing lawlessness, inhumanity and hypocrisy, the United Nations has plunged into an abyss from which there is no exit. Just as the demise of the League of Nations began when it bowed to force and aggression, so the sun appears to have set on the United Nations when so many in this debate joined in worshiping the Moloch of murder and international banditry.

This will not affect Israel. The Jewish people has learned over the ages not to be submerged by iniquity and decadence. Throughout history, the Jewish people and, since its independence, the State of Israel have known how to defend their rights and uphold their ideals without much support from others. We have never had any qualms or regrets about remaining faithful to our values, even when few were with us. We always understood that strength lies in quality, and not in numbers. Justice stands by itself. Truth speaks for itself.

The resolutions adopted by the General Assembly are products of iniquity and decadence. They have been initiated by the PLO. They reflect the PLO views. They encourage the PLO to pursue its goals and methods, which are contrary to the United Nations Charter, to international law and morality. They deal another grievous blow to the peacemaking efforts in the Middle East, in which Israel has placed its hope and trust—efforts intended also to bring about satisfaction of the needs of Palestinians.

These resolutions have obtained the usual mechanical majority, but those who reject them will add strength to the cause of peace. History has proved, time and again, that it is the few who are right that prevail in the end. The Bible says: "Thou shalt not follow a multitude to do evil." Israel will not follow the multitude. It will treat the resolutions for what they are and deserve to be: utterly contemptible and devoid of legal and moral worth.

Israel will not follow the multitude. It will not be deterred from its course. All it has done and achieved in the struggle for independence, in the defense of its heritage, its freedom and its sovereignty, in the construction and development of its homeland, in the ingathering of its exiled and oppressed brethren has been the fruit of the Jewish people's resolve, unity and tenacity maintained despite the ill wishes and designs of its enemies. Not resolutions expressing the belligerent views of Israel's opponents, but Israel's determination to safeguard its rights, fortified by the understanding and solidarity of people of goodwill everywhere, have shaped the realities of the situation.

Thus it shall continue to be. At no time has the people of Israel felt more certain of the justice of its cause than now. At no time has it been more steadfast and more united in warding off the assault of the forces of darkness than today. Israel looks to the future with confidence strengthened by its past and inspired by the ideals it has always cherished.

4 The Territories Under Israeli Control and the Palestinians: A Laboratory for Peace

I

Excerpts from a statement delivered in the Security Council on September 20, 1968, during a debate on the situation in the territories under Israeli control. The session had been requested by Senegal and Pakistan.

Any reference to areas under Israeli control is meaningless without recalling why Israeli forces are stationed today on the Suez Canal, why Israeli troops guard the crossings on the Jordan River and patrol the cease-fire line in the Golan Heights.

We stand where we stand today because the Arab States did not let us live in peace where we were before June 1967. We are where we are today because, having spilled our blood and drained our strength for nineteen years, the Arab States mounted last year the onslaught that was to bring about Israel's final annihilation. Israel found itself in control of these territories because it survived and dislodged the Arab armies from their bases of aggression.

Thus, resulting from Arab aggression, Israeli presence in these areas is imposed by the vital exigencies of security. However, the meeting for the first time since 1948 between Israelis and Arabs has demonstrated that peaceful coexistence between the two peoples is now possible and that both peoples want peace. It is Israel's hope that this coexistence will prove to be a bridge to final peace with the Arab

States. It is regrettable that the Arab Governments appear to be guided so far by different aspirations, that they manifest unhappiness at the normalization of life and growing understanding between the Jews and the Arabs, that they continue warfare, incite to hatred and hostility, and encourage incidents of violence and terror. However, neither these incidents nor the security measures which they engender change the general picture in the Israeli-administered territories.

The well-known neutral organ of a neutral country, the *Neue Züricher Zeitung,* wrote on June 8, 1968:

Life in the occupied Arab areas has, for all practical purposes, returned to complete normality . . .

. . . also the Israeli armed forces are distributed through the area in as unobtrusive a manner as possible. In the larger towns one hardly encounters Israeli soldiers . . .

The system of occupation built up by the Israelis in the occupied areas is able to function thanks solely to the far-reaching cooperation that prevails between them and the local Arab administration. The Israelis have made it a cardinal principle to interfere as little as possible in the Arabs' internal affairs. At the head of the various communities, nearly everywhere, are still the same people as before June 5, 1967.

Law and order are maintained locally by an Arab police force, which has hardly changed in composition since the war.

Israel endeavors to maintain the occupation strictly according to international law. That is why local law has remained in force.

The courts, too, have hardly been touched by the upheaval of June 1967.

The school system was subjected to a minimum of interference as a result of the occupation. The schools are being run with the same teaching personnel and the same instructional material as before.

The occupied territories have not produced an indigenous underground movement.

The terrorists brought in from the outside hardly found support among the indigenous population.

The impressions of thousands of other visitors have been the same. Their reports have appeared in the press, radio and television all over the world. The isolated exceptions, simply repeating hackneyed Arab propaganda, merely emphasize by their rarity and anomaly to what extent the true picture varies from their accounts. This applies, of course, also to the Amman-inspired and fabricated trash submitted this morning by the Jordanian representative. He seems to have forgotten one thing—the truth about the situation in the areas under Israeli control is freely accessible to all and does not depend on Arab propaganda stunts.

I am authorized to state that any person present at this Security Council table who wishes to come to Israel would be welcome and we would be happy to facilitate his visit to the territories under Israeli control so that he can form his own impressions. We would be glad to assist him in becoming personally acquainted with the situation. However, what we cannot accept is a deliberate disregard for the fate of Jews who are in distress. This consideration touches our innermost feelings. Respect is due to it, if not from the Arab Governments, at least from the United Nations and its organs.

II

The following statement was made in the Security Council on April 4, 1968, in reply to allegations voiced by the Jordanian representative regarding the situation in the territories under Israeli control.

The representative of Jordan has joined the chorus of those who express unhappiness about the relations between Israelis and Arabs in Israel-controlled areas. The object of his particular interest is the West Bank, an area occupied by Jordan in 1948 in defiance of the United Nations, an area kept under occupation for nineteen years without the world, including the Arab States, recognizing Jordan's rights to it. For nineteen years this was a hotbed of political ferment, of social unrest and resistance to the Amman authorities. Riots, strikes and military repressive measures against the local population, and arrests were a daily occurrence.

It is sufficient to recall the record of public disturbances and the drastic measures adopted by the Jordanian authorities to suppress them during 1966.

In January 1966 the Jordanian authorities arrested two hundred persons in Jericho; in April they arrested two thousand persons in the West Bank. In May mass demonstrations took place in east Jerusalem, Hebron and Ramallah. The police used force, closed down schools and arrested hundreds of persons.

In July disturbances and mass demonstrations broke out in Nablus. The Jordanian police used tear gas; twelve persons were wounded and 250 arrested.

That November saw a series of stormy disturbances and clashes between civilians, police and army forces, with numerous casualities. On November 21, shop and business strikes broke out in the Ramallah area. The Army was called in to intervene and employed tanks. The Jordanian authorities imposed a curfew and closed all schools. Similar events reoccurred through November and December in most other towns. On November 24 the Jordanian Army again employed tanks and tear gas. Twenty demonstrators were killed and many more wounded. On December 8, 1966, a general business strike was put down by force by the police and the Jordanian Army.

On January 13, 1967, the population of Nablus rose up, and barricades were put up in the streets. The Jordanian Army had to surround the city and suppress resistance by force.

With an army composed mainly of Bedouin from the East Bank, the Jordanian Government succeeded in retaining its military hold over the West Bank. The Jordanian authorities knew, however, that the West Bank was at best only a stepchild, not a member of the family; they knew well that the heart of the Arab inhabitants of the West Bank was not with them. The Amman Government treated the West Bank accordingly.

The area had almost half of Jordan's population, but it accounted for only one third of the output. Per capita average income in the East Bank was $335 annually; in the West Bank, only $216. The East Bank enjoyed priorities of development and investment out of all proportion to the size of the population and the economic potential of the area. In the years of Jordanian rule, not a single investment was authorized for the West Bank that amounted to more than 10,000 dinars. Of the $884 million invested in 1966, two thirds went to Transjordan, that is, to the East Bank, seat of all the country's sizable industries, such as oil refining, cement and phosphates. The West Bank was relegated to agriculture. The Government gave East Bank merchants priorities in such matters as import quotas and buying privileges. It even blocked loans to West Bank projects, resulting in a steady exodus of economic concerns and persons eastward. This left the West Bank with only 22 percent of Jordan's industry and 16 percent of its transport.

In the light of this, it is not surprising at all that the Jordanian representative, like certain other Arab representatives who preceded him, voiced unhappiness with Israel's efforts to encourage and assist West Bank development. I can well understand that he would have preferred the present situation there to be one of chaos as in the days of Jordanian rule—one of economic deterioration or at least stagnation, as before June 1967.

One thing must be clear. Whatever the political views and desires of the Jordanian representative, the Arab population on the West Bank does not want war and conflict with Israel. It wants peace and coexistence. In the same manner as thousands and thousands of Arab inhabitants began to frequent Israeli hospitals when the doors were opened to them after the cease-fire, so did scores of thousands of Arab farmers ask for Israeli machinery and Israeli instruction in agriculture. When Israeli authorities recently helped the farmers in the Jenin area to increase by three times the land under tobacco growth, it was, of course, not expected that this would please the rulers in Amman. They in the last eight years had gradually limited the area under tobacco growth on the West Bank from 7,000 dunums to only 2,000, while at the same time extending tobacco cultivation on the East Bank.

No; what concerns the Arab rulers today is perhaps less the fact that Israel has successfully repelled their aggression than the fact that in areas under Israel control it has been proved that Israelis and Arabs can live together, work together and understand each other. Those who want the war to continue cannot be happy with this situation. They cannot find much pleasure in the fact that local Arab authorities have continued to function uninterruptedly, that schools, courts, public services are operating normally, that hundreds of trucks with vegetables, fruit and other produce are daily crossing the Jordan bridges, that trade between the East and West Banks is today at the same level as before June last, that Arabs are free to move in all parts of Israel, that thousands of them are visiting their families and friends and calling on Jordanian Cabinet members and the King himself and then returning peacefully to their homes on the West Bank.

The foreign editor of *The Financial Times* of London, Mr. J. D. E. Jones, has the following to say on the situation in the February 28 issue of that newspaper: ". . . the fact remains that for the first time ever the Arabs are travelling in large numbers to and fro between Israeli and Arab territory. . . . It is a development arguably more important than any of the other aspects of the Middle East situation . . ."

5 The Refugees: Arab and Jewish

I

*Statement delivered November 17, 1969, in the United Nations Special
Political Committee during the annual debate on the Palestine refugees.*

The war unleashed against Israel in 1948 gave rise to two waves of
refugees. There was a large-scale movement of Arabs out of Israeli
territory. There was a general exodus of Jews from the Arab States.

The world remembers both these waves of human beings, one
flowing out of the country, the other into it. We in Israel remember
the Arab refugees. We are conscious of their plight. We understand
their suffering. But at the same time that we remember them, we also
remember the Jewish refugees wending their way through deserts and
mountains, across frontiers, and over the seas and through the air.
They came in hundreds of thousands: men, women and children,
destitute and miserable, haunted by memories of fear and grief.

They were in flight from homes in which they and their ancestors
had lived for centuries, even thousands of years. Entire communities
were uprooted. It was in Israel, the home of their fathers, that they
found refuge. Forcibly deprived of their property, crowded into huge
refugee tent camps, they were entirely dependent on others for food,
clothing, work and shelter.

TREATMENT OF JEWISH AND ARAB REFUGEES COMPARED

There were no deliberations in the United Nations about their plight. No relief agencies were established by this Organization to help in their rehabilitation. Israel was left to do it by itself with whatever outside help it could muster. We supplied the refugees with food and clothing, with medical assistance and educational services. We constructed houses for them and created places of work. Today, these Jewish refugees from Arab States and their children, totaling close to a million persons, are full-fledged, fully integrated citizens.

They are not the only ones for whom new lives had to be created by Israel. The refugees from Arab lands joined hundreds of thousands of Jewish refugees from Europe, remnants of the Holocaust, survivors of concentration camps and gas chambers, those whose six million brethren were barbarically murdered for being Orientals, for being of an Asian race and a Semitic civilization. They were all welcomed by their brethren in Israel. They were not allowed to linger for long in refugee camps. Their wounds were healed. Their lives were reconstructed. The Government and people of Israel saw in them human beings, not political pawns, and treated them accordingly.

The movement of Arab inhabitants out of Israel took place at the same time as this influx of Jewish refugees into the country. Most of the Arab refugees departed at the urging of their own leaders. All of them found refuge in the midst of their own kin. The great majority never left Palestine and simply moved from Jewish-controlled areas to those under Arab jurisdiction. Their transition from one side of the Armistice Line to the other did not constitute a change more radical in nature than the movement of Jews from Arab lands to Israel. Yet the treatment meted out to them was entirely different from that accorded Jewish refugees in Israel. They became wards of the United Nations. The Relief and Works Agency was set up to assist in their rehabilitation. For twenty-one years the General Assembly held special debates on their situation and organized international pledging conferences at which member States were invited to contribute to their maintenance.

The most striking difference, however, was in the attitude of the Arab Governments toward their own brethren. The refugees were to become, above everything else, instruments in the continued belligerency of the Arab States toward Israel. Their misery was to be perpetuated and exploited in the campaign of unabated political and military hostility against Israel. Development plans to resettle the refugees and provide them with work were rejected by the Arab Governments. The word "works" in UNRWA's title ceased to have any meaning. Offers to admit refugees into immigration countries were turned down by the Arab Governments. Refugees who wished to go abroad, attracted by opportunities of rehabilitation and resettlement, were barred from doing so. Attempts by refugees to reintegrate themselves and become self-supporting within the host countries were discouraged. In the Gaza area they were not allowed even to travel to Egypt, the occupying power. The design appeared to be as simple as it was sinister. The refugees were to remain refugees, unsettled and unrehabilitated, to serve as a battering ram that would be thrust back into the body of the State of Israel and bring about its destruction.

No attempt was made to conceal this goal.

ARAB REFUGEE QUESTION: AN EXCEPTION

The Arab States' callous attitude toward the Arab refugees differed drastically not only from the attitude of the Israel Government to Jewish refugees, but also from the policies followed by Governments all over the world in regard to refugee questions which confronted them.

In all ages, on all continents, man's failure to free himself from the scourge of war has resulted in the uprooting of people, in the flight of innocent civilians, in the search for new homes and new life.

In the wake of World War I there were nearly a million refugees from Russia. There were approximately 200,000 Armenian refugees, more than a million and a half Greek and Turkish refugees and numberless others of whom there is no international record. The rise of Nazi and Fascist regimes brought new waves of refugees, mostly Jewish.

In the period since World War II forty million people were displaced from the countries of their residence and found themselves on the refugee trail.

All these problems were solved by integration of the refugees in the countries of refuge. The annual reports of the United Nations High Commissioner for Refugees illustrate with what relative speed and efficiency such problems can be solved in our time, when there is a will to do so. None of these questions was resolved by trying to prevent the resettlement of refugees and by turning them into an instrument of continued warfare in an international conflict. The only exception, in the entire world, are the Arab refugees from Palestine.

ARABS TO ISRAEL: HELP US DESTROY YOU

The exceptional handling of the refugees by the Arab Governments has been reflected in the equally exceptional argumentation put forward by these Governments in discussions of the Arab-refugee problem.

It is a generally known fact that had the Arab States accepted the United Nations resolutions affirming the Jewish people's right to independence, and had they refrained from invading Israel in defiance of the United Nations Charter, there would have been no Arab-refugee problem. Yet the Arab Governments have never ceased to delude themselves that this basic fact could be ignored or forgotten and responsibility for the refugee problem shifted to Israel.

The General Assembly resolution most frequently referred to in discussions on the Palestinian refugee questions is Resolution 194 (III) of 1948. That resolution called for a negotiated peace between Israel and the Arab States that would include economic cooperation for the development of the region. The resolution as a whole, with its fundamental objective of peace, has been relegated to oblivion by the Arab States, the only exception being made for its paragraph 11, which dealt with refugees. However, even this paragraph was postulated on peace and a readiness to live at peace to which it refers in so many words. While providing for the alternative of return or resettlement, the paragraph made it clear that only those ready to live at peace with Israel would be eligible for permission to return. Disregarding this premise, the Arab States again put forward a strange, exceptional claim. For two decades they have waged unabated warfare against Israel. At the same time, however, they came year after year before the United Nations, demanding, tongue in cheek, that Israel agree to receive those who were being maintained, indoctrinated, trained as a spearhead of aggression against Israel. Israel had no right to live, they claimed; war against Israel will continue, they brazenly informed the United Nations. Yet the United Nations must insist, they demanded, that Israel introduce into the country the very bomb readied to blow it up.

This dismissal of fact and reason is especially apparent in the Arab stand on persons displaced by the 1967 hostilities. As early as September 1967 the Arab States decided in Khartoum to reject peace with Israel and pursue warfare against it. Since then war against Israel has continued despite the cease-fire. Fighting is raging incessantly. Egypt has repeatedly announced that there is no solution to the conflict but war. Only a few days ago President Nasser promised the region "fire and blood." Syria has refused to pay even lip service to the notion of peace. Jordan is toeing Cairo's line and has turned its territory into the principal base for terror operations against Israel. Lebanon is being pressed to follow suit. Instead of seeking peace, the Arab Governments are organizing for continued war. Their regular forces are engaged in constant armed attacks along the cease-fire lines. Their irregular forces are trying to intensify their operations of murder for murder's sake. Israeli houses are blown up and their tenants killed in sleep. Israeli civilians are bombed in crowded marketplaces and on their way to worship. Israeli children are threatened by mines planted in schools and on school buses.

At the same time, as if none of this were happening, the Arab States appear here and say to us, Take them all back, with the saboteurs we have trained and implanted in their midst, with the assassins we have taught to murder your women and children, with those we have indoctrinated to direct all their efforts to Israel's downfall. We shall continue to attack you, the Arab Governments tell us, to kill you and to undermine your people's existence, but you must not defend yourselves. In fact, you must help us to destroy you.

There is much illogic in the Middle East conflict, there is considerable unreasonableness in the Arab attitude toward Israel, but there is no obligation upon us, or upon others, to accept it. We understand fully the concern of men of goodwill for the difficulties of ensuring adequate and expeditious supplies to refugees, for the fact that there are dwellings in refugee camps on the West Bank which remain unutilized, for the wintry weather which brings additional hardship. We understand and sympathize with the vicissitudes confronting the Arab refugees; we feel most strongly that they must be alleviated. We cannot, however, forget for a single moment the struggle imposed on us by the Arab Governments' continued belligerency. It is not a struggle for better food or shelter, but for our life. It is not a problem how to protect our citizens from rain or cold, but how to save them from enemy bullets and shells, how to put an end to the monstrous bloodlust that has surrounded us for twenty years.

In these circumstances it is not enough to see only one aspect of the situation. In these circumstances it is unjust to take into account the problems and needs of one side only. In these circumstances views and resolutions which disregard the overall picture and overlook the right of one of the parties to safety and security could only be harmful. We must do all to bring relief to the refugees. We must explore all avenues to bring about a solution of their problem. We must, however, bear in mind at all times that the refugee problem is a consequence and a function of Arab aggression against Israel and that Israel is still trying to defend itself against this aggression.

WARFARE AGAINST ISRAEL PREVENTS SOLUTION, HAMPERS
IMPROVEMENT

The problems of displacement in 1948 and 1967 were caused by war stemming from Arab belligerence against Israel. They can fully be resolved only in the context of peace.

As regards the 1948 refugee problem, that view was implicit in the inclusion of paragraph 11 in a resolution which called for a general peace settlement. It was on that assumption that the Palestine Conciliation Commission's peace efforts were based in the period from 1949 to 1951. For many years after that, Arab efforts were made to deal with paragraph 11 in isolation from the rest of Resolution 194 (III)—i.e., to deal with the refugee problem as if it existed in a vacuum and disregard its background of continued Arab belligerence. This approach proved sterile, and the Security Council resolution of November 22, 1967, drew the necessary conclusion by recognizing the refugee problem as one element in a comprehensive peace "package."

The same reasoning applies to the displacement of 1967. It would be unreasonable to believe, as suggested in the UNRWA report and in Resolution 2452 A (XXIII) of last year, that a large-scale and unrestricted repatriation of persons dislocated by hostilities can take place while hostilities are still continuing and without any relation to the actual political or security circumstances, or to the progress, if any, toward a peace settlement.

The Israel delegation stated the following on this matter at the meeting of the Special Political Committee on November 26, 1968.

The extent and rapidity with which a return can be facilitated is inevitably affected by the political and security conditions on the spot. We still live in a situation that officially rests on a cease-fire but that is in practice marked by continuous border warfare and by efforts to promote violence and disrupt orderly administration within the Israel-held areas. The Jordanian Government, which foments and supports all these activities, is itself making any large-scale repatriation as difficult and as sensitive as possible. . . .

Pending a peace settlement, Israel is doing its best to reconcile the return of displaced persons with responsibility for the safety, welfare and security of the local population and the security of the State itself. A program for an influx of returnees obviously needs to be carefully regulated, though it can be reviewed and expanded as the situation permits.

In appraising the degree to which the return of displaced persons can be facilitated in accordance with Security Council and General Assembly resolutions, it is essential to take also into consideration the fact that certain Arab Governments in the Middle East have since June 1967 continued to persecute ruthlessly the Jewish minorities in their countries, in flagrant violation of the selfsame Security Council and General Assembly resolutions. Invocation by Arab Governments of United Nations resolutions at the very time that these texts are being trampled upon by the Arab States makes a farce of Arab arguments regarding their implementation. The Charter of the United Nations binds member States to a mutuality of obligations. There can be no implementation on one side and complete violation on the other.

RETURN OF PERSONS DISPLACED BY 1967 HOSTILITIES

In spite of these considerations and difficulties, the Government of Israel has continued to the best of its ability to facilitate the return of persons who left the West Bank in the June 1967 hostilities. This has been done in full cooperation with the Arab local authorities in the area, and in the context of family reunion, hardship cases, and the reissuance to other applicants of entry permits not utilized by their original recipients.

It is pertinent at this stage to make two general observations. First, the majority of persons that crossed from the West Bank to Jordan after the end of the June 1967 hostilities cannot be regarded as "displaced persons who have fled the Israel-occupied areas." They were persons who left the area of their own will, in an orderly fashion, and without being obliged to do so. This is undoubtedly the reason why so many who have been granted permission to return have not availed themselves of this possibility.

ECONOMIC INTEGRATION SUBSTANTIAL

Our direct contacts with large numbers of refugees in Israel-held territories bear out the fact reported by the Commissioner General to successive sessions of the Assembly that, despite political obstacles, there has been over the years substantial economic absorption of the refugees. As far back as five years ago the Commissioner General reported that 50 to 60 percent of the registered total of refugees were economically independent or partially self-supporting.

Three years ago Mr. Michelmore stated:

With the passage of time and changes in the economic circumstances, the rations have become for many of the recipients a modest economic subvention from the international community to assist them in their struggle to support themselves and improve their economic conditions. The Commissioner-General believes that it would be misleading to attach undue importance to the number of ration recipients as an index of the dependence or independence of the refugees on international aid.

According to a study carried out by a research team from the Hebrew University of Jerusalem of one of the large refugee camps in the West Bank, the average family income and level of employment were nearly equal to local standards, and even a little higher, when adding the cash value of UNRWA rations. Moreover, very few of the original refugees were left in the camp, and a number of local inhabitants had gradually moved in.

The refugees have to a large extent merged with the indigenous population. Even if we include the special case of the Gaza Strip, only a third of the refugees live on camps at all. The camps themselves have in the intervening years evolved into villages, small townships and urban quarters. The original homes have been expanded into family dwellings by the refugees from their own resources.

It is to be observed also that the majority of names on UNRWA lists today are those of children and young people who were born after the events of 1948 that created the refugee problem. The proportion will be even larger when the lists catch up with the undisclosed deaths.

Thus, behind the smokescreen of political propaganda, the natural absorption into the local life and economy of the Arab refugees is quite advanced, despite the political designs of the Arab Governments and despite the difficulties arising from the persistence of Arab warfare.

The accurate assessment of the degree of this absorption is complicated by the fact that UNRWA's working rule has in effect been "Once a refugee, always a refugee." As my delegation indicated last year and in previous sessions, even those persons who become self-supporting and no longer receive the agency's help remain registered with it as refugees and are included in its refugee totals. According to the Commissioner General's report the number of persons in this category is as high as 148,004. There are undoubtedly many more who are self-supporting but continue to receive relief. This perpetuation of the refugee status is also encouraged by UNRWA's assumption in practice that such status is handed down from the original refugees to their children and their children's children and all subsequent generations. Indeed, an adjustment of the UNRWA rolls continues to be essential, especially in view of the financial difficulties that burden UNRWA today.

As the Commissioner General points out in his report, UNRWA's relief to refugees and their integration into normal life, like Israel's own efforts to improve their condition, have been hampered by "the persistence of sporadic hostilities and a general heightening of tension in the area." Indeed, the persistent warfare waged by the Arab States against Israel has made UNRWA's operation considerably more onerous. Arab terror operations have sometimes been directed against the refugees themselves, causing many dead and wounded. On the other hand, the Israel authorities, in the exercise of their responsibility for security and safety in areas under their administration, find it necessary from time to time to take measures to prevent acts of violence and punish the perpetrators and their accomplices. The picture of the resultant situation as painted by Arab propaganda is grossly exaggerated, but the grave problems and additional difficulties created by the pursuance of aggression against Israel confirm that the key to the settlement of the refugee problem is peace.

LOOKING TO THE FUTURE

It is not sufficient to wait for peace. It is possible to begin to plan and work for it right now. It is with this in view that the Government of Israel has proposed immediate action toward an overall solution of the refugee question. In his statement in the plenary session of the General Assembly on September 19, 1969, the Foreign Minister of Israel declared, "I propose that a Conference of Middle Eastern States should be convened, together with the governments contributing to refugee relief and the Specialized Agencies of the United Nations, in order to chart a five-year plan under regional and international responsibility for the solution of the refugee problem in the framework of a lasting peace and the integration of refugees into productive life."

A similar proposal was made by my delegation in this committee last year and two years ago. We are still awaiting the response of Arab Governments.

The Arab-refugee problem was born of war. It will be solved by peace. It is time to make peace.

The Arab-refugee problem has been exploited since 1948 as an instrument of continued warfare against Israel. It is only when this warfare ceases that substantial progress toward a full solution of the refugee question will become possible. It is time to end this warfare and to make such progress toward a solution.

II

Statement delivered November 25, 1970, in the Special Political Committee during the annual debate on the Palestine refugees.

More than any other aspect of the Middle East conflict, the refugee problem has over the years become enveloped in passion and acrimony. Facts have become secondary to arguments. Belligerency has overshadowed constructive thinking. Humanitarian concern has been replaced by political reckoning and invective.

A solution to the refugee problem is not only desirable, indeed vital, but also possible. Its attainment would require an attitude of understanding and cooperation on the part of the Arab States, an attitude long overdue if it is truly the welfare of the refugees that they seek. No issue arising out of the Middle East situation has ever been resolved or brought nearer solution through confrontation and discord. It must be evident to all that only agreement between the parties is capable of achieving a settlement. The Security Council has recognized this fundamental truth, and Resolution 242 adopted by the Council on November 22, 1967, affirmed the necessity of achieving a settlement of the refugee problem within the context of agreement on a just and lasting peace. The Government of Israel has suggested accelerating the efforts toward a settlement of the refugee problem and has proposed to convene at an early date an international conference of the contributing Powers, the Arab States and Israel to agree on a five-year plan for solving the question. The Arab States have refused.

There was no reason, no logic, in this refusal. With goodwill it is possible to remove the obstacles which have stood in the way of a solution of the refugee problem.

Nations in other parts of the world have demonstrated how this could be attained. Since World War II fifty million refugees have had to leave their homes and move to other lands. As in Palestine, these movements resulted from war. Many of them involved large ethnic, religious or national groups. All of them created deep grievances and sharp claims and were accompanied by loss of property and deprivation of human and political rights. Most of them could have developed into highly inflammatory international disputes. Yet all these problems have been settled quietly and constructively, the refugees absorbed in the countries of refuge and given new life in new surroundings.

This has happened also in the Middle East itself. Jewish refugees from Arab lands, equal in number to the Arab refugees from Israel, have been received by Israel and rehabilitated within the Jewish State. Today, almost half of the population of Israel is composed of refugees from Arab countries and their families. A virtual exchange of population has taken place between Israel and the Arab States, with the acquiescence of the Arab Governments. This is a fact basic to any consideration of the Arab-refugee problem. If we are to pursue the search for a possible settlement, we cannot think in terms of reversing these two parallel movements of large masses of people, but must guide ourselves by the successful experience gained in all parts of the world with the integration of refugees in the societies in which they had found refuge. The criterion applied in assisting refugees to rebuild their lives has always and everywhere been where they could best live in peace and harmony with society, and not necessarily where they were born.

UNITED NATIONS EFFORTS TO RESETTLE ARAB REFUGEES

Efforts in this direction have also been made by the United Nations in respect of the Arab refugees.

In 1948 the United Nations sent to the Middle East the Economic Survey Mission to devise projects for regional economic development which would enable resettlement of refugees in various parts of the region.

The mandate of UNRWA itself was defined by the General Assembly in Resolution 302 of December 8, 1949, as follows:

a. To carry out in collaboration with local governments the direct relief and works programs as recommended by the Economic Survey Mission.

b. To consult with the interested Near East Governments concerning measures to be taken by them preparatory to the time when international assistance for relief and works projects is no longer available.

In 1951 UNRWA formally proposed to the Government of Egypt to settle seventy thousand from the Gaza Strip in Sinai.

In 1952 the General Assembly adopted Resolution 521, which established a $200-million fund for the reintegration of refugees and suggested that the administration of relief be transferred to the host Governments, allowing UNRWA to concentrate on reintegration projects.

In 1959, the Secretary General submitted to the General Assembly a report recommending to integrate the refugees in the economy of the Middle East countries in general.

All these plans, projects, resolutions were rejected one by one by the Arab Governments. Their attitude was explained in the January–March 1957 bulletin of the Research Group for European Migration Problems, which stated:

The Arab Governments have been applying to the refugees an abstract and inhuman policy for the purpose of maintaining a menacing population on the frontier with Israel. These Governments have systematically rejected all organization and employment for the refugees. Their attitude is one of seeking to prevent any sort of adaptation and integration because the refugees are seen as a political means of pressure to get the greatest number of concessions.

On January 17, 1960, King Hussein of Jordan declared, "Since 1948 Arab leaders have approached the Palestine problem in an irresponsible manner . . . They have used the Palestine people for selfish political purposes."

REFUGEES: AN INSTRUMENT OF BELLIGERENCY AGAINST ISRAEL

The Arab Governments did not confine themselves to frustrating international plans for dealing constructively with the refugee problem. They turned the refugees into an instrument of continued warfare against Israel. When they realized after 1948 that they were unable to crush Israel by regular military forces, they resorted to terror warfare. The Egyptian Army organized the so-called *fedayeen* squads and sent them into Israel with explicit instructions to murder civilians. The refugees served as a reservoir of manpower for these acts of aggression. Later Syria established in a similar way and for the same purpose the Al Fatah organization. These organizations have increased in number and intensified their activities since 1967. Their aim is clear, and they proclaim it without equivocation—it is to destroy Israel. Their method is murder of innocent citizens. They have claimed credit for the murder of children on school buses, for killing and maiming students at university, for exploding dynamite charges in crowded markets and stations, for hijacking airplanes and detaining their passengers as hostages. Gradually the refugee camps became centers and bases for such activities while United Nations assistance continued to flow into them as usual.

Emboldened by this situation, the Arab Governments now suggest that the terror organizations grouped in the so-called Palestine Liberation Organization be given an advisory status with UNESCO and UNRWA. Indeed, the advice that these organizations could offer on the propagation of hatred and bloodshed, on the killing of helpless civilians, on the hijacking of planes, on the rejection of all United Nations resolutions, would be most impressive. On one hand the international community desperately gropes for ways to cope with the criminal activities of the terror organizations; international organs including the United Nations adopt resolutions condemning air terror and hijacking. On the other hand, UNRWA is being asked to further boost these groups, and this, of all fields, in education. This is an irresponsible suggestion fraught with dire implications.

The attitude toward Israel's right to independence adopted by these Palestinian organizations, their total rejection of peace with Israel, their continued warfare against Israel, and the support they enjoy from Arab Governments are adequate to explain the impossibility of moving large numbers of refugees into territory under Israeli jurisdiction. The 1948 resolution of the General Assembly made any return of refugees conditional on peace. The Arab Governments and the Palestinian organizations have, however, made the refugees a tool in their continued aggression against Israel. The 1967 Security Council resolutions called on Israel to ensure the welfare and security of the inhabitants in Israeli-held areas. The Arab Governments and the Palestinian armed organizations have been conducting an uninterrupted assault on the welfare and security of the civilian population in these areas.

Despite these impediments, Israel has admitted over the years approximately fifty thousand refugees displaced by the 1948 hostilities.

The Israel Government is prepared to take certain security risks for the sake of the refugees. However, there are limits beyond which an influx of refugees could become a direct threat to the welfare and security of the population.

The caution required in dealing with this matter is best illustrated by the statement made by the late President Nasser on September 1, 1961: "If the refugees return—Israel will cease to exist."

Speeches delivered by certain Arab representatives during the Twenty-fifth Session of the General Assembly indicate that this design has not been abandoned. The recent hostilities in Jordan have strengthened even further the need to weigh most carefully the effect that the return of refugees in large numbers would have on public order and security.

Attempts have been made to cloak the terror activities of the Palestinian organizations in the mantle of a struggle for Palestinian rights. The truth of the matter is, however, that the aims which these organizations pursue are as destructive as their means. Their objective was defined by Yassir Arafat, head of Al Fatah and the PLO, on March 29, 1970, as follows: "The goal of our struggle is the end of Israel and there can be no compromises or mediations, whether our friends like it or not . . . Peace for us means Israel's destruction and nothing else."

Indeed, the primary objective of the terror organizations is to deprive the Jewish inhabitants of Palestine of their legitimate rights. However, the legitimate rights of the two peoples, Arabs and Jews, who inhabit Palestine are not irreconcilable. The Arabs exercise them in the Palestinian State of Jordan established within the borders of mandatory Palestine; the Jews, in Israel. The Arabs are free to determine the structure and character of the Arab State. The Jews are equally at liberty to do so in their State. To question the right of Jews to freedom and sovereignty in their ancient homeland simply because they had been conquered and exiled from it by foreign invaders is untenable historically, legally and morally.

INTEGRATION OF REFUGEES PRACTICABLE

The fact that integration of Arab refugees into the local economies is possible has been demonstrated throughout the years.

A significant comment on this is to be found in the Lebanese daily *Al Hayat,* which wrote more than ten years ago:

Here we have a further example of our hypocrisy. For is there an Arab country in which there has been a greater absorption of refugees than in Lebanon? Of the 120,000 refugees who entered Lebanon, not more than 15,000 are still in camps. Taking into account a natural growth of 15,000, we may conclude that 120,000 refugees have been absorbed in Lebanon and have become an integral part of her population, her society and her economy . . . Yet we "reject" settlement; we brand every stranger who dares to use the word "resettlement" as being guilty of treason, imperialism and plotting—even if he wants to do us, or the refugees, a service.

The Swiss *Review of World Affairs* reported in its November 1961 issue:

It seems probable that the refugees in Syria have made the best adaptation to the host country's standard of living. Since the refugees make up only 4.5 percent of the total population, they were more readily absorbed . . .

The fact that nearly all the Palestinians in Syria receive UNRWA rations does not necessarily mean that they have no other source of income. But the authorities in Syria prevent the organization from carrying out any investigations regarding the income of the refugees.

Integration is a natural process in particular because the majority of Arab refugees had never left the territory of Palestine. They moved only a few kilometers, settling down anew among their kinsmen and friends.

The UNRWA report indicates that only one third of the registered 1948 refugees live in camps. Two thirds reside in the midst of the general population. Of the total number of 1948 and 1967 refugees, 60 percent live outside camps. Moreover, it is to be borne in mind that the rolls remain inflated by names of persons long dead and by refugees who have in the meantime become self-supporting. Hundreds of thousands of refugees earn a living, and for them UNRWA relief is merely a source of additional income.

This was confirmed already six years ago by the Commissioner General, who reported that 50 to 60 percent of the registered total of refugees were economically independent or partially self-supporting.

Four years ago Dr. Michelmore reported:

With the passage of time and changes in the economic circumstances, the rations have become for many of the recipients a modest economic subvention from the international community to assist them in their struggle to support themselves and improve their economic conditions. The Commissioner-General believes that it would be misleading to attach undue importance to the number of ration recipients as an index of the dependence or independence of the refugees on international aid.

The continuation of the process of economic integration and self-support after 1967 is reflected for instance in the fact, reported by UNRWA, that although expenditure for education has increased and become the main item of UNRWA's budget this year, the relief program and other sources of livelihood have made it possible to maintain nutrition and health at the same level as in the past.

INTEGRATION IN ISRAEL-ADMINISTERED AREAS

The potentialities of economic integration and self-support have been substantiated by the experience in Israel-administered areas. The Israel authorities have found that by removing obstacles to the refugees' inherent human aspiration to lead normal lives within the structure of economy and society in which they live, it is possible to make considerable progress.

There are nearly a million Arab inhabitants in these areas. About a quarter of them live in refugee camps on the West Bank and in the Gaza area. UNRWA rolls include, however, 300,000 more names of persons who live outside the camps.

The objectives of Israel's policy are to ensure the normal course of life, encourage economic development and restrict security measures to those indispensable for safeguarding public law and order. It is the Israel Government's view that while UNRWA continues its activities, Israel should do all that is possible to improve the refugees' living conditions and to offer them opportunities to become productive and self-supporting. For that purpose Labor Exchange offices have been established throughout the Israel-administered areas. These not only channel applications for employment but also protect Arab workers from exploitation. The Israel authorities are promoting governmental and private economic activities in agriculture, construction, trade, industry and public works. Employment is also offered in Israel itself. At present more than thirty thousand workers from the administered areas, a considerable part of them refugees, earn relatively high wages in Israel.

The result of this policy has been a sharp decline in unemployment, which is now on a very small scale and does not exist at all in certain seasons of agricultural activity.

On March 4, 1970, Radio Cairo reluctantly took note of this situation. It said: "Immediately after the June war, the enemy opened labor exchanges and took steps to promote the economy."

The *Guardian* of April 26, 1970, stated: ". . . by and large the Israeli presence has boosted rather than depressed the economy of Judea and Samaria."

Indeed, since 1967, agricultural production has expanded in Israel-administered areas by 20 percent, industry by even more than that.

The refugees, treated by the Israel authorities as an integral part of the local economy, have thus found their standard of life rising, with resultant improvement in housing, food and clothing.

The *Wall Street Journal* reported on March 6, 1970: "Israel is coming to grips with one of the most explosive problems in the Middle East—Arab refugees. . . . Now Israel is starting to move, by setting up rehabilitation and assistance programs that include expanded education and vocational training and by simply providing work for the refugees."

As part of the policy of improving general public utilities and service, the Israel authorities have also undertaken improvement projects in refugee camps. These include installation or amelioration of water, electricity and sewage facilities, the paving of streets and construction of new roads, the development of playgrounds. Such projects are usually carried out in coordination with the residents and local councils.

EDUCATION IN ISRAEL-ADMINISTERED AREAS

During the year under review there has been improvement and expansion of education services in Israel-administered areas. As reported by the Commissioner General, Israel authorities have spent in the course of this period nearly U.S. $1,500,000 on education services for refugee children in public and private schools subsidized by the Israel Government. The above sum is only a fraction of the total expenditure by the Israel Government on general education in Israel-held territories. While 85,000 refugee children attend UNRWA/

UNESCO schools in these areas, 24,000 study in public and private schools.

According to the Commissioner General's report the education of refugee children in areas administered by Israel has proceeded in improved conditions.

The report states in paragraph 112: "The school year on the West Bank has been relatively good in so far as work and attendance are concerned."

With regard to the situation in the Gaza area, the Commissioner General declares in paragraph 113: "The UNRWA/UNESCO school system continued to operate with acceptable results."

This situation is particularly significant as compared with the known interferences with schoolwork in the neighboring countries, as mentioned in paragraph 24 of the report.

The difficulties concerning the import of textbooks from Arab countries have, to a large extent, been resolved. This was reported by the Commissioner General in his statement to the Committee on November 18, 1970.

Of 118 textbooks submitted by UNRWA, the Government of Israel has by the end of October 1970 granted permits for the importation of 103. Israel is consulting with the Director General of UNESCO on the question of the remaining fifteen textbooks.

The Government of Israel objects to the use of these books in UNESCO/UNRWA schools because they contain derogatory passages regarding Jews and Israel. For instance, an Egyptian book for the fourth elementary grade, *Al Tarbiyah Al Deeniyah,* says: "The Jews are traitors and are plotting against every person who has money in order to take it away from him." It is regrettable that such texts are still in use in UNRWA schools in Arab States. It is a primary responsibility of United Nations organs not to lend themselves to the dissemination of incitement to national, religious or racial hatred.

Israel's attitude toward the education of refugee children is demonstrated in the continuous efforts made to facilitate to the utmost the normal functioning of the school system, even when security risks are involved. In paragraph 107 of the UNRWA report we read:

The organization by UNESCO in August 1969, with the active col-laboration of the United Arab Republic and Israeli authorities, of secondary school certificate examinations for some 7,000 students of both sexes in the Gaza Strip was a remarkable example of international cooperation in very unfavorable circumstances. This operation, which was supervised in Gaza by local government and Agency staff working under the control of a team of international experts from UNESCO and UNRWA, resulted in 5,109 students passing the United Arab Republic certificate examination, and in 1,031 subsequently crossing the Canal zone in five convoys, conducted by the International Red Cross, to take up university scholarships offered by the United Arab Republic Ministry of Higher Education. This constructive action has brought fresh hope to thousands of young Gaza residents, most of them registered refugees. The Israeli Defence Department has given an undertaking to permit these students to return to Gaza during the long vacation and at the end of their university education.

In his statement of November 18, 1970, the Commissioner General added, with reference to paragraph 107: "The Director-General of UNESCO was successful in making similar arrangements again this year and in late September about 8,000 Gaza students were again able to take the examination."

This is the general picture of the refugee situation in Israeli-admin-istered areas. It is a situation not lacking signs of progress and im-provement, indicating that when constructive attitudes are adopted it is possible to advance satisfactory solutions.

SECURITY MEASURES TO PROTECT POPULATION

It is natural that even under the most constructive policies difficul-ties do arise from time to time. However, such difficulties cannot overshadow the overall situation.

This is the case, for instance, with security measures which Israel is at times compelled to take. These measures have decreased with the improvement of security conditions. In any event there is no comparison between them and the drastic security actions which Governments in neighboring host countries have resorted to.

The measures undertaken by Israel are unavoidable, especially in view of the fact that Palestinian terror organizations exert great efforts to mobilize and activate saboteurs from among the refugee population. Refugee camps are considered by these organizations as ideal bases and hideouts. In their efforts to enlist collaborators, the terror organizations regard Arab staff members of UNRWA as being of special interest and use. This is, of course, the reason why some of these local employees of UNRWA have been affected by the security measures.

It is important to note, however, that the refugees themselves are frequently targets and victims of the terror operations. From 1967 until November 10, 1970, Arab terror attacks have resulted in 2,000 dead and wounded. Of these, 1,204 were Arabs, refugees and non-refugees, killed or injured by Arab saboteurs. Indeed, Arab terrorists have thrown more grenades on Arab buses, exploded more dynamite charges in Arab marketplaces, fired more often into Arab classrooms than on Jewish targets. This was explained by Radio Damascus on March 26, 1970, as follows: "The death of a starving Arab in the conquered land will arouse international wrath against the enemy."

There could be no more cynical an admission of the sinister objectives of the terror organizations.

An analysis of the operations by agents of terror organizations in the last three years in Israel and Israeli-administered territories demonstrates that the security steps Israel is obliged sometimes to take are as vital for the protection of the Arab population, including the refugees, as for the safety of Israeli civilians. This applies, as already explained, to the regulation of admittance from Arab-controlled territory of refugees, and in particular of persons displaced by the 1967 hostilities.

In conclusion, my delegation would like to associate itself with the words of appreciation addressed by other representatives in this Committee to the Commissioner General and his collaborators and to assure them of our continued cooperation.

War has given rise to the Arab-refugee problem, and peace will solve it. Whether in the search for an overall solution within the context of a just and lasting peace, or in the efforts to assist the refugees to rebuild their lives before final peaceful settlement is attained, it is essential to abandon warfare, to forgo belligerency and bloodshed and to begin to think of peace and act for peace. We appeal from here to the Arab Governments to start addressing themselves to the Arab-refugee problem in terms of peace and understanding with Israel. We call on them not to add to hostility and discord, not to make the road to peace and settlement of the refugee problem more difficult. Of the Committee we ask to encourage mutual understanding between Israel and the Arab States, to avoid creating new obstacles to agreement, to help remove the blocks that have been placed in the way to settlement.

It is for the good of the refugees and of all peoples in the area that the counsel of harmony and accord should prevail in this debate.

6 The War Has Not Ended—
the Struggle for Peace Goes On

I

Address made in New York, April 15, 1975, on the occasion of the twenty-seventh anniversary of Israel's independence.

This is a day of thanksgiving for the gift of life in these momentous times, for partaking of the present; for remembering the past, for being able to shape the future; for being Jewish.

This is a day to sing of the glory of the Jewish people, the grandeur of its civilization, the indestructibility of its faith, the vision of its existence.

Today we are celebrating the Jewish people's triumph in history, the vindication of its age-long struggle, the justification of generations of suffering and sacrifice, dedication and perseverance.

Israel's renewed independence and sovereignty revolutionized the laws of time and space, challenged the unchallengeable, gave new meaning to national creativity.

The world said it was not possible. We proved that it was. The world advised us not to resist fate. We did. The world was ready to watch us go under the waves of hatred and violence. We refused and emerged victorious to rise to new heights.

By this act of rebellion and resurgence the Jewish people reasserted its ability and determination to be master of its own destiny. Its own willpower, its own judgment, its own perception of the nation's interests were to guide it in its hours of trial and triumph.

It was in November 1947 that the family of nations recognized the Jewish people's right to sovereignty. However, no sooner had the Arab States started to oppose it by force than the international community abandoned the Jewish people and prepared to place Palestine under a United Nations trusteeship. It was in defiance of this attitude that the people of Israel proclaimed its independence. We said no to the world of indifference and shortsightedness.

If we had done what others wanted us to do, there would have been no Jewish State. Israel is the expression of the Jewish resolve to live by what is good and just for the Jewish people and not by what finds favor in the eyes of others.

If we had hearkened to outside advice, Israel would not have taken in hundreds of thousands of new immigrants in its very first act of sovereignty. It was against such advice that we opened the gates to all our brethren, because we knew that this was our Jewish obligation, because we knew that this was the fulfillment of the nation's timeless dreams.

If we had lent our ears to the views and prejudices of others, Israel would not have warded off Arab onslaughts as it has, with all the wrath and might that it could muster. When we put to naught Arab aggression, when we destroyed invading armies, when we hit out at terrorist bases, it was not the displeasure in various parts of the world that counted, but our own interests and our own decision.

If we had yielded to the weaknesses and hesitations of others, we would not have struggled for the rights of our brethren in the Soviet Union and the Arab States in the way that has brought redemption to so many of them.

This is the principal lesson of the years of Israel's independence.

Our destiny lies in our own hands. We ourselves must determine what is right for the Jewish people and the Jewish State. We ourselves must choose the course we shall follow. We need and we desire the understanding and the support of others, but in the hour of decision it is our judgment and our resolve and our vision that must guide us. In the Jewish people's long titanic struggle there must be daring which we can ask only of ourselves; there must be self-sacrifice which we can demand only of ourselves; there must be responsibility which we can assume only ourselves.

The struggle is far from over. Those who fought against Jewish independence in the past continue to fight it at present. Those who tried to prevent the emergence of a sovereign Jewish State are attempting to undermine it now. Those who sought to deprive the Jewish people of its fundamental rights are battling us till this very day. Those who didn't lift a finger to save the millions of our brethren from death in the Holocaust are not aroused when the blood of innocent Jewish women and children is being shed again.

Thus the Jewish people's struggle continues unabated, one of the greatest epics of history, one of the most inspiring sagas of national liberty and equality. A struggle carried on through millennia, waged against tyrants and oppressors in all parts of the world, a struggle for the right of a whole nation to live, a struggle of an entire civilization to survive. The English- and French- and Spanish-speaking peoples, the Protestant and Catholic and Moslem nations, the peoples of all continents and all beliefs and all cultures and all social and political regimes are represented in the family of nations by numerous sovereign entities. The Arab nation alone has twenty sovereign States, including the Palestinian Arab State of Jordan. The only Jewish State, Israel, still has, however, to defend its right to freedom and independence. The Jewish people still has to bleed for its right to live. But live it shall, for there are enough people all over the world, and you amongst them, who are determined that it should live and thrive and create and inspire.

Because ours is a struggle which galvanizes and beckons to all. It is the cause of life itself, the cause of basic human rights. The cause of the boldest and most tenacious revolution in the annals of mankind. Yet also the cause of preserving fundamental and immutable values. A struggle carried on in storm and fire, yet aiming at peace and construction.

That is why all who are associated with it know that there is no struggle more justified, none more inspiring, none more rewarding.

Throughout the ages, one aspiration has permeated the Jewish people on its eternal trek—the longing for peace.

At no time has this longing been more fervent than since Israel's independence. To Israel peace means welfare and happiness, growth and strength. Israel emerged into independence appealing to its neighbors for peace. Israel has persisted in its call for peace, offering its hand to the Arab States again and again. The aspiration to peace has dominated Israel's entire existence. It has shaped the policies of all Israeli Governments. The Arabs have persistently reacted, however, with a single sinister voice—the voice of war. They never made any secret of their objective—to eradicate the Jewish State and annihilate the people of Israel. They never renounced this objective.

They are still motivated by it today. For Israel there can be only one way—defend itself, resist, strike back until the Arab States abandon their gruesome designs on Israel's existence and become ready to make peace with us. Peace must be attained in the Middle East. Peace can be attained in the Middle East. It will come, however, only when the Arab States change their basic attitude toward Israel and accept Israel's sovereignty, and that change will occur only when the Arab Governments are convinced that Israel is strong enough to thwart any attempt on its independence. Israel will not weaken in the pursuit of this goal. Its firmness, its tenacity, its determination are essential to temper Arab extremism and advance the region toward peace.

Those are the considerations which guided Israel in the recent talks with Egypt conducted through Secretary Kissinger. The issue in those negotiations was not a few square kilometers of territory. The issue was peace. The question was whether Egypt was ready to take the first step in the direction of peace. Egypt was not, and the negotiations broke down. Egypt wanted territory, but was not prepared to abandon the path of war and to begin to construct peace together with Israel. If Israel had acquiesced in Egypt's position, if Israel had yielded to Egypt's demands, it would have opened the Middle East to a process of Vietnamization. Israel will not allow this to happen. Israel will not be deterred by lack of understanding or by unfounded criticism. It will not be swayed by charges that determination to attain peace is intransigence. It will not be impressed by the misguided view that

Egypt's refusal to end war constitutes moderation. Israel will not bow to pressure, from whatever quarter it may come. Israel will continue its struggle, steadfast and resolute, until its rights are fully vindicated.

Those who support peace in the Middle East will support Israel. Those who seek peace in the Israel–Arab conflict will strengthen Israel. A strong Israel means stronger prospects of peace. Reducing support for Israel would mean reducing the chances for peace.

We live in a world in which weakness has brought mortal disaster to nations. In recent years mankind has watched Czechoslovakia succumb to a powerful neighbor, Pakistan torn apart by the force of arms, and now Cambodia and South Vietnam overrun and shattered. Israel is not Czechoslovakia or Cambodia. Israel is one of the few countries in the democratic world determined to stand up for its rights, prepared to safeguard, at all cost, its independence and the ideals by which the free world lives. If the free world wants to discourage aggression, if the free world does not intend to abdicate its international responsibilities, it will welcome Israel's resilience and steadfastness. It will cherish and encourage Israel's constancy of purpose and resoluteness. Those who are concerned by the fact that the forces of tyranny and totalitarianism are on the march while democracy is in retreat will give their backing to Israel, not coerce it, while Israel is defending its right to life and to peace.

One of the greatest dangers to the future of enlightened mankind stems from the tide of despotism, extortion and arrogance, fed by oil power, which is threatening to sweep across the world. Mankind owes a debt of gratitude to Israel for showing that this destructive tide can be resisted even by small nations.

The Jewish people's history is measured in thousands of years. The present is a mere prelude to the future. Though Israel's reestablished independence has not solved all the problems confronting the Jewish people, it has provided us with the instrument for their solution. That is why we face the future with hope and confidence. The difficulties of today should not be more than transitory. There is enough dedication and strength within the Jewish people to overcome these difficulties.

The challenges of today, economic and military, are grave, but it is within the power of the Jewish people to meet them. We have been through more trying days and succeeded. Let us, therefore, unite in one great national endeavor to see Israel through these crucial times. Beyond the horizon stands a Jewish State larger in population, more advanced in science, agriculture and industry, more powerful militarily, more secure in its sovereignty. Beyond the horizon looms a world freed from the shackles of the oil Moloch, a world in which natural resources serve all mankind and not the lust and greed of the few.

In the immediate future Israel will pursue peace and probe every possibility of attaining understanding with its neighbors. It will consent to methods and accept agreements that will further peace. It will turn down demands for gratuitous Israeli concessions which would undermine the peacemaking effort. At the same time Israel will continue to build and develop and to offer shelter to all who wish to live and work and create in the midst of their own people. Israel and the entire Jewish people will continue to struggle for the redemption of our brethren who are still oppressed in the lands of darkness. We shall not rest till the Jewish State and Jewish people everywhere enjoy the rights of all States and all peoples.

This is the credo of the Jewish rebirth, and Israel shall live up to it.

So many centuries of hope and prayer have gone into Israel's independence. So much suffering, so many tears, so much blood have forged the state. So much yearning, pain, love and sacrifice have built the nation's resolve, its tenacity and its strength. It has been in the most trying hours of its existence that the Jewish people has reached the heights of its greatness. This is the way it has been throughout our history. This is the way it has been throughout the years of independence. This is the way it shall continue to be. All together we shall make certain that the Jewish people remains a great people. All together we shall make certain that Israel's years of strife and sacrifice, which have borne such bountiful fruit of glory and achievement, lead into years of joy and peace for the Jewish State and the Jewish people everywhere.

II

Excerpts from an address before the Conference of Presidents of Major American Jewish Organizations, May 26, 1975, in New York.

A constructive policy on the Middle East will be guided at all times by one central consideration: how can genuine progress be made toward peace between Israel and the Arab States? Consequently every attitude adopted, every action undertaken, every assessment of policy should be judged by its ability to contribute tangibly to progress toward peace. Peace is the principal objective. Peace must be the overriding criterion.

When in its struggle for peace Israel adopts a position that in its view strengthens the prospects of peace or opposes a development it regards as detrimental to the search for peace, can there be any justification to find fault with it? After all the years of Israeli endeavors to attain peace, and Arab warfare and negation of peace, can there be any doubt that there is nothing that Israel desires more than peace with its neighbors? On one hand there is the State of Israel, its desire for peace unquestionable. On the other hand there are the Arab Governments, some of which continue to reject a pacific settlement with Israel while others pay lip service to the concept of peace. Even the less extreme of the Arab Governments support the PLO with its Nazi attitude toward the Jewish State and the Jewish people. Even the allegedly moderate Arab leaders demand the restitution of the so-called inalienable rights of the Palestinians—a euphemism for replacing Israel by a Palestinian Arab State with a Jewish minority.

Is it not evident, then, that in these circumstances Israel must be persistent and vigilant in its efforts to persuade the Arab States to abandon their course of hostility and war? Is it not clear that Israel must not miss any opportunity to try to commit the Arab States to a process of peace? Is it not imperative that the territories which have come under Israeli control in the struggle to repel Arab aggression must be used, with the greatest of circumspection, as instruments for peace? It is common knowledge that the Arab Governments are prepared to affix their signatures to agreements providing for Israeli withdrawals. This is not the issue at all. The question is whether the Arab Governments would be prepared to conclude agreements containing the political elements of peacemaking.

If the search for peace in the Middle East is to be serious and effective, Israel must insist that every new arrangement between itself and its neighbors should be a concrete step in the direction of peace. Israeli territorial concessions without Arab commitments to peace would stall and undermine the peacemaking efforts. The attainment of peace is too great and too historic a responsibility for Israel to make light of these facts. Neither should others.

Thus, support for the cause of peace in the Middle East requires support for Israel's painstaking efforts to ensure that every new diplomatic development should bring us nearer to peace. To weaken Israel is to weaken the forces of peace in the region. Assistance, especially military aid, to the Arab States in their belligerent confrontation with Israel is harmful to the interests of peace. When Israel's entire existence is postulated on the aspiration and pursuit of peace while the Arab attitude toward peace is at the very best a dubious one, it is right to favor Israel. It is wrong to place Israel at a disadvantage in its ceaseless, tenacious drive for peace.

This is not a matter of sympathy for one side or the other, but a question of realistic understanding of the fact that reduction of support for Israel encourages Arab intransigence, retards the peace effort and increases the danger of war.

Under these conditions the Arab call for evenhandedness toward Israel and the Arab States must be seen for what it is—a demand to treat on an equal footing Israel's unrelenting search for peace and Arab policy that is still keeping the Middle East in a state of war after twenty-seven years of conflict.

There are manifold expressions of support. But it is evident that the support for Israel necessary at this juncture to reinforce the prospects of peace is not the declaratory underwriting of Israel's survival.

Israel's survival is not in doubt. Israel can and will ensure its existence and sovereignty. Israel will live because the entire Jewish people wants it to live. The problem is whether Israel's strength will be maintained at a level that will give it security, deter Arab aggression and enable Israel to attain peace with its neighbors, including the establishment of defensible boundaries—a prerequisite for lasting peace.

Israel's goal of peace is clear. Israel is determined to advance toward it. Israel is prepared to try each and all the roads that could hopefully lead to it.

It is ready to resume the talks on a limited agreement with Egypt from the point at which they were suspended. Such agreement, which would contain a commitment on the nonuse of force, is still possible, especially if its validity is established for a longer period of time.

Israel is also prepared to discuss a broader agreement involving more extensive territorial changes accompanied by termination of belligerency. An end to belligerency short of peace and short of the delineation of final boundaries is realistic and not unprecedented in international relations. It has been resorted to both in Europe and in the Far East.

Israel is also ready that, after necessary preparations are made, the Geneva Conference be reconvened.

There is one thing, however, that Israel cannot do. The Government of Israel cannot abandon the responsibility to appraise meticulously and test with care every idea, proposal or move by its ability to promote peace in the Middle East.

It is in this light that Israel's tactical moves must be understood. Israel will agree to withdrawal coupled with an Arab commitment to advance on the path to peace. It will reject withdrawal if it leaves the Arab party immovable in its negativism toward peace.

In the framework of comprehensive peace negotiations Israel will seek a solution for the needs of Palestinian Arabs. Israel will not undermine the peace prospects by any contact with a murder organization which is not representative of the Palestinians, not concerned with their true needs, denies the Jewish people's right to self-determination and independence and does not constitute a factor of real import in the Middle East situation.

Israel recognizes the right of every people in the region to independence, but it will not endanger the structure of peace by countenancing the creation of a second Palestinian Arab State, in addition to Jordan, a development which would open the door to irredentism and perpetual conflict.

When peace treaties and state boundaries are under negotiation Israel will put forward precise plans, formulations and maps. It will not create, however, further difficulties for the peacemaking process by indulging in premature finalization and disclosure of such proposals, inviting their inevitable outright rejection by the Arabs and thus bringing about deeper entrenchment of Arab intransigence.

Recent events, such as the letter of support for Israel addressed by seventy-six Senators to President Ford and Syria's agreement to renew the mandate of the United Nations forces for another six months, contribute to a more hopeful atmosphere for the pursuance of diplomatic efforts. The success of these efforts in the forthcoming months will depend on a number of developments.

First: Will the Arab Governments, and especially Egypt, realize that if peace is to be built in the Middle East every new agreement must, from now on, possess the political elements essential for the construction of peace?

Secondly: Will all concerned realize that if another attempt is to be made to reach an interim agreement between Egypt and Israel, it is incumbent upon Egypt to soften its position? Will it be understood that if progress is to be achieved Egypt must be persuaded to take a concrete step toward peace paralleling its demand for an additional Israel withdrawal?

Thirdly: Will the Arab States take the road of constructive peacemaking, or will they continue to shatter the hopes for mutual confidence and understanding by acts such as assistance to terrorism and extreme hostility in international arenas and organizations?

Fourthly: Will the reassessment of United States policy on the Middle East be concluded by a reaffirmation of support for Israel's peace struggle and by reinforcement of Israel's economic and defensive strength? This would facilitate not only the search for agreement between the parties but the United States role in it as well.

Fifthly: Will the idea that the two superpowers could ever, jointly or separately, chart for the parties the outline of a peace settlement remain safely interred? In 1973 the United States vetoed a resolution in the United Nations Security Council which aimed at imposing on the parties the Jarring proposals, based in turn on the plan known by the name of Secretary of State Rogers. The reasons which prompted that veto at the time are valid today. The way to end the conflict and reach stable agreement is to allow the parties themselves to work out the terms of settlement, even if they are assisted by others, and to bind themselves, of their own accord, to such a settlement.

Finally: Will the Soviet Union steer a more constructive course than in the past and refrain from encouraging Arab intransigence and belligerency?

All these developments will have a significant bearing on the course of events. On the evolution of some of them we can have an influence. One factor, however, remains at all times dependent entirely on ourselves. It is our faith, our resolve. This will be decisive in our struggle. It is said that only they conquer who believe they can. We believe that we can meet the challenges that confront us. Our faith comes from our Judaism, from the history of the Jewish people, from the Jewish vision of the future. Our resolve is rooted in our age-long struggle, in the tragedy and triumph of our existence, in the knowledge that this time we cannot afford to fail.

We know that we shall succeed, for you and we have within us the vigor, the dedication and the readiness for sacrifice that bring success.

III In the Face of the Nations

1 Israel and the United Nations

I

Excerpts from the first statement in the Security Council, convened March 21, 1968, at Jordan's request following an Israeli action against terror bases in the Jordan Valley.

I would be remiss in my responsibilities if in this first statement to the Council I did not bring before you certain misgivings which fill the hearts of the people of Israel and its Government as we engage in another debate in this Council. Time after time we turned to the Security Council in appeal for action and assistance to preserve peace. In the somber hours of the last twenty years we have repeatedly come before the Council in plea, in hope and in expectation. The Council has failed us again and again. For the past fifteen years this organ has found itself paralyzed whenever Israel has had recourse to it. The "veto" was cast to avert a reaffirmation of Israel's right to free navigation. It was cast to torpedo even the mildest of requests to Arab States to cease their warfare against Israel. It crushed all attempts at evenhandedness and made resolutions recognizing Israel's rights a near impossibility. The people of Israel, indeed the entire world, watched in dismay and trepidation how the doors of the Security Council were in effect shut before Israel. As I survey the Council table, this situation appears today in rather dramatic form. Five * of

* In 1975 eight of the members of the Security Council have no diplomatic relations with Israel.

the members of the Security Council have no diplomatic relations with Israel. All five have identified themselves unreservedly with the position of the Arab States. Two of them deny Israel's right to exist. One has participated in the war against Israel and refuses to accept the cease-fire ordered by the Security Council.

In these circumstances it is not surprising that questions are being posed with regard to the Council's attitude in the Israel–Arab dispute. We hope that the Security Council will rise above these disabilities and be guided by the desire to bring peace and security at long last to the Middle East. We shall judge this debate in the light of its contribution to the attainment of these goals.

II

On May 21, 1968, the Security Council adopted a resolution which called urgently on Israel to rescind all measures already taken which tended to change the legal status of Jerusalem, and to desist forthwith from further action of that nature.

The following statement was made in the Council after the adoption of the resolution.

The Security Council has ended its deliberations on Jerusalem. Through the morass of acrimony and abuse, the truth about Jerusalem emerges more clearly than ever. Jerusalem faithful to its history, Jerusalem at peace at last, reunited again, Jerusalem where Christian, Moslem and Jew live side by side, work together and create together. Jerusalem of the Holy Places, venerated and secure, beckoning to worshipers and pilgrims of all faiths, from all parts of the world. Jerusalem the workshop of understanding and coexistence between Israeli and Arab. Nothing can tarnish the truth about Jerusalem. Nothing can change its reality. Nothing can overshadow its glory.

Fully conscious of its international obligations, respectful of the universal interests in the city, inspired by Jerusalem's rejuvenation, the Government of Israel will do all in its power to ensure the welfare of the city and the happiness of its people.

The principles of the Charter, the precept of equality of all member States, the fundamental right to peace and security will guide us with regard to the resolution adopted today by the Security Council. The resolution is neither practical nor reasonable. It ignores reality and disregards Israel's basic rights. It seeks to violate the natural unity of Jerusalem and to overlook the interests of Jerusalem's inhabitants and their welfare. It advocates the return to the nightmare of separation and religious discrimination. It does not contribute to the attainment of peace. On the contrary, it is designed to serve as a weapon in the pursuance of Arab belligerency against Israel. It does not bring closer the prospects of understanding between the parties, but further deepens the abyss between them.

When, in 1948, the Arab States took up arms in defiance of the United Nations and launched their aggressive attack against Israel and Jerusalem, little international concern was expressed; when Jerusalem was shelled and bombarded and its population brought to starvation, the Security Council remained silent. When for twenty years there existed an occupation by Jordan resulting from aggression, when for twenty years access to the Western Wall was barred, when ancient synagogues were deliberately destroyed by the Jordanian Government, when any idea of agreement with world religious interests was rejected by the occupying Power, the Security Council remained silent.

Where was the Security Council in those hours of trial and agony? Where was the Security Council when Jordan again launched an onslaught against Jerusalem last June? Where was it when Jordan refused to make peace? Where was the Security Council when Jordan openly declared the intention to continue its warfare against Israel by raid and terror?

Now, a whole year after the barriers fell in Jerusalem, now when Jews and Arabs live side by side in peace and work together in coexistence, when reconstruction and restoration are well on their way, and, above all, when, for the first time in twenty years, access to the Holy Places is universal and complete, guaranteed by law and open to constructive dialogue with the universal religious interests involved, the Security Council hastens to evince concern.

To be of any consequence, a resolution must first of all be realistic and equitable. Is the world really to believe that there is an international principle whereby Jerusalem must be divided against the wishes of its citizens, its Jews and Arabs separated, access to some of the Holy Places denied? The resolution would have us reinstall the barbed wire and mine fields which have been removed and rescind measures which have brought normality and peace to a city artificially bisected for nineteen years.

It is, of course, regrettable that some still find it possible to support the revival of military confrontation and chaos in Jerusalem. The people of Jerusalem, however, cannot be expected to welcome the weird idea that they should be amputated and sacrificed on the altar of belligerency. To suggest this to them would be contrary to all the principles of international law, of morality and justice.

At this point I should like to reiterate Israel's intention to ensure fully the universal character of the Holy Places themselves, Christian as well as Moslem, and to seek arrangements to this effect with the authoritative representatives of the faiths concerned. This policy has been repeatedly enunciated by Israel and is being pursued constantly in practice.

We appreciate the attitude of the member States that have dissociated themselves from the resolution.

In the past I have had occasion to draw attention to the disabilities of the Security Council when it comes to dealing with questions of the twenty-year Arab war against Israel. The resolution now adopted does not change or add to the known pattern of Security Council resolutions on the Middle East situation. It adds, however, to the determination of the people of Israel to gird themselves with even greater fortitude for the defense of their rights and the pursuit of peace and security, despite the malice of those who have injured us and despite injustice born in error.

After twenty years of war it is evident beyond any doubt that peaceful and accepted settlement rather than Security Council resolutions will resolve the Israel–Arab conflict. Indeed, the choice lies once again with the Arab States: the choice between continued acrimony and the search for understanding; between contests of public debate and quiet constructive effort; between warfare by terror, threat, in-equitable resolutions on the one hand and agreement on the other; the choice between impasse and solution. We hope to be able to make progress toward agreement and peace. We still await, however, an indication from the Arab States that they too are ready to join in a common effort in this direction.

III

On December 29, 1968, the Security Council was summoned into urgent sessions at the request of both Lebanon and Israel, the day after Israel defense forces took action against the Beirut international airport. The action was carried out three days after an Arab terror attack on an El Al airliner in the Athens airport.

The following statement was delivered December 31, 1968, after the Council had adopted a resolution which ignored Beirut's responsibility for terror operations against Israel.

By ignoring the fundamental principle of the United Nations, equality of all member States, the resolution now adopted by the Security Council is contrary to the United Nations Charter and cannot therefore be considered as applicable. A resolution which fails to take account of Israel's rights under the cease-fire, disregards the right of its citizens to be free from Arab attack, overlooks and slights Israeli dead and wounded, is an affront to the basic values of the United Nations. The resolution reflects the moral, political and juridical bankruptcy of the Security Council in respect of the Middle East situation. It cannot but raise the question asked by the Psalmist in the Bible: "How long will ye judge unjustly, and respect the persons of the wicked?"

The people of Israel will see in today's decision another sign that the strength to vindicate their rights and protect their legitimate inter-ests must come from within themselves. This is the world we live in. The troubles and grief and suffering of a nation frequently remain of limited concern to others. We have recently witnessed an entire people enslaved and then almost forgotten. Massacres of human beings are still taking place in some parts of the world without evoking undue anxiety. Thus it has also been in the Middle East. The central and gravest fact in that region—the Arab war of aggression relentlessly pursued against Israel since 1948, the continued Arab warfare in violation of the cease-fire of 1967—is frequently lost sight of or relegated to the background.

However, the people of Israel cannot afford the luxury of such callousness. There is a daily struggle for life, a continuous titanic contest with death. Let no one misjudge their mood and their resolve. Let no one make the mistake of thinking that the people of Israel might be swayed by inequitable pronouncements. Let no one make the mistake of thinking that the fate of the people of Israel can be decided by others; not the fate of a people with a four-thousand-year history; not the fate of a people which has reestablished its sovereignty after twenty centuries of subjugation, exile and dispersion; not the fate of a people that has been subjected to genocide; not the fate of a people that has waged a war of defense and survival for twenty years.

That is why the attitude and actions of the Governments in the area, not Security Council resolutions, will determine the destiny of the Middle East. That is why Israel's action in Beirut, taken in defense of its rights, should make the Arab Governments understand the full depth of Israel's determination to ensure its right to peace and security. When the Arab States realize that determination, become persuaded by its tenacity and draw the appropriate conclusions, there will be peace in the Middle East. There is nothing that the people and Government of Israel desire more. There is nothing that depends more on the Governments of the Arab States.

IV

On August 26, 1969, the Security Council adopted a resolution condemning the air attack by Israel against terror bases in southern Lebanon, ignoring the intensification of armed attacks against Israel from

Lebanese territory. The following statement was made in the Security Council after the vote.

It is regrettable that the resolution now adopted joins a long list of similar texts which have reflected, again and again, the chronic inability of the Security Council to address itself to the Israel–Arab conflict with the necessary equity and effectiveness. The facts of the situation discussed by the Council are unmistakably clear. In recent months Lebanese territory has become a base for terror operations against Israel. The last few weeks have witnessed a grave intensification of these attacks, directed primarily against the civilian population of Israel. Terror warfare of this kind is an old method employed by the Arab States, in violation of international law and the United Nations Charter, throughout the twenty-year Arab war on Israel.

Faced with the duty to protect its citizens from armed attack, the Government of Israel resorted, on August 11, to its inherent and inalienable right of self-defense and took action to disable encampments of the irregular forces in southern Lebanon, from which the acts of aggression against Israel were being carried out.

These facts have been fully confirmed by published statements made on behalf of the joint command of the terror organizations; they have been freely announced by Lebanese personalities and the Lebanese press, widely reported by international media of information, and are fully established by many eyewitnesses of unimpeachable integrity. The Lebanese representative has made only perfunctory attempts to question these facts, and when he does question them, as he did today, he finds himself at odds with reality.

For instance, according to the Beirut daily *Al Nahar* of August 18, 42.4 percent of the Lebanese citizens questioned in a special Gallup poll consider the presence of saboteur groups on Lebanese soil and their operations against Israel as the cause for Israel's action on August 11.

The resolution of the Security Council inexplicably ignores these facts. A number of members of the Council have condemned unequivocally the armed attacks carried out from Lebanon against Israel, and rejected the Lebanese Government's denial of responsibility for violations of the cease-fire. However, the resolution, although it proscribes all violent incidents in violation of the cease-fire—and, therefore, obviously the armed attacks by irregular forces from Lebanon—fails to single out those attacks for strong and specific censure. On the other hand, it does censure the Israel defense action against those attacks.

Now, such a double standard may encourage the aggressor. It will strengthen the defender in the opinion that the Security Council is, unfortunately, unable to recognize the defender's legitimate rights, whatever the understanding, and indeed knowledge, of some of its members may be.

Matters have reached such a point that even a formal reference in the preamble of the resolution to the Lebanese letter to the Council cannot be balanced by a similar reference to the Israeli letter; and at the same time room is found in the preamble to recall the ghost of the Armistice regime, nullified by the Arab refusal to respect it and finally voided by Arab aggression. The defects of the resolution are further expressed in the fact that, while terror organizations and the Lebanese press and Lebanese leaders have openly admitted that Israel's action was directed against saboteur encampments, the resolution speaks of reprisal on Lebanese villages; and the exclusion at Arab insistence of a direct and explicit call by the Security Council to the parties to observe the cease-fire is a striking example of the resolution's inadequacy.

Here I would observe that my Government's reluctance to invite the Security Council to consider Israeli grievances flows from considerations such as these and not from those repeatedly alleged by Arab spokesmen, including the representative of Lebanon, and their supporters. Members of the United Nations and the representatives in the Council who know of the high esteem and personal friendship in which we hold them will undoubtedly understand that resolutions on the Middle East adopted by the Council in these circumstances must be regarded as being primarily a reflection of the arithmetical vagaries of the vote, always dominated by the fact that of fifteen members of the Council no fewer than six have no diplomatic relations with Israel or deny Israel's right to independence and sovereignty.

The difficulties which the Security Council faces in producing balanced, equitable, realistic resolutions on the Israel–Arab conflict are becoming a matter of increasingly grave concern to the Council itself and to all to whom the ideals of the United Nations Charter are dear. These internal difficulties, however, do not affect basic tenets of law and justice, and their unhappy results cannot be interpreted as prejudicing the legitimate rights of a State which has been continuously resisting implacable aggression for more than two decades.

V

On December 8, 1970, the United Nations General Assembly adopted a resolution which declared that the Palestinians are "entitled to equal rights of self-determination," disregarding the rights of the Jewish people.

The following statement was delivered after the adoption of the resolution.

Today's vote on Draft Resolution C is a further illustration of the causes behind our Organization's continuing loss of prestige and effectiveness. When rules of procedure are set aside and Charter provisions are violated in order to push through texts unacceptable to the majority of member States, United Nations actions become valueless.

The goal of the United Nations is not to offer a forum to the kind of distortions and falsifications that the General Assembly heard today from the representative of Jordan. A country which on its admission to the United Nations accepted all the obligations under the Charter has repudiated every single one of them in relation to Israel, and still has the audacity to come before this organ and offer advice on behavior in accordance with United Nations principles.

The goal of the United Nations is not to offer opportunities for voting contests, but to encourage member States to reason together, to seek understanding, to harmonize their differences, to strengthen friendly relations among States. The vote on Draft Resolution C makes mockery of these objectives. Indeed, the Arab States have once again perverted the United Nations into an instrument for the pursuance of their hostile policies toward Israel.

The resolution was supported by a minority of States; the majority refused to give it its approval. The fact that it will nevertheless be recorded as having been adopted is due to procedural manipulations whereby its sponsors established that it is not an important question. Israel will treat it accordingly as a text of no import, and the Government of Israel cannot be expected to attach to it greater importance than the Assembly itself, which, at the instigation of the sponsors, has decided that the matter is not important.

The resolution reflects the well-known views of a group of States concerned, apparently, more with the vagaries of vote mechanics in this Organization and with paper achievements than with peace in the Middle East. If part of the effort expended by the Arab delegations to accumulate votes in support of continued enmity were devoted by them to utilizing the United Nations for the attainment of peace, the interests of all of us in the United Nations and the peoples of the Middle East would be better served.

The States which have initiated and supported this resolution will recall that Jewish history is the story of a people that has remained faithful to its ideals and has not faltered in its struggle for equality, justice and independence, though it has always confronted nations more numerous than itself. In all epochs, expressions of belligerency have strengthened our unity and our determination to vindicate our rights. It is clear that a Middle East settlement will not be encouraged by votes in the United Nations reflecting controversy, hostility and a narrowly partisan approach. The only way to contribute to a settlement is by promoting agreement between Israel and the other parties to the conflict. Israel will continue to struggle for its right to peace and security, and this struggle is in conformity with the true principles of the United Nations.

VI

On December 13, 1972, the General Assembly adopted a resolution which affirmed "that the people of Palestine are entitled to equal rights and self-determination," while completely ignoring the rights of the Jewish people to national existence, freedom and self-determination.

The following statement was delivered in the General Assembly after the adoption of the resolution.

For twenty-five years the General Assembly has been adopting resolutions which gave satisfaction to Arab belligerency but in no way advanced the settlement of the refugee problem. Again today a series of resolutions has been brought before this plenary session, almost all reflecting the usual expressions of Arab animosity toward Israel. Ignoring facts, perverting truth, distorting legal precepts, injecting issues extraneous to the refugee problem such as the positions adopted by Palestinian terrorist organizations, those texts, as in the past, are inequitable and detrimental. As in the past, Israel will oppose them. By their one-sided and acrimonious nature, these resolutions reemphasize the known inability of the United Nations to discuss objectively any aspect of the Middle East situation and to contribute constructively to its solution.

Utilizing their parliamentary advantage, the Arab Governments have throughout the years confined their efforts in the United Nations to obtaining unbalanced resolutions, inimical to Israel, ignoring its legitimate rights and interests. They have thereby virtually deprived the United Nations of the possibility of playing a useful role in the advancement of peace in the area. The only way the United Nations could play such a role is, first, by replacing sterile polemical debates with serious, constructive exchanges of views; secondly, by adopting resolutions arrived at through consultation with and consent of the parties directly concerned; and thirdly, by encouraging the parties to seek agreement between themselves through negotiation.

As long as the United Nations continues on its present course of acrimonious verbiage, it will inevitably remain outside the arena of effective peacemaking efforts. Israel, on its part, in accordance with the principle of sovereign equality of all States as enshrined in the Charter, will be guided only by texts which are formulated in consultation with it and which give due consideration to its rights and its views.

The victims of the Arab States' policy in the United Nations are first and foremost the Palestinian refugees themselves. Instead of assisting them in reconstructing their lives, the Arab Governments have been feeding them, year after year, with United Nations resolutions which reflect the views of notorious violators of international law and morality such as Syria, Libya and Algeria, but not even the actual opinions of all those who vote with them, because of the parliamentary mechanics of our Organization.

Instead of giving the refugees hope of a solution to their problem, the Arab Governments have been offering them, again and again, hackneyed slogans of hate and hostility. Instead of attending to and respecting the concerns of the Palestinians, the Arab Governments have been representing in the United Nations the interests of Palestinian terror organizations, initiated, supported and controlled by them. Those professional thugs, numbering a few thousand and assisted by foreign mercenaries, are no more representative of the refugees and of the Palestinian Arabs in general than the Assassins who appeared in the Arab lands in the Middle Ages were representative of the Arab world at that time. The Arab people, including the Palestinian refugees, know that their future lies in agreement with Israel. Indeed, the first indication that Arab Governments are seriously concerned about their fate will come when those Governments cease pressing for the adoption of texts such as those before us today and begin seeking agreement with Israel. It is time to end the annual recitals of calumny which lead nowhere, and to enter on the path toward agreement and the solution of the problems besetting the Middle East.

VII

*Excerpts from a statement delivered April 17, 1973, in the Security
Council, convened at Lebanon's request to discuss Israel's action against
terrorists in Beirut.*

Is not the United Nations Charter based on the sovereign equality of
all its member States? Why, then, is one Arab representative after
another permitted, as they have been again today, to come before the
highest organ of the United Nations and openly reject Israel's right to
independence? Why are they permitted to claim here that all peoples
in the world have a right to national identity, to freedom and self-
determination, but not the Jewish people? Why are Arab representatives allowed to turn the Security Council Chamber into a forum
where slander and falsehood are constantly trotted out, where truth
and history are turned into mockery, where law and equity are cynically distorted? Is it not a travesty of elementary justice when the
Jewish people's age-long struggle to restore its independence in its
ancient homeland is calumniated and dismissed, while the descendants
of Arab conquerors of this land and people, the great majority of
whom had immigrated into Palestine from abroad in the same years
the Jews returned to it, are referred to as indigenous, as they were by
some representatives again at the present meeting?

How long will the United Nations have to hear what the world
knows to be a total untruth: that the problem of a million Palestinian
refugees, out of more than forty million refugees in all parts of the
globe who have been resettled a long time ago, is the source of Arab
terrorism, which began long before there was a single Palestinian
refugee in the world?

Those who have been listening to the statements made in the Council today and yesterday must have been pondering and wondering over
a number of questions. Does not international law, do not United
Nations resolutions, prohibit the organization and the support of ter-

rorist acts from the territory of one State against another, as provided for, for instance, in the Declaration * I cited? Why then does not the Security Council do something about the maintenance of terrorist bases and the initiation of terrorist acts on the territory of Lebanon and other Arab States? Why does the Council listen passively to Arab Governments justifying their identification with terror and atrocities and demanding a license for continuing in this criminal attitude?

Is there or is there not a fundamental Charter principle recognizing the right of every State member of the United Nations to self-defense, a right transcending all other principles and obligations? Why, then, is there criticism of Israel's action against the terrorist bases from which savage attacks have been launched against its territory and its citizens? Is it merely because this action was carried out by Israel? Does not the principle of self-defense apply to Israel as it does to other countries? Is not the entire enlightened world engaged today in combating international terrorism? Why does not the Security Council do something about it?

What is the advice that we hear at the Council table? From Arab representatives it is simple: disappear from the world and then there will be peace. Well, the Jewish people has rejected such advice for several millennia; it does not intend to heed it now, especially when it comes from such paragons of international law as Arab representatives or the representative of Indonesia, which thought nothing of massacring half a million Chinese citizens only a few years ago. Where was the Security Council then?

What alternatives do those who have expressed dissatisfaction with Israel's action against the terrorist bases have to offer to us? Address ourselves to the United Nations? Has not our Organization proved helpless to take effective action against terrorism? Have we forgotten what happened only a few months ago at the General Assembly session? Turn to the Security Council? How many times is it necessary to do so in order to prove that the Council, because of its structure, its composition, its voting procedures, is unable to take an equitable

* General Assembly "Declaration on Friendly Relations and Cooperation Between States" (A/8028).

stand on Middle Eastern questions? How many more meetings of the Security Council are necessary to remind the world that in its entire history this organ has not adopted a single resolution—not a single resolution—condemning the murder of Israeli citizens, and that time and again such resolutions have been voted down or vetoed?

Have we already forgotten how, when in 1967 Egypt chased out the United Nations Emergency Force (UNEF) from Sinai and Gaza, imposed a war blockade in the Strait of Tiran, massed its forces for attack along Israel's borders and began shelling Israeli villages, the Council found itself in a mire of polemics, incapable of taking any action?

What is then the course of action against the barbaric campaign of Arab terrorism that is being proposed to us here? Nothing, nothing at all. Since the beginning of the Al Fatah/Black September atrocities in 1970, eighty Arab terrorists have been caught in Western countries—some of them in States represented in this Council, including States whose representatives have spoken today. All of these terrorists—all of them—have been released. Now, is this the way to combat terrorism? Is this the example set for Israel? In another country, Yugoslavia, only a few days ago, an Israel table-tennis team participating in an international tournament was compelled by the Yugoslav authorities to leave because those authorities gave in to the threats of Arab terrorist organizations to attack the Israeli sportsmen. Now, is this a policy to be emulated? Do nothing? Surrender to the menace of savage bloodshed? Release criminals engaged in it?

A Jewish citizen of the USSR recently wrote a letter to the Secretary General of the United Nations explaining his suffering, his despair, his longing to live as a free man in Israel. Recalling Jewish history—the Inquisition, the pogroms, the Nazi Holocaust—he wrote: "In the heart of every Jew there is a cemetery." Yes, we have not forgotten and we shall not forget. We have not forgotten the six million barbarically butchered, the two million Jewish children led to gas chambers and crematoria, while the world stood by in silence. We have not forgotten how in those dark years of persecution and murder we were being told that there are principles of sovereignty, of domestic jurisdiction, of vital State interests which prevented intervention, which prevented effective action to save six million Jews.

The advice given us today—sit still, do nothing about the murder of Jews in our times, because there are questions such as those of sovereignty—cannot but bring back the echoes of the past.

The problem before the Security Council is clear. Egypt and Lebanon and their supporters are asking for a license to continue international terrorism. Israel submits to the Council that, in the absence of any readiness by Arab Governments to abide by their obligations and put an end to the use of their territory for murder operations, in the absence of any effective measures by the United Nations to curb international terrorism, Israel has no choice but to protect its people with its own means. The cycle of violence is not of Israel's making. When Arab violence ceases, when Arab terrorism ends, there will be no need for Israeli countermeasures, and an effort toward understanding and agreement can be made.

VIII

Excerpts from a statement delivered April 21, 1973, in the Security Council following the adoption of a resolution in connection with Israel's action against terrorists in Beirut.

The adoption of the text just voted upon confirms a number of known facts. It demonstrates once more that the Security Council, like other United Nations organs, cannot, because of its structure and composition, its voting procedures and their preordained results, deal equitably with questions pertaining to the Middle East situation. If it cannot examine and at least pronounce itself fairly and adequately on the murder of innocent men, women and children by Arab terrorist gangs, if it cannot recognize Israel's inherent right to defend itself against sanguinary attacks, it is obviously not the body capable to act on any of the complex issues of the Arab–Israeli conflict.

The adoption of the resolution confirms that there is international law on the one hand and that there are words produced in the Security

Council on the other, and the twain rarely meet. In this Passover season, one is tempted to say that the forceful exodus of the Israelites from ancient Egypt would have been condemned by this Security Council had the Egyptians asked for it.

The resolution also confirms that in the absence of meaningful United Nations action against international terrorism it is incumbent upon responsible governments to combat this scourge by their own means. The Government of Israel, in accordance with its inalienable rights and its international obligations, will continue to protect the people of Israel from Arab murder attacks.

The debate has given Israel the opportunity publicly to restate its case. We appreciate this, although we knew in advance that the Security Council was not able to consider it on its merits. Ours is a just case, and we are fortified in our conviction that this is so not only by the unity of the people of Israel in the defense of its rights but also by the support of enlightened public opinion all over the world, by the stand adopted by international organizations capable of taking a more balanced view of the situation than the Council and by the attitude of international personalities who, unlike Government representatives guided by political considerations, can assess problems on the basis of principles of law, justice and morality.

IX

Statement delivered in the Security Council August 15, 1973, following the adoption of another one-sided resolution in connection with Israel's action against terror bases in Lebanon.

The resolution adopted by the Security Council is the customary one-sided text this organ has been producing on the Middle East situation. It closes its eyes completely to the grave menace of Arab terrorism which necessitated Israel's defensive action on August 10.

This is not unusual for the Council which, during the entire twenty-five years of the Middle East conflict, has been unable to make up its mind even once that armed attacks against Israel by Arab States or from the territory of Arab States constitute transgressions against the United Nations Charter and international law. This is not exceptional for the Council which has never, not even once, brought itself to condemn the murder of Israeli children, men and women.

In these circumstances, the precise wording of the resolution is of lesser import than its primary significance—namely, that the United Nations is unable to cope with international terrorism in general and with Arab terrorism in particular. Indeed, no member of the Security Council has challenged that basic fact. No one has suggested that States should abdicate their duty to combat terrorism and leave the struggle against that scourge to the helpless organs of the international community. No one could have suggested that Israel should rely on the Security Council or the General Assembly to take effective measures against the Arab campaign of violence and bloodshed. No one had a word of explanation why Governments, including those of States members of the Security Council, have been and still are releasing without trial, or even after conviction, Arab terrorists who were caught redhanded in the perpetration of their criminal acts.

Nothing has been said in the course of the Security Council's debate that could weaken the incontrovertible tenet of international law and the United Nations Charter whereby the Arab States must be held responsible for the use of their territory by murder organizations to wage an open campaign of barbaric atrocities against innocent human beings in various parts of the world. Nothing said here was capable of derogating from the evident truth that by harboring those organizations, by supporting them politically, financially and militarily, the Arab Governments are guilty of persistent violation of Israel's sovereign rights under the Charter and the cease-fire, and in particular of the right to security from armed attack.

No member of the Council could plausibly show that a State which violates the sovereign rights of a neighboring country could at the same time substantiate the claim that its own rights bar the injured country from defensive action. Not a single tenable argument has been put forward that in this situation Israel could be denied the right to self-defense. Nobody has questioned the well-known fact that other

States—among them, permanent members of the Security Council—
have in similar conditions exercised their right to self-defense in the
same manner as Israel.

It is obvious to everybody that there must be one law for all, and
that Israel will not be an exception. No member of the Security Council has dared to challenge Israel's judgment that the life of a single
Israeli child is more sacred than any claim of the inviolability of territory serving as a base for aggression. Law exists for men, not vice
versa. The criminal individual or the State violating law cannot seek
refuge behind it. Everywhere and at all times the protection of innocent lives takes precedence over solicitude for the alleged rights of
those who endanger human life.

Consequently, those who hope that the world will be rid of the murderers of defenseless men, women and children, those who pray that
massacres such as those of Lod, Munich, Khartoum and Athens should
never happen again, can rest assured that Israel will not fail them. The
Government of Israel will continue in its struggle against Arab terrorism with determination and unswerving firmness. It will continue to
protect the lives of its citizens. It will give no quarter to the ruthless
killers of the innocent. It will pursue them and strike at them until
mankind is free of their bloodthirsty savagery.

In striving toward that goal, Israel will cooperate with all responsible Governments and all competent international organizations which
seek to ensure international security and the safety of world communications.

X

*Excerpts from address at a meeting with young Jewish leaders on May 15,
1975, in New York.*

As I sat in the chambers of the United Nations and listened to
representatives of the most totalitarian Governments in the family of
nations preach of the freedom of peoples and individuals; as I heard

delegates of States which know not what elementary democracy is speak of human rights; as emissaries of countries where more than ninety percent of the population is illiterate quoted Shakespeare and admonished the world on education, I found myself thinking, What a hoax, what a sham.

Of 138 States members of the United Nations, approximately one hundred have no parliamentary regimes. The majority of the States deny basic human rights to their own citizens. Many oppress the ethnic or religious minorities within their borders. In international relations a great number of these States are guilty of grave violations of the United Nations Charter and some of the most flagrant aggressions of our times. Yet these are the States which, because of their membership in such groupings as the Arab, Soviet and nonaligned blocs, are able to muster an automatic majority on every issue, and thus appear to be mankind's mentors on law, justice, morality and human rights. This is not merely the tyranny of the majority. This is tyranny of the unprincipled and lawless, of the aggressors and oppressors. Without understanding that, one cannot understand how Yassir Arafat, his hands covered with the blood of countless innocent victims, could be invited into the United Nations and welcomed with loud cheers and applause. Without understanding that, one cannot comprehend how UNESCO could have excluded Israel from its activities.

How can the UN, in these circumstances, command respect? How can its discussions and resolutions be given credence? Even a schoolchild watching its work must feel shocked by the violations of the Charter principles, the distortions of truth and the perversion of values that take place daily within the walls of the Organization.

The UN is in a state of tragic decline. It is in a state of deterioration reminiscent of the decomposition of the League of Nations. It is dominated today by the twenty Arab delegations, which, by virtue of their predominance in the so-called nonaligned group that, together with the Soviet bloc, disposes of some one hundred votes, are running amok in the United Nations. What we are witnessing is a veritable "Aminization" of the Organization, the wielding of power by the irresponsible and the extremist. If this process continues, the United Nations, already unable to deal constructively with international conflicts and situations, will inevitably become completely incongruous to international developments.

To avert the demise of the UN, a fundamental change in the methods of its work is essential. It is not a question of amending the Charter. The principles and the purposes of the Organization enshrined in the Charter remain as valid and inspiring today as they were at the time of the establishment of the United Nations. What is necessary, however, is for the Organization to abandon its present system of adopting resolutions by means of automatic majorities. The result of this system is one-sided, ineffective and sometimes absurd resolutions, to which responsible sovereign Governments cannot subordinate their vital national interests. Instead, discussions in United Nations organs should aim at agreement and understanding acceptable in the first instance to the parties directly concerned. In other words, the UN must see to it that, as a first step, the parties to a conflict or dispute are brought together to negotiate and to reach agreement between themselves. When such understanding is attained, the approval of the entire membership could be sought. This would mean utilization of the novel, multilateral parliamentary framework which the UN is, together with the application within that framework of the traditional method of bilateral diplomacy. Only such a blend of the new and forward-looking with the tested and proven methods of quiet diplomacy could salvage the United Nations from the fate which befell its predecessor, the League of Nations.

2 Israel and the Superpower Adversaries— the USSR and China

I

Israel voted in 1971 for the admission of the People's Republic of China to the United Nations. The following brief statement was made in the General Assembly on October 26 in explanation of Israel's vote.

The Israel delegation voted for it, since the central purpose of the resolution is to clarify that the Government of the People's Republic of China is entitled to represent China in the United Nations.

In casting its vote the Israel delegation was guided by the principle that this is a vote which gives recognition to the right of the Government of the People's Republic of China to represent China, a member of the United Nations, and not a vote for the expulsion of a member State.

Israel's fundamental attitude is based on the principle of universality of the United Nations, on recognition of the right of all States to be represented by their Governments and on the membership in the United Nations of every peace-loving State that applies for it.

II

A reply to the representative of China. (Excerpts from a statement made in the Security Council, June 23, 1972.)

This is the first time I have heard the representative of China address himself to the Israeli problems. As he undoubtedly knows, I have a special sentiment for his country and his people which is shared by all my countrymen, and I should therefore like to make a few observations about his statement.

Only three days ago, the Security Council adopted a decision expressing grave concern at the threat to the lives of passengers and crews arising from the hijacking of aircraft and other unlawful interference with international civil aviation, condemning such acts and calling upon States to take appropriate measures to deter and prevent such acts and to take effective measures to deal with those who commit them. The decision was adopted unanimously. It represented the consensus of all members of the Security Council. What value is to be attached to that decision if members who supported it a few days ago now come out in defense of organizations and movements responsible for the most serious and atrocious attacks in the air and on land? If one condemns the hijacking of aircraft, can one find attenuating circumstances for the massacre of innocent and defenseless passengers by Arab terror squads or condone the murder of civilians perpetrated by the same Arab terror squads on land? It is as though one professed respect for the Ten Commandments but rejected the injunction "Thou shalt not kill."

The premeditated murderous attacks carried out by Arab terror organizations against civilians on land and in the air, such as the ambushing of school buses or the massacre at Lod, are barbaric crimes which only the demented or most cowardly are capable of committing or initiating, and the criminality of those attacks is not diminished but aggravated by their motivation. They are being perpetrated as part of the campaign directed against the right of the Jewish people to self-determination, freedom and equality among nations. The Arab terror attacks are carried on under the banner of an openly avowed design to bring about the destruction of a member State of the United Nations and of its people. Therefore no usurped slogans or semantic contortions used by those organizations can conceal this basic fact.

No one denies the Arab people's national rights. Indeed, no people has vindicated its rights more impressively and extensively. The Arab people's right to self-determination and independence is expressed in the sovereignty of eighteen Arab States members of the United Nations—all part of the Arab nation, all speaking the same language, professing the same faith, bound by the same culture. Even if each one of those States is to be considered a separate branch of the Arab people, there is today no part of the Arab nation that has not attained independence and sovereignty, and that applies equally to the Arab people of Palestine. In Palestine there does exist the Arab State of Jordan, Palestinian in its geography, Palestinian in its population. In 1948 another Arab State could have been established in Palestine on the West Bank of the River Jordan if the Arab States had not prevented its creation by invading the West Bank and Gaza in defiance of the United Nations. When peace is attained in the Middle East, it will be up to the Arab people of Palestine to decide what the constitutional structure of the Arab State or States in Palestine should be and whether that entity or those entities would continue to be designated by the name of the River Jordan which flows through the center of Palestine or use the name Palestine itself.

The rights of the Arab people to independence and sovereignty in Palestine cannot derogate from Israel's rights as a sovereign member of the United Nations, and especially not from the right of the Jewish people to liberty and independence in its homeland. All peoples have a right to live and create in freedom. Surely that is also a prerogative of the Jewish people, one of the most ancient in the world, which has preserved its identity, its civilization and its faith during thousands of years even after it was conquered and uprooted from its land by foreign invaders practicing imperialism and colonialism not unlike those that other nations have had to face in modern times.

The Chinese people, whose history, like that of the Jewish people, dates back thousands of years, and whose civilization, like that of Judaism, has given birth to other great cultures and faiths, knows that history cannot be erased. Surely the Jewish people's right to defend its existence and sovereignty is not inferior to that of other nations only because the conquest of Israel by Imperial Rome took place not two or three hundred years ago but nineteen centuries before our time.

The Jewish people's right to struggle against the consequences of that conquest have not been reduced by the fact that it was not only conquered but also taken into bondage by the invaders and carried off by them to foreign lands. If anything, the tenacity and perseverance which the Jewish people have shown and the suffering and sacrifice they have known in their struggle through the ages should command greater respect and sympathy. At a time when almost all the States represented at the Council table were still absent from the firmament of history two States were already there—China, on the easternmost edge of the Asian continent, and Israel, on the western shores of Asia.

III

A reply to the representative of China. (Excerpts from a statement in the Security Council, April 16, 1973.)

I remember hearing as a child the Chinese story of the blind man and laughter. Apparently a blind man was standing near a crowd of people who were in a jocular mood, and suddenly he heard them burst into laughter; he joined them and laughed as well. Asked one of the men in the crowd, "Why do you laugh, blind man, not knowing what it is all about?" And the blind man replied, "As you are all laughing, there must be something worth laughing about, and therefore I laugh, too." What the blind man did not know was that the crowd was laughing at him.

To the representative of the People's Republic of China, who is relatively new in this Organization, I would say: Make no haste in joining the chorus of those who attack Israel by distorting basic international concepts, and by falsifying fundamental principles regarding peace and war and aggression, and the right of Israel, a victim of twenty-five years of Arab aggression, to defend itself against terrorism. One day these same distortions of values and precepts might be turned by their proponents against you.

But I would leave it to the founder of the Chinese Republic, Sun Yat-sen, to reply to the substance of the Chinese representative's statement.

On April 24, 1920, Sun Yat-sen wrote a letter to a Zionist leader in Shanghai, Mr. N. E. B. Ezra, in which he said:

DEAR MR. EZRA,

I have read your letter and the copy of *Israel's Messenger* with much interest and wish to assure you of my sympathy for this movement, which is one of the greatest movements of the present time. All lovers of democracy cannot help but support whole-heartedly and welcome with enthusiasm the movement to restore your wonderful and historic nation, which has contributed so much to the civilization of the world and which rightfully deserves an honorable place in the family of nations.

It is time for the Government of the People's Republic of China to ponder those words.

IV

A reply to the representative of the USSR. (Excerpts from statements in the Security Council, December 31, 1968.)

A meeting of the Security Council without a verbal skirmish between the Soviet representative and myself would be considered unusually dull. I would be the last one thus to detract from the drama of our deliberations. Therefore allow me to refer, first of all, to the statement made today by the representative of the Soviet Union.

On May 21, 1948, the Soviet representative in the Security Council and present Minister for Foreign Affairs of the USSR stated, "The USSR delegation cannot but express surprise at the position adopted by the Arab States in the Palestine question, and particularly at the fact that those States—or some of them, at least—have resorted to such action as sending their troops into Palestine and carrying out military operations aimed at the suppression of the national liberation movement in Palestine."

On May 28, 1948, the representative of the Ukrainian Soviet Socialist Republic stated, ". . . we do not know of a single case of invasion of the territory of another State by the armed forces of Israel, except in self-defense, where they had to beat off attacks by the armed forces of another State on Israel territory. That was self-defense in the full sense of the word."

The war that was described in 1948 as a war of Israel's defense is still continuing. It is still the same war that the Arab States are waging against Israel today. It is the same war that the Arab States still refuse to end.

History, truth and fact do not change at the whim of the winds that blow through the cold corridors of the Kremlin. As long as this Arab war of aggression against Israel continues, Israel will insist on its right to defend itself in the best way it finds necessary and possible, whether the guardians of international law in Moscow are pleased by it or not. That is especially so as the United Nations itself has already established, in particular in Resolution 2131 (XX) of December 21, 1965, that the organization of, assistance to, fomenting, financing, inciting or tolerating of terrorist activities directed against another State is to be regarded as aggression. It is to be observed that that resolution was initiated by the Soviet Union, which in all its definitions of aggression has always included indirect armed attacks by irregular forces and terrorist groups. Thus, in a draft resolution submitted by the Soviet delegation to the General Assembly on January 5, 1952, we read:

The General Assembly,

Considering it necessary to formulate directives for such international organs as may be called upon to determine which party is guilty of aggression,

Declares:

1. That in an international conflict that State shall be declared the attacker which first commits one of the following acts: . . .

(f) Support of armed bands organized in its own territory which invade the territory of another State, or refusal, on being requested by the invaded State, to take in its own territory any action within its power to deny such bands any aid or protection.

Surely that definition applies to the operations of terror organizations against Israel from the territory of Lebanon and other Arab States.

The time has come for the Soviet Union to stop giving advice on how to conduct and how not to conduct military activities, especially when these activities are undertaken in self-defense. The time has come for the Soviet Union to help in securing peace in the Middle East by terminating its unilateral support of Arab aggression.

For months now we have been treated to the Soviet representative's expertise on the concept of aggression. I should like to tell him, in the words of an ancient Hebrew saying, "Taunt not your neighbor with your own blemish." It is a wise saying that has stood the test of centuries. Soviet concepts are new, and time has not always been kind to them. I would suggest that the Soviet representative and his Government ponder over this Hebrew saying: "Taunt not your neighbor with your own blemish."

I shall not prolong the discussion with the Soviet representative, but I should like to leave him with one thought to ponder over.

A quarter of a century after a desperate fight for life against Hitler's Nazi hordes, the Soviet Union finds itself today completely identified in the Middle East with aggressive Arab Governments which are the only ones in the entire world that still publish and still distribute Hitler's *Mein Kampf*. Twenty years after supporting, in the words of Mr. Gromyko, "the Jewish national liberation movement in Palestine," the Soviet Union now gives succor and encouragement to Arab terror organizations openly proclaiming as their aim the destruction of the Jewish State and the annihilation of its people. I have no doubt that the time will come when the Soviet Government and the Soviet people will look with a blush of shame upon this disgraceful chapter of Soviet history.

V

A reply to the representative of the USSR in the Security Council, October 11, 1973.

To the representative of the Soviet Union I would like to say, I wish
he and his Government contributed just part of the effort to achieve
peace in the Middle East that it does to the extent and thickness of the
protocols of the Security Council. One thing is clear after his observations, and that is what the Soviet Union wants under the present circumstances. One thing is clear after listening to the representative of
the USSR, and that is that his Government supports the renewal of
aggression by the Arab States on October 6. I take note of that
fact.

Ambassador Malik spoke of responsibility for war now and even
before, he said. I have here a list of statements made by him, by his
present Foreign Minister, and by other representatives of the Soviet
Union in the Security Council and the General Assembly at the time
when the conflict in the Middle East first started in 1948. And at that
time the representatives of the USSR had no hesitation at all in saying
very clearly who the aggressor was and pointing their fingers at the
Arab Governments. Now, history and fact are not going to be changed
with every statement in the Security Council delivered by representatives of the Soviet Union. The war to which the Middle East has been
subjected by the Arab States since 1948 is the same war of aggression
initiated by them at that time. There was a period of truce followed by
a period of armistice, and now, since 1967, a period of cease-fire. And
today we heard the theory that even the cease-fire was nonexistent and
invalid. But there was never a time of peace. It is the same war; it is
the same aggression. Those responsible for its initiation are the same
today as in 1948. Those who are defending their right to live in peace
and security—in fact, their life, in fact their right to exist as other
nations do—are the same today as in 1948, when Ambassador Malik
spoke in this very Security Council of Arab aggression, and was supported by Mr. Gromyko, Mr. Tsarapkin and Mr. Tarasenko. Facts
and history cannot change. And when the Nazis were at Stalingrad
they were aggressors. When the Soviet Red Army threw them back to
Berlin, they remained the aggressors and the Soviet army was the defender. Can you imagine, Ambassador Malik, someone getting up in
those days of 1944 and 1945 and telling your Government that you
have become aggressors because you have defended yourselves suc-

cessfully and pushed back those who wanted to turn you and your peoples into slaves?

I have listened carefully to your definition of what criminal, barbarian military actions—especially air attacks—are. Well, let me tell you one thing—and I challenge the Soviet press to publish it and Soviet international lawyers to reply to this: By this definition which you threw at us, all the Soviet marshals and generals and officers and soldiers who defended themselves against the Nazi aggressors in the Second World War should be considered criminals and barbarians— and no one, I think, in his right mind would suggest that. But there is one law, if there is law at all in this world, and it will be the same for the Soviet Union and its military forces and its leaders as it is for Israel and its Government and its armed forces.

VI

A reply to the representative of the Byelorussian Soviet Socialist Republic in the Security Council, April 18, 1974.

I have asked to speak in order to exercise my right of reply to the representative of Byelorussia, a country which is encouraging Arab aggression against Israel, and to the representative of Iraq, which will go down in history as the country where innocent Jews were hanged in a Baghdad square and where the population was called upon by the Iraqi Government to feast and revel in that barbaric spectacle.

On December 31, 1968, the representative of the Union of Soviet Socialist Republics in the Security Council, at that time representing also Byelorussia, said in a debate concerning Israel's action against terror warfare from Lebanon, "If a State helped armed bands to enter another State, that was an act of aggression. However, Israel had produced no evidence to show Lebanon's responsibility and Lebanon denied any responsibility."

Has not enough evidence been accumulated since 1968 to establish very clearly what is going on in Lebanon, what is happening in Beirut? Is it a secret that their bases are located in various parts of Lebanon, especially the southern region of the country? Is it a secret that their agents travel freely from Beirut in various directions into all parts of the world, carrying Lebanese passports and suitcases with bombs and explosives to kill innocent people? Is it a secret that they send letter bombs to innocent citizens of various countries, some of them represented at the Security Council table? Is any additional evidence required to that already presented by me in the course of the previous meetings, evidence not only gathered from facts reported by me but even based on statements made by Lebanese Government leaders, by leaders of Lebanese parties in the Parliament in Beirut?

If any other additional evidence is required by the representative of the Byelorussian SSR, may I add the following. Kamal Jumblatt, leader of the Lebanese Progressive Socialist Party, a personality well known in the Soviet Union, a gentleman who has paid several visits to Moscow, a man who does not hide his support for Arab terrorism carried on from Lebanon—even he found it necessary to say the following only yesterday, April 17, 1974: "I oppose operations directed against civilians and in particular children. I am not one of those who believe that the cause justifies the means. Certain Palestinian organizations were not faithful to the promises that Lebanese territory will not be used as a departure point for Fedayeen operations."

Now what else has to be said at this Security Council table to prove not only that those who murdered eighteen innocent civilians in a little Israeli townlet only one kilometer from the Lebanese border came from Lebanese soil, but that Lebanon is in truth a center of terrorist activities in the Middle East and in other parts of the world?

Is it not clear, Mr. Representative of the Byelorussian SSR, that by permitting the existence of such centers of armed attacks, of acts of aggression against a neighboring State, Lebanon is in fact, to use the term used by the Soviet representative, aiding these attacks against Israel, Israeli territory and Israeli civilians, and, according to the Soviet statement quoted by me, is therefore guilty of these continuous acts of aggression perpetrated from Lebanese territory?

These observations obviously apply also to the grotesque illegal theory which we heard from the representative of Iraq, that a Government is not responsible for what goes on within its territory, that

Lebanon cannot be held responsible for permitting the continuation, for years now, of the open operation of terrorist bands on and from its soil against a neighboring member State of the United Nations.

The representative of the Byelorussian SSR spoke of liberation of occupied territories. We know who the liberators are. The entire world knows who gentlemen like Arafat and Habash are. We still remember when they used to say, "It does not matter whether our *fedayeen* kill men, women or children, as long as they kill Jews."

These are statements in the records of this very Security Council. These are the leaders of the movement which the representative of the Byelorussian SSR chooses to define as a liberation movement: killers of children, murderers of defenseless innocent human beings. And it is these people, these assassins, that are being received, with honor, in Moscow and in Minsk. It is these murderers who are being received for medical treatment in Soviet hospitals. Soviet scientists are being sent to mental homes. Innocent Jews begging to leave for Israel are being incarcerated in labor camps. But murderers of children are being treated in Soviet hospitals.

I should like to add that the official representative of the Palestine Liberation Organization—the umbrella association of all the terrorist organizations, the organization headed by Arafat, received so joyously and honorably in the Soviet Union—a man called Said Hammami, wrote the following letter to *The Times* of London, a letter which was published in *The Times* on April 16, 1974, and had the following comment about Kiryat Shmona, the murder of the innocents, an act called here by the representative of the Byelorussian SSR an act of liberation: "The death of 18 Israelis and 3 Arabs in that settlement last Thursday carries different lessons to different parties. To the Palestinians, especially those in refugee camps, it has one obvious meaning: if the world is going to forget about us, we are going to ignore it and carry on our suicide missions."

This is the kind of movement we are dealing with. This is what we in Israel have to confront. I have spoken at previous meetings about the denial by the Palestine Liberation Organization and its various branches of Israel's fundamental right to be independent and sover-

eign, the denial to the Jewish people of its basic right to self-determination and national liberation. And here we have the representative of the Byelorussian SSR who has the audacity to come before the
Council and to say that the massacre of Kiryat Shmona is an act of
liberation, but that Israel's response to it is comparable to the fascist
actions of the Second World War. Not the killing of eighteen innocent
civilians, not the murder of defenseless men, women and children is
an act comparable to fascist nazi barbarism, but the destruction of
bricks after the inhabitants of the twenty houses have been evacuated
from them.

The general representative of the International Union of Resistance
and Deportees' Organizations had the following to say on April 15,
1968, about this kind of blasphemy: "We denounce those who insult
the memory of the Jewish dead, of the camps and the resistance, by
comparing the children of Israel of today to the Nazi oppressors or
by likening the terrorists who attack innocent men, women and children to the heroes of the European Resistance."

At its plenary session in Brussels, held from April 3 to 7, 1968,
with the participation of distinguished delegations from countries like
Belgium, France, the United Kingdom, Austria, Cyprus, Denmark, the
United States, Luxembourg, Israel, Italy, Norway and the Netherlands, the International Union of Resistance and Deportees' Organizations adopted the following resolution:

No one can compare the spirit of resistance to the terrorist activities and odious and blind crimes intended to provoke fear and insecurity, to give rise to violence, when all possibilities are openly offered
for an open discussion, or try to compare to the resistance against
Nazism the fanatics surrounded by former Nazi criminals who merely
prolong the Hitler genocide and thereby offer an insult which is felt
deeply not only by the citizens of Israel, who courageously fight for
their right to life, but by all those who resisted and who remain true to
themselves.

I would add to that statement and to that resolution that the comparison made by the representative of Byelorussia with fascists, with

Nazis, is an insult not only to those who spoke as they did on behalf of the international resistance movements and deportees, not only to the children of Israel, not only to the entire Jewish people, who lost six million brothers and sisters in the Nazi Holocaust; it is an insult also to Byelorussia and to its people and to its resistance fighters, among them many Jews, who fought heroically against Nazi occupation in the Second World War.

Why does the representative of Byelorussia come here with such eagerness to speak at such length in the language of slander and calumny? Perhaps the answer is to be found in a cablegram which reached me only today and which reads as follows:

WITH GREAT PAIN WE RECEIVED THE NEWS OF THE TERRORIST ATTACK ON THE PEACEFUL RESIDENTS OF ISRAEL KILLING WOMEN AND CHILDREN. OUR HEARTS GO OUT TO THE PEOPLE DURING THIS DIFFICULT TIME. WE ARE WITHOUT RIGHTS IN THE SOVIET UNION AND ARE TREATED LIKE PRISONERS. THEY ARE WITHHOLDING OUR RIGHT TO EMIGRATE. OBVIOUSLY THE JEWISH PEOPLE ARE DESTINED TO SUFFER MUCH.

The cablegram which I just read out is signed by the following citizens of Novosibirsk: Alexander Roizman, Raya Roizman, Isaac Poltinnikov, Irma Bernstein, Victoria Poltinnikova and Gimel Manuel Feinberg—citizens of the USSR. Therefore I shall end my reply to the representative of Byelorussia by saying simply: As long as you encourage Arab aggression against Israel, as long as by your acts and pronouncements you give succor to the murderers of innocent Israeli children and women and men, as long as your country provides weapons to kill defenseless Jewish civilians, as long as it provides SAM-VII missiles which turn up in Rome aimed at international civil aircraft, your advice on how Israel should defend itself is not only inappropriate but completely worthless.

The fundamental right of every people, of every State, is also the fundamental right of the people of Israel and of the Jewish State, and that is the right to self-defense, to self-preservation and to survival. It is in accordance with this right that Israel will continue to act to protect its territory and its citizens.

VII

Excerpts from a reply to the representatives of the USSR and China in the Security Council, April 16, 1974.

There was nothing new in the Soviet representative's statement. We have heard the same unfounded charges, the same distortions, in years past. They have always reflected the most unhelpful role played by the USSR in the Middle East, a role that hampered the attainment of peace and encouraged Arab aggression. It is significant that in these very days, while Syrian acts of aggression are taking place along the cease-fire line, it was in the course of a visit to the capital of the Soviet Union that President Assad of Syria declared that as far as his country is concerned the October War is still continuing. That was on April 11, 1974. On April 15, 1974, Radio Damascus quoted President Assad as having said on the same day, also in Moscow, "Syria is determined to continue the war until Israel is defeated."

Listening to the statement of the representative of the USSR, one could not but wonder, Will there really be not a single constructive word or thought in the entire pronouncement? There was none. Not a word about the right of every State to be free from armed attacks by irregular forces, by murderous gangs, organized and operating from the territory of neighboring States. Not a word about the right, under the Charter of the United Nations, of every State to self-defense. Not a word about the Declaration on Principles of International Law Concerning Friendly Relations and Cooperation Among States, initiated, I think, by the Soviet Union and stating: "Every State has the duty to refrain from organizing, instigating, assisting or participating in . . . terrorist acts in another State or acquiescing in organized activities within its territory directed toward the commission of such acts, when the acts referred to in the present paragraph involve a threat or use of force."

There was not a word in the Soviet representative's statement about Lebanon's obligation to put an end to a situation which is contrary to the principles of the Charter, to the provisions of the Declaration on Principles of Friendly Relations, to scores of resolutions adopted by the General Assembly.

The Soviet concept, according to Ambassador Malik, is that while international terrorism should be disapproved, Israel should do nothing at all to protect itself against the attacks by the terrorists. The people of Israel desire peace, and they have sought peace throughout the years of Israel's independence. It is because they desire it that they shall defend themselves against Arab aggression, whether it comes by means of regular armies or through the use of irregular terrorist bands.

If the Soviet representative wished to indicate his country's interest in peace in the Middle East, he should have spoken of measures to stop terrorism, first of all in the Middle East, but also in the world at large, and not of steps to be taken against those who are victims of international terrorism.

The Soviet representative was followed by the Ambassador of China, to whom I would say that slogans cannot be a useful contribution to the examination of any situation, especially when such slogans are based on distortion. When those who speak in almost Kafkaesque terms—and this applies to both speakers to whom I have just referred —when those who consider that an Arab antiliberation terror directed against the very life and liberty of the Jewish people is a liberation movement, and also slander Israel as an aggressor, enlightened public opinion and Israel know for certain that the very opposite is true. To both these statements, I shall therefore answer with an ancient Chinese fable. Two men were nearsighted, but, instead of admitting it, both of them boasted of keen vision. One day they heard that a tablet was to be hung in a temple, so each of them found out beforehand what was written on it, and when the day came they both went to the temple. Looking up, one said, "Look, aren't the letters, the characters, 'brightness and courage'?" "And the smaller ones there, you can't see them, but they say, 'Written by so-and-so in a certain month on a certain day,' " said the other. A passerby asked what they were looking at. And when told, the passerby laughed and said, "The tablet has not been put up yet, so how can you see the characters on it?"

You are like those two shortsighted gentlemen, Ambassador Malik and Mr. Representative of China, competing with each other without seeing or wanting to see what is really going on in the Middle East situation. Now, so that my use of a Chinese fable should not, Heaven forbid, bring about, as it did on another occasion, a Soviet accusation of an Israeli-Chinese conspiracy, let me add also a Russian proverb in response to both these statements, a proverb which says: "Slander, like coal, will either dirty your hand or burn it."

3 To Stand Alone Is Not to Be Isolated

Excerpts from a reply to the representative of the USSR in the Security Council, April 16, 1974.

I should like to refer to one point raised by the representative of the USSR. He found it advisable to speak of Israel's alleged isolation in the international community. I wonder whether those who make such statements realize the meaning of isolation in general, and in respect of Israel in particular. Do they realize, for instance, that in all democratic countries, even in those whose Governments, for reasons of material expediency, sometimes do lean toward the Arab States, the peoples, as demonstrated in public opinion polls, are squarely on Israel's side? I would even venture to say to the representative of the USSR that if such a free public-opinion poll were allowed also in his own country the results would be the same, and the support of the peoples of the Soviet Union for Israel's struggle would be as strong as in other parts of the world.

As for the attitude of the Governments themselves, we attach great significance to it. But it is no secret that this attitude is frequently influenced by such considerations as the number of Arab votes in international organizations, the size of Arab territories and of Arab populations, and the need for Arab oil. These considerations have, of course, no relation whatever to the merits of Israel's position and to the righteousness of its course.

Moreover, this situation is not new. It is not new for Israel; it is not new for the Jewish people. We have always been a small nation, devoid of large territory or vast riches. Our strength has always been in the realm of the spirit, in our faith, in our civilization, in the values of morality and justice which we have enunciated and upheld through the ages.

But those who held different beliefs, those who disagreed with us, those who opposed us, have always been more numerous than ourselves. Yet throughout history, we have always remained faithful to our heritage and have always refused to abandon it and to join the majority. We knew at all times, in all periods of history, that it was easier to yield, to give in and to give up, and to become part of the multitude. We chose not to do that.

Have those who speak of Israel's isolation, as the Soviet representative did, given any thought to the question, What would have happened if at the time the Jewish people was the only one with a monotheistic religion it had discarded it because the entire world rejected the idea of one God? What would have happened to the birth of Christianity and Islam, both rooted in Judaism? What would have happened to the vision of the Hebrew Prophets inscribed at the gates to the United Nations—the vision of a world at peace, of swords being turned into plowshares—if the Jewish people had said to itself, "We are isolated because all nations believe in war. Let us therefore join them in the glorification of war, and stop preaching peace"?

The Jewish people was isolated when, three thousand years ago, it proclaimed the concept that all men are born equal because they are all created in the image of one God. The Jewish people was all alone when, thirty centuries before the abolition of slavery, it established by binding law that slaves must be freed after seven years of servitude. When the Crusaders massacred entire Jewish communities, including those in the land of Israel, when the Inquisition burned Jews at the stake, when pogromists butchered Jewish women and children, when the Nazis annihilated them in gas chambers and crematoria, we were isolated. Do not, therefore, throw at us the epithet of isolation when our children and women are again being murdered—this time by Arab terrorists. Do not taunt us with isolation when we are still defending, as we have been for centuries, our very right to life as individuals and as a people, different but equal with others.

We shall not be impressed nor deterred. The Jewish people has never betrayed itself and never will, small as it is, surrounded by those who are more numerous, as it has always been. That has been our strength in all ages: isolation from injustice, isolation from a refusal to distinguish right from wrong; isolation from the belief that material power, numerical strength and the power of violence are supreme. That is a condition about which the Jewish people has never had any regrets. In fact, it is not isolation at all but a conscious choice, a conscious preference for and alliance with the right and the just and the humane even in times when only a few uphold those tenets.

For thousands of years, our people has found in this situation sufficient strength and inspiration to persevere and even to outlive its detractors, because the Jewish people has always known that its ideals and values, its identity, the protection of its heritage, the righteousness of its cause, are more precious than the plaudits of others. That is true also today.

4 Resolution 242: The Beginning of Peacemaking

I

Statement delivered in the Security Council on June 11, 1973. The Council was convened at Egypt's request with a view to imposing on Israel the Arab interpretation of Resolution 242. *

After twenty-five years of Egyptian warfare against Israel, Egypt now seeks to impose on Israel Egypt's *Diktat* to restore insecurity and vulnerability of the past, to change Resolution 242 (1967)—the only basis for United Nations peacemaking efforts accepted by both parties —and to reject negotiations between the parties, the only method that could lead to agreement between them.

I regret to say that even as we have been deliberating here in the Council chamber, the Egyptian governmental press has been, day after day, confirming our worst fears regarding the Egyptian position. Thus I indicated here that when demanding Israel's withdrawal to the 1967 lines, Egypt seems to continue to consider that this will be only the first stage in the struggle against Israel that will go on. In our view, Minister Zayyat confirmed that when he declared that Israel's recognized boundaries were those of 1947.

Mr. Hassanin Heykal once more made the Egyptian view more explicit in his weekly article in the semiofficial *Al Ahram* of June 8, in which he wrote: "Israel in its present position, composition and character has no future in the region and is an entity which is histor-

* See Appendix, p. 283, for the text of this resolution.

ically doomed to extinction. Israel thus constitutes an additional attempt at colonialism, which is out of place."

In my previous interventions I also submitted that Egypt's refusal
to negotiate with Israel is not a matter of procedure, nor is it motivated by Israeli occupation of Egyptian territory, for the refusal pre-
dates that occupation, but emanates, it would seem, from Egypt's
denial of Israel's fundamental, legitimate rights. On June 6, the very
day on which the Security Council opened this debate, *Al Ahram*
confirmed this and wrote: "The Arab refusal to negotiate with Israel
conceals their insistence on the rejection of a racial and colonial
entity."

Finally, I drew attention to Egypt's attempt to change Resolution
242 (1967) by proposing the dismemberment of Jordan. *Al Ahram*
again confirmed this. Only yesterday it published an article stating
that it is essential that the world should recognize a Palestinian State,
as proposed in the Security Council by Egypt's Foreign Minister. I
do not believe there is need for any further comment on my part on
these matters.

At the Security Council meeting last Friday, June 8, I said that the
multiplicity of Arab statements in this debate is in fact beneficial. One
could almost say today, the more the merrier. No one could demonstrate more convincingly the justice of the Israeli position and the
extremism of the Arab attitude than the Arab spokesmen themselves.
No member State of the United Nations except Israel is surrounded by
enemies which openly proclaim in the United Nations that their objective is to eradicate it, as reaffirmed today with a greater or lesser
degree of explicitness by the representatives of Kuwait, Algeria and
Sudan.

It is well known that these are not mere words. One does not, for
instance, mount a campaign of barbaric slaughter of innocent men,
women and children unless one thinks and acts in terms of total annihilation. Algeria has served as the haven of Arab terrorists and air
pirates. According to press reports, Sudan, apparently out of sympathy
for the murder of guiltless civilians by Arab terrorists, has decided not
to put the assassins of Khartoum on trial. Kuwait is one of the princi-

pal sources of financial support for the Arab terror organizations, as well as a supplier of military equipment and arms to them.

Algeria's attitude toward Israel was formally expressed by its President, Boumédienne, as follows: "The true freedom of the entire homeland must be won through the liquidation of the State of the Zionists." Algeria's Foreign Minister today gave expression to the same view when, *inter alia,* he spoke of the "original sin" of creating Israel and of Israel's being an artificial State.

Sudan's position was defined by President Numeiri, as reported by Reuters on June 2, 1969: "The military leader of Sudan, General Al-Numeiri, today stated that his regime will work for the strengthening of the Arab nation with the purpose 'to annul the results of aggression and put an end to Israel's existence on Arab soil.' "

Kuwait's fundamental policy has been expressed by its rejection of the Security Council's cease-fire resolutions and of Resolution 242 (1967). On February 17, 1969, the Kuwaiti Foreign Minister declared that his Government rejected all peaceful solutions of the Palestine issue. At the plenary meeting of the General Assembly on November 4, 1970, the following declaration was made on behalf of Arab States, including Algeria and Kuwait:

Israel is composed preponderantly of transplanted, alien settlers, who have forcibly dispossessed and subjugated the indigenous Palestinian people and conquered and usurped its homeland. To contend, as the draft resolution does, that the recognition of the claims of Israel to the attributes and prerogatives of statehood is indispensable for the achievement of a just peace is tantamount to contending that the legitimization of a gross injustice is a prerequisite for the attainment of justice and peace. We reject this thesis as well as the principle on which it is predicated;

Our respective Governments have categorically rejected, and continue to reject Security Council resolution 242 (1967) . . .

These are the defenders of international law and of the United Nations Charter. These are the Arab States which came today before the Security Council to speak of respect for the Council's resolutions and their principles.

The Security Council cannot ignore this attitude of the Arab States. Israel will not ignore it. The Government of Israel would be amiss in its international and national obligations if it did not remain at all times alert to the fact that Arab States continue to strive for the liquidation of the only independent Jewish State and preach this in the United Nations.

How secondary must appear some of the questions touched upon in our discussion, at a time when the entire situation is overshadowed by the Arab objective to deprive the Jewish State of its freedom and equality with other nations.

It has been said that the Security Council is the only forum where all the parties of the conflict have been able to meet in the same room. If today's appearances of Kuwait, Algeria and Sudan, and the Algerian Minister's insistence that he should not be contaminated by the presence of the Israeli representative, are examples of such meetings in the same room, I am certain that those really desirous of peace would rather forgo them.

At the meeting of June 7 I stated:

Egypt's Minister for Foreign Affairs asked . . . that the Security Council change Resolution 242 (1967), and in particular: (a) replace the establishment in agreement between the parties of secure and recognized boundaries by the Egyptian *Diktat* to restore the insecure provisional old line of 1967; and (b) to replace the call for a just settlement of the refugee problem, which appears in Resolution 242 (1967), by a provision referring to the so-called Palestinian rights, implying in effect, as we heard yesterday, the dismemberment of Jordan, a member State of the United Nations.

It is important that we have a closer look at that resolution. A principal architect of Resolution 242 (1967), Ambassador Arthur J. Goldberg of the United States, declared in a speech in Washington on May 8 of this year:

The record shows that even before the Six-Day War the Arab States were opposed, as they are now, to direct negotiations with Israel to settle their differences and to conclude a peace agreement.

Today, this unwillingness to engage in direct negotiations is explained on the ground that Israel is in occupation of Arab territories. A commitment by Israel for total withdrawal is insisted upon by Egypt, in particular, as a precondition to any form of negotiation—direct or indirect.

It is a simple fact of international life, however, that a refusal to negotiate on this ground is unprecedented and contrary to international custom and usage . . .

Ambassador Goldberg continued to explain Resolution 242's crystallization:

The unanimous support for Resolution 242 (1967) was the product in considerable measure of intensive diplomatic activity by the United States . . . The United States went all out diplomatically because we still hoped, first, to get a resolution, and second, to have all parties, pursuant to the resolution, negotiate an agreed and accepted settlement before positions congealed.

Then he defined the resolution as follows:

Resolution 242 (1967) does not explicitly require that Israel withdraw to the lines occupied by it before the outbreak of the war. The Arab States urged such language; the Soviet Union, as I have already mentioned, proposed this at the Security Council, and Yugoslavia and some other nations at the Special Session of the General Assembly. But such withdrawal language did not receive the requisite support either in the Security Council or in the Assembly.

Resolution 242 (1967) simply endorses the principle of "withdrawal of Israel's armed forces from territories occupied in the recent conflict," and interrelates this with the principle that every State in the area is entitled to live in peace within "secure and recognized boundaries."

The notable omissions—which were not accidental—in regard to withdrawal are the words "the" or "all" and "the June 5, 1967, lines." In other words, there is lacking a declaration requiring Israel to withdraw from "the" or "all the" territories occupied by it on and after June 5, 1967.

There were two major attempts by the Arab States to gain the Security Council's approval for their demand that Israel should withdraw from all the territories. One attempt was made in June 1967, the other in November 1967. In both instances the Council refused to endorse the Arab demand. Thus it rejected demands that Israel should withdraw its troops "behind the armistice lines" or "to the positions held before June 5, 1967." Equally, demands that withdrawal should be "from all the territories" failed to gain the Council's support. Even a formula that spoke of withdrawal "from the territories" was rejected.

In view of all these abortive efforts it is clear that the absence of the word "all" or even of the definite article "the" from the withdrawal phrase is significant and purposeful. On June 13, 1967, the USSR representative submitted a draft resolution to the Council which said *inter alia:* "The Security Council demands that Israel should immediately and unconditionally remove all its troops from the territory of those States"—that is, the United Arab Republic, Jordan and Syria—"and withdraw them behind the armistice lines and should respect the status of the demilitarized zones as prescribed in the General Armistice Agreements." This Soviet draft was rejected by the Security Council.

On November 7, 1967, the UAR asked for an urgent meeting of the Council. The Council met on November 9, and the discussions that started then ended on November 22 with the adoption of Resolution 242 (1967). The note to the President of the Council in which the United Arab Republic, today Egypt, asked for the urgent meeting said *inter alia:* "I have the honor : . . to request the convening of the Security Council in an urgent session to consider the dangerous situation prevailing in the Middle East as a result of the persistence of Israel not to withdraw its armed forces from all the territories which it occupied . . ."

Thus, at the core of the UAR application was spelled out clearly, explicitly, the demand that Israel withdraw "from all the territories."

In his opening address at the Council meeting the Egyptian representative urged that it was the "duty" of the Council "to force the Israeli forces to return to the positions held before June 5."

A comparison of the Egyptian demands as presented to the Council with the resolution actually adopted by the Council demonstrates the dimension and finality of the dismissal of the Arab demands.

On November 7, 1967, India, Mali and Nigeria submitted a pro-Arab draft resolution which, on the subject of withdrawal, required the following: "Israel's armed forces should withdraw from all the territories occupied as a result of the recent conflict."

On the same day, the United States also submitted a draft resolution which, on the subject of withdrawal, spoke of "withdrawal of armed forces from occupied territories." It further spoke of "respect for the right of every State in the area to . . . secure and recognized boundaries."

For a few days, discussions went on in the Council and behind the scenes without any version gaining enough votes for adoption.

The Arabs eventually realized that the Council did not support their insistence on withdrawal from all the territories. This opened the way for the British draft, which spoke of withdrawal from "territories," without the definite article, and without the word "all."

The following is an account of the days preceding November 22, 1967. On November 16, 1967, Lord Caradon, the representative of the United Kingdom, submitted his draft resolution.

On what happened immediately after the Council's meeting in which Lord Caradon had submitted his draft, we read in *The UN and the Middle East Crisis, 1967,* by Arthur Lall, a former Ambassador of India to the United Nations:

V. V. Kuznetsov at once met with the Arab delegates, who told him that the formulation on the withdrawal of Israeli forces in the first operative paragraph of the British draft was not acceptable to them. They insisted that the wording read either that Israeli forces would be withdrawn from "all the territories," instead of "territories" occupied by Israel, or that Israel would "withdraw to the positions of June 4, 1967." In addition the Arabs were unwilling to accept the phrase "recognized boundaries" also occurring in the first operative paragraph.

. . . The Arab States met on the morning of November 17 and took a dramatic decision . . . The Arabs concluded that it was better to get a resolution backed by all 15 votes in the Council than to insist on a resolution which might not be adopted or which might obtain the bare minimum of nine votes. Several of them discussed matters with Caradon. Could he not use the formulation "all the territories" instead of "territories" in relation to the clause requiring Israel's withdrawal? Caradon's response was that his draft represented a delicate balance which would be upset by any changes.

On November 20, 1967, four days after the British draft had been submitted, the USSR representative submitted his own draft resolution, which, on the subject of withdrawal, said: "The Security Council . . . (2) urges that . . . (a) the parties to the conflict should immediately withdraw their forces to the positions . . . held before June 5, 1967." This USSR draft once more attests how wide is the gap between the pro-Arab demands and Resolution 242 (1967) that was ultimately adopted, and which speaks of withdrawal "from territories."

Before the vote, Lord Caradon, sponsor of the draft about to be adopted, affirmed:

. . . the draft resolution is a balanced whole. To add to it or to detract from it would destroy the balance and also destroy the wide measure of agreement we have achieved together. It must be considered as a whole and as it stands. I suggest that we have reached the stage when most, if not all, of us want the draft resolution, the whole draft resolution and nothing but the draft resolution.

The foregoing was the basis for the following summary made by Professor Eugene V. Rostow, professor of law and public affairs at Yale University, who, at the time of the adoption of Resolution 242 in 1967, was United States Undersecretary of State for Political Affairs:

. . . paragraph 1 (i) of the resolution calls for the withdrawal of Israel armed forces "from territories occupied in the recent conflict," and not "from the territories occupied in the recent conflict." Repeated attempts to amend this sentence by inserting the word "the" failed in the Security Council. It is, therefore, not legally possible to assert that the provision requires Israeli withdrawal from all the territories now occupied under the cease-fire resolutions to the Armistice Demarcation Lines.

Addressing the Security Council moments after the adoption of the draft resolution, Mr. Abba Eban, Israel's Minister of Foreign Affairs, declared: "For us, the resolution says what it says. It does not say that which it has specifically and consciously avoided saying."

Of particular interest are the following statements reflecting the views of members of the Security Council regarding the withdrawal provision of Resolution 242 (1967).

On November 15, 1967, Mr. Arthur Goldberg, the United States representative, said in the Security Council:

To seek withdrawal without secure and recognized boundaries, for example, would be just as fruitless as to seek secure and recognized boundaries without withdrawal. Historically there have never been secure or recognized boundaries in the area. Neither the armstice lines of 1949 nor the cease-fire lines of 1967 have answered that description, although the . . . Armistice Agreements explicitly recognize the necessity to proceed to permanent peace, which necessarily entails the recognition of boundaries between the parties. Now such boundaries have yet to be agreed upon. An agreement on that point is an absolute essential to a just and lasting peace just as withdrawal is. Secure boundaries cannot be determined by force; they cannot be determined by the unilateral action of any of the States; and they cannot be imposed from the outside. For history shows that imposed boundaries are not secure and that secure boundaries must be mutually worked out and recognized by the parties themselves as part of the peacemaking process.

On September 10, 1968, President Lyndon Johnson declared:

We are not the ones to say where other nations should draw lines between them that will assure each the greatest security. It is clear, however, that a return to the situation of June 4, 1967, will not bring peace. There must be secure and there must be recognized borders. Some such lines must be agreed to by the neighbors involved.

On July 1, 1970, President Nixon stated: "Israel must withdraw to borders, borders that are defensible."

On July 12, 1970, the Assistant Secretary of State, Mr. Joseph Sisco, declared:

The Security Council did not call for unconditional Israeli withdrawal to the Armistice Lines as had been the case at the time of the 1956 war in Sinai. Rather, it called for "withdrawal . . . from territories occupied" in the 1967 war as part of a package settlement in which the parties would agree to respect each other's right to live in peace within secure and recognized boundaries. The Security Council resolution established principles; it did not establish borders or define precisely the obligations of peace and security.

The United Kingdom, as the Council knows, was the sponsor of Resolution 242 (1967). On March 17, 1969, Mr. Goronwy Roberts, Minister of State, Foreign and Commonwealth Office, in a reply to a question in Parliament said:

The Security Council resolution lays down certain principles which are required for the establishment of a just and lasting peace. These include "withdrawal of Israel armed forces from territories occupied in the recent conflict" and the right of every side in the area to live in peace within "secure and recognized boundaries." These boundaries will be determined in the context of a general statement.

On November 17, 1969, Mr. Michael Stewart, Secretary of State for Foreign and Commonwealth Affairs, in reply to the following question in Parliament, "What is the British interpretation of the wording of the 1967 resolution? Does the Right Honourable Gentleman understand it to mean that the Israelis should withdraw from all territories taken in the late war?," replied, "No, sir. That is not the phrase used in the resolution. The resolution speaks of secure and recognized boundaries. Those words must be read concurrently with the statement on withdrawal."

On December 9, 1969, the same Mr. Michael Stewart, Secretary of State for Foreign and Commonwealth Affairs, in reply to the observation by Sir Alec Douglas Home that "the House should be told whether or not this resolution requires the complete withdrawal of the Israelis," replied, "As I have explained before, there is reference, in the vital United Nations Security Council resolution, both to withdrawal from territories and to secure and recognized boundaries. As I have told the House previously, we believe that these two things should be read concurrently and that the omission of the word 'all' before the word 'territories' is deliberate."

Mr. George Brown, British Foreign Secretary in 1967, at the time of the adoption of Resolution 242 (1967), said in January 1970:

I have been asked over and over again to clarify, modify or improve the wording, but I do not intend to do that. The phrasing of the resolution was very carefully worked out, and it was a difficult and complicated exercise to get it accepted by the Security Council. I formulated the Security Council resolution. Before we submitted it to the Council we showed it to Arab leaders. The proposal said Israel will withdraw from territories that were occupied and not from "the" territory, which means that Israel will not withdraw from all the territories.

Mr. Harold Wilson, head of the United Kingdom Government that put Resolution 242 (1967) to the vote, stated on December 27, 1972: "The Israel interpretation of the resolution was fully consistent with what the then British Government had meant. If our Government had meant 'all,' we would have said 'all.' We would have never wanted to say it anyway, and if we had it wouldn't have been passed."

Finally, in an interview on February 10, 1973, just a few months ago, Lord Caradon, the principal architect of Resolution 242 (1967), declared:

Withdrawal should take place to secure and recognized boundaries, and these words were very carefully chosen: they have to be secure, and they have to be recognized. They will not be secure unless they are recognized. And that is why one has to work for agreement. This is essential. If we had attempted to draw a map, we would have been wrong. We did not. And I would defend absolutely what we did. It was not for us to lay down exactly where the border should be. I know the

1967 border very well. It is not a satisfactory border, it is where troops had to stop in 1947, just where they happened to be that night. That is not a permanent boundary.

On November 9, 1967, Mr. George Ignatieff, the Canadian representative in the Security Council, declared in the Council, "If our aim is to bring about a settlement or a political solution, there must be withdrawal to secure and recognized borders . . ."

Again on November 9, Mr. Otto R. Borch, the Danish representative in the Security Council, speaking in the discussions which preceded the adoption of Resolution 242 (1967), quoted a public statement of the Danish Minister for Foreign Affairs, Mr. Hans Tabor, as follows: " 'As we see it, the full implementation of these principles would include the withdrawal of Israeli troops, the safeguarding of the territorial and political integrity of all States in the area, including a final settlement of the borders in the area . . .' "

On November 22, 1967, Mr. Geraldo de Carvalho Silos, the Brazilian representative, said, "We keep constantly in mind that a just and lasting peace in the Middle East has necessarily to be based on secure permanent boundaries freely agreed upon and negotiated by the neighboring States . . ."

The views of those who criticized certain provisions of Resolution 242 (1967) also throw light on the meaning of the resolution. Thus, the Soviet representative, Mr. Kuznetsov, said in the discussion:

. . . phrases such as "secure and recognized boundaries." What does that mean? What boundaries are these? Secure, recognized—by whom, for what? Who is going to judge how secure they are? Who must recognize them? . . . there is certainly much leeway for different interpretations which retain for Israel the right to esablish new boundaries and to withdraw its troops only as far as the lines which it judges convenient.

Egypt's Minister for Foreign Affairs has come to the Security Council to suggest in fact that Resolution 242 (1967), which provided for the establishment of secure and recognized boundaries through negotiation and agreement, either meant the very opposite of what it said or was illegal and has to be modified. All those who interpreted the resolution as members of the Security Council that sponsored and adopted it, and even those who criticized it, did were in his view wrong. That is, of course, an utterly groundless thesis, especially as Resolution 242 (1967) was accepted by both parties. Even if Governments that had voted for the resolution were to modify their political views regarding one or another aspect of the situation, they could not now change the meaning of the resolution without destroying it.

Negotiation and agreement to determine secure and recognized boundaries where none had existed is a necessity. Negotiation and agreement on border changes, even when secure and recognized boundaries do exist, is not unusual. That is particularly so in a situation of war. That is especially so when changes in the old lines are required by the State that did not initiate the war but has been subjected to it for twenty-five years and now desires to agree on boundaries that would take into account its vital security needs. I find few States around the Security Council table that have not applied these tenets in their own relations with other countries. It is obvious that Israel cannot be deprived of the same right. States that try to alter or unilaterally reinterpret Resolution 242 (1967) and to exclude from it the call to establish through agreement between the parties, for the first time in the Middle East, secure and recognized boundaries take upon themselves a grave responsibility, for such an attitude will surely undermine the prospects of agreement between Israel and the Arab States and make progress toward peace more difficult. It is to be hoped, therefore, that members of the Security Council will not tamper with the only existing basis for agreement on a just and lasting peace in this region.

True, progress toward such agreement has been slow. But this is not a justification for destroying the only common ground, unless, of course, one wishes to create a void that would entail also the undermining of Israel's commitments on the basis of Resolution 242 (1967). Giving verbal satisfaction to a partisan view in disregard of its merits may be a valid consideration in ordinary situations. It is not in questions of war and peace, especially when an effort is being made to terminate the most protracted war in this century in the entire world. Such an effort requires patience and circumspection, a search for that which unites, and not the creation or solidification of divisive elements.

Every State member of the Security Council has its individual interests in the Middle East. Israel appeals to all members of the Security Council to allow the paramount interest of peace to prevail. None of you carries the burden of a two-thousand-year struggle to retrieve freedom and equality and restore independence. None of you has known what it means to be under constant assault for twenty-five years. None has had to face for a quarter of a century an enemy seeking total destruction and annihilation of his nation. Do not make it more difficult for us to terminate this war. Do not make it more difficult for us to establish secure boundaries, which had never existed before between Israel and the Arab States, so that there can be peace at long last in the Middle East.

II

Excerpts from a statement in the Security Council, June 13, 1973.

The representative of France referred to the continuation of the Israeli presence in territories held since 1967. In connection with that, it is necessary to bear in mind the following:

First, Israeli forces find themselves in the areas which came under Israel's control in 1967 as a result of a war of aggression pursued by the Arab States against Israel since 1948 and as a result of the attempt made in 1967 by Egypt and by other Arab States under Egypt's direction to liquidate Israel, as announced at the time by President Nasser.

Second, the Israeli forces remain on the present cease-fire lines in accordance with the Security Council's cease-fire resolutions.

Third, the provision for withdrawal from those lines is, as indicated also by the representative of France, linked to and contingent on the provision regarding the establishment of secure and recognized boundaries.

Fourth, those boundaries are to be established under Resolution 242 (1967) by agreement between the parties. There has thus far been no Arab willingness to negotiate such agreement without prior conditions with Israel.

Fifth, the requirement to determine for the first time between Israel and the Arab States secure and recognized boundaries is of a general character. It does not exclude Egypt. All the armistice agreements with Jordan, Syria, Lebanon and Egypt specified that the armistice lines were provisional lines and should not in any way prejudice the rights, claims and positions of either party in the ultimate settlement. The Egyptian-Israeli Armistice Agreement went further. It stated specifically that the demarcation line "is not to be construed in any sense as a political or territorial boundary."

There could be no more unequivocal a formulation. Israel and Egypt have clearly undertaken not to regard the old military lines as a territorial boundary. Israel cannot be expected twenty-five years later to give a different interpretation to that commitment and to accept that there was a territorial boundary between Israel and Egypt when the existence of such a boundary was specifically declared by both parties not to be.

I took note of the observation made by the representative of France regarding the possibility of agreed changes in the old lines. But I took particular note of the specially significant statement made by the representative of the United Arab Emirates that in fact the Arab delegations were told and knew in November 1967 that Resolution 242 (1967) provided for the possibility of such changes in the old lines. This is the fundamental, the decisive principle. The determination and precise extent of those changes must, of course, come through agreement between the parties. It is good that we found corroboration of this central principle of change of the old lines in the statement of an Arab representative.

5 The Principle of Negotiations

Excerpts from a statement delivered in the General Assembly in a debate on the situation in the Middle East, November 29, 1972.

There is a way that can lead to peace between the parties: a dialogue between them. All other means have been tried already and have failed. This is the method that has been followed in other parts of the world.

This is the method of negotiation between the parties, of nonintervention from the outside, of respect for the principle of nonimposition. This is the method in which agreements are the outcome of negotiation and not of commitments demanded as a precondition to negotiation. This is the method Israel proposes. (It has achieved peaceful solutions of other conflicts. There is no reason why the Middle East should be an exception. The Middle East cannot be an exception if the conflict which has enveloped it for so long is to be brought to an end.)

"Negotiation is not an act of 'humiliation' or 'surrender' for anybody, as some Arab leaders have said," declared Israel's Foreign Minister in the General Assembly on September 28. "It is a supreme assertion of national sovereignty and of international responsibility. Courage in leadership does not belong to the battlefield alone; it can be put to the service of conciliation and peace."

Indeed, there is humiliation, but that is when nations are allowed to languish in war, when cities and towns linger in desolation because leaders refuse to talk peace. Negotiation is not surrender. It should be an exchange of views leading to mutual adjustments of positions.

Israel's desire for peace, Israel's hopes for peace, the prayer for peace that is in the heart of every Israeli are manifest to all who genuinely wish for progress toward peace in the Middle East and shun hollow polemics.

The Government of Israel is ready to negotiate peace without any preconditions, in accordance with the principles expressed in its official statements, including the statement in this year's general debate.

The Government of Israel is prepared to engage in proximity talks on an agreement to reopen the Suez Canal, as proposed to it.

I am also authorized to reiterate that Israel does not seek to freeze the existing situation or to perpetuate the cease-fire lines, but to replace them in peace with secure and agreed boundaries to be established through negotiation with each of its Arab neighbors.

Israel has no ultimative maps delineating the peace boundaries. The only thing that Israel has refused was to accept in advance Egypt's position regarding these boundaries. History knows of no instance of successful negotiations under such a *Diktat*. Israel for its part does not demand that Egypt should accept any Israeli position as a precondition for negotiation.

This attitude offers the possibility of an honorable and meaningful negotiation between Israel and Egypt. To malign it is utterly groundless. To reject it is to reject the possibility of peace.

II

Excerpts from a statement in the Security Council, June 12, 1973.

The only agreements ever concluded and signed by Israel and the Arab States were achieved through negotiations. At the time, the Security Council played an important role in bringing about those negotiations. On November 10, 1948, the Acting Mediator, the late

Dr. Ralphe Bunche, reported to the Security Council on the situation in the Middle East and suggested that an armistice be established between Israel and the Arab States. The delegation of the Union of Soviet Socialist Republics proposed that the central provisions of the resolution based on Mr. Bunche's report should read: "The Security Council . . . calls upon the parties directly involved in the conflict in Palestine, in order to eliminate this threat to peace, immediately to begin negotiations, directly or through the good offices of the Acting United Nations Mediator in Palestine, . . . [for] the establishment of formal peace."

At its 381st meeting, on November 16, 1948, the Security Council adopted a resolution which contained the basic idea of the USSR text, calling, however, for the establishment of an armistice. The Council called "upon the parties directly involved in the conflict in Palestine, as a further provisional measure under Article 40 of the Charter, to seek agreement forthwith, by negotiations conducted either directly or through the Acting Mediator [on Palestine]."

In the course of the debates which preceded the adoption of that resolution, representatives around the Council table addressed themselves to the mechanism of negotiation and its advantages in promoting the cause of peace. During one of his interventions in the debate the representative of Egypt, Mahmoud Fawzi Bey, declared, "I cannot agree with the observations made by the representative of the USSR in connection with the principle of negotiations . . ."

At the 380th meeting of the Security Council, on November 15, 1948, Ambassador Yakov Malik, today the President of the Security Council, replied:

As a result of a preliminary exchange of views, most members of the Security Council as well as the Acting Mediator have recently stated that they were in favor of general talks between the two parties involved in the Palestinian conflict and that these talks might develop into the next stage on the way to a peaceful solution to the situation in Palestine . . . it was indeed time for the parties in Palestine to begin negotiations directly or through the Acting Mediator.

In view of that, it would be impolitic to adopt any decision on details that might complicate these bilateral negotiations. Needless to say, in the course of such negotiations any question may be discussed.

At the same meeting, Ambassador Malik also declared, "In our view, it would be preferable to adopt fewer decisions, but when adopted they should be such as to be effective and helpful in securing a genuine settlement by peaceful means . . ."

The Ambassador went on in words most pertinent to the present situation under discussion by the Security Council:

Thus the bitter lesson of events in Palestine teaches us that all the means so far employed for solving this problem have proved fruitless. The situation now is such that probably none of us would be surprised if the interested parties themselves, impelled by their own interests, were suddenly to cease to heed what was being imposed on them from outside and entered into direct negotiations with the object of settling all the outstanding questions, thus confronting the Security Council and the Mediator with a fait accompli.

The USSR delegation feels that those who genuinely desire a peaceful solution of the Palestinian problem in the interests . . . of Palestine would welcome this turn of events and would do all in their power to bring it about.

Then he added:

The USSR delegation considers that the wisest and most expedient proposal would be to offer the parties concerned the opportunity to try to settle all outstanding questions by direct negotiations or negotiations with the assistance of the Acting Mediator.

Speaking on the draft resolution, the representative of the United States declared, "The effect of this new resolution if adopted by the Council would be to suggest a new direction for those negotiations."

The representative of Belgium stated *inter alia,* "The text is quite explicit. It says that negotiations should take place either directly between the parties or through the Acting Mediator."

The representative of Canada observed, "I associate myself with these remarks of the Belgian representative."

The Syrian representative, Mr. Faris El-Khouri, explained at the 381st meeting of the Security Council of November 16, 1948, why the Arab States rejected the method of negotiations, and I quote from the statement of Mr. El-Khouri:

Such negotiations as have been called for—and the Arabs have been invited to enter into direct negotiation with the Jews—would be possible only if there were no dispute between them regarding the essence of the situation in Palestine. Broadly speaking, negotiations would take place between two States in conflict over any matter such as frontiers or any other things, but negotiation implies mutual recognition of the sovereignty of both States; but in this case, this does not exist. We should understand the question from the beginning: not this year, or last year, but for a quarter of a century, or even for thirty years, since the Balfour Declaration was made known in November 1917, the Arabs have never accepted immigration into Palestine on a large scale.

Now, the negotiations which are intended, either by the Security Council or by other parties inviting the Arabs to enter into negotiations, would entail recognition by the Arabs of the state of things as it stands, the consideration of the Jews in Palestine as a State, and that they should negotiate regarding frontiers, economic matters, communications, transport, or any other matters which may arise between two sovereign States. But this is the focal point of the dispute. The whole dispute in Palestine hangs on this point: whether or not there is to be a Jewish State in Palestine.

The Egyptian representative offered the same explanation:

I shall stop here for a moment on this point. In so far as negotiations are concerned I have already stated more than once to the Council my point of view and the determination of my Government not to negotiate with the Zionists. We do not recognize them as a party. We will stand by our position which was upheld by the United Kingdom Government more than once. As I have mentioned to the Council before, in London, although we were all there, we usually used to call them the London Conferences. The British were negotiating with the Jews and with the

Arabs, but the Jews and the Arabs were not negotiating through the British. This to some people might seem a mere technicality, but it touches the very crux of the whole matter.

If there are negotiations at all, we certainly welcome the idea that they should be carried out with representatives of the United Nations. We not only encourage them but we welcome negotiations with representatives of the United Nations; however, we should not be forced to negotiate with people with whom we do not want to negotiate and whom we do not recognize as a party.

Here was, therefore, the same Arab opposition to negotiations as today. The Arab delegations at the time were perhaps somewhat more explicit in indicating the motivation of their refusal to negotiate. It is precisely the motivation which, we submit, lurks also behind the present refusal—unwillingness to abandon definitely and unequivocally any claims on Israel's fundamental right to exist as a sovereign State.

It is for this reason that readiness to enter into negotiations is not merely a question of applying the only method that could bring agreement between the parties, but a test of the Arab States' genuine desire for real peace with Israel.

The most important development in the 1948 experience was that despite the strong Arab opposition to negotiate with Israel, the Security Council adopted the resolution which called for negotiations. That was a bold and decisive move. In the wake of the resolution the Arab States dropped their objections and entered into the talks that led to the Armistice Agreements.

Following the adoption of the Security Council resolution on November 16, 1948, the Acting Mediator, Dr. Ralph Bunche, stated, "Negotiations, either directly or through a United Nations intermediary, are to be promptly undertaken."

On the next day, November 17, 1948, he sent a letter (S/1090) to the Provisional Government of Israel and to the Governments of Egypt, Iraq, Lebanon, Saudi Arabia, Syria, Transjordan and Yemen in which he stated *inter alia:*

I wish to reiterate my sincere belief that the interests of all parties to this dispute would be best served by direct negotiations undertaken by the parties themselves. But whether the parties decide that the negotiations should proceed directly or through a United Nations intermediary, the services and good offices of myself and staff are at their disposal for every possible assistance in the effort to achieve peace in Palestine.

In his report to the President of the Security Council dated January 6, 1949 (S/1187), the Acting Mediator wrote:

I have the honor to inform you that the Government of Egypt and the Provisional Government of Israel have notified my representatives in Cairo and Tel Aviv, respectively, of their unconditional acceptance of a proposal providing for a cease-fire to be immediately followed by direct negotiations between representatives of the two Governments under United Nations chairmanship.

In his cablegram (S/1205) dated January 12, 1949, also addressed to the President of the Security Council, Dr. Bunche reported the arrival of the Israeli and Egyptian delegations in Rhodes. He said:

BOTH DELEGATIONS ARE EMPOWERED TO NEGOTIATE . . . I SHALL HOLD FURTHER MEETINGS WITH EACH DELEGATION TOMORROW MORNING, JANUARY 13, AND THE FIRST JOINT MEETING UNDER UNITED NATIONS CHAIRMANSHIP IS FIXED FOR 3:30 P.M. ON THE SAME DAY.

And in another cablegram (S/1209) dated January 13, 1949, he states:

THIS AFTERNOON, JANUARY 13, THE FIRST JOINT MEETING WAS HELD. AT THIS MEETING THE DELEGATIONS WERE INTRODUCED. MEETINGS WILL NOW PROCEED ON THE SUBSTANTIVE ITEMS ON THREE LEVELS AS FOLLOWS: (1) PRELIMINARY DISCUSSIONS SEPARATELY WITH EACH DELEGATION; (2) INFORMAL MEETINGS BETWEEN HEADS OF DELEGATIONS AND UNITED NATIONS; (3) JOINT FORMAL MEETINGS OF THE TWO DELEGATIONS. THE CONCILITORY SPIRIT OF BOTH PARTIES AND THE PROGRESS MADE IN MATTERS OF PROCEDURE CONTINUE TO INSPIRE HOPE FOR SUCCESSFUL RESULTS.

In a telegram (S/1225) dated January 25, 1949, he insists: "THAT THE PROCEEDINGS OF THE NEGOTIATIONS ARE NOT TO BE RELEASED IN

ANY WAY"—I repeat, "the proceedings of the negotiations are not to be released in any way"—"UNTIL THE NEGOTIATIONS ARE CONCLUDED."

Dr. Bunche, as we all know, succeeded in bringing about the conclusion of four Armistice Agreements between Israel and Egypt, Jordan, Lebanon and Syria.

On March 3, 1949, Ambassador Malik commented in the Council on the Israeli-Egyptian agreement as follows:

The USSR delegation notes with satisfaction the successful outcome of the negotiations between Egypt and the State of Israel, which it regards as a most favorable development in the Palestine question. Ever since the Palestine question first arose, the USSR delegation has maintained that direct negotiations between the two parties were the best way of settling the disputes which have arisen between the State of Israel and the Arab States.

Events have justified this stand. Only direct conversations have enabled both sides to bring the negotiations to a successful close, and thus, to a certain extent, to take the first step toward the settlement of their disputes.

When all four of the Armistice Agreements were signed, Dr. Bunche reported to the Secretary General by letter of July 21, 1949, in which he said, *inter alia,* "The negotiations leading to these agreements were, in each case, tortuous and difficult. But they demonstrate that once the parties could be brought together, they could, with United Nations assistance, be led to reasonable and honorable agreement."

That was the only Security Council experience with the Middle East situation in twenty-five years which bore fruit. The 1948 Council call for negotiations between the parties produced the only step toward peace that Israel and the Arab States ever took together. It was not a big step. It did not bring about the final peaceful settlement which the Arab States undertook to reach with Israel. Yet it was a significant step in the right direction.

If Egypt and the other Arab States really desire to attain genuine peace with Israel, there can be no reason, no reason whatever, that would justify their refusal to enter negotiations with Israel without preconditions as they did in response to the 1948 Security Council resolution.

Egypt's Minister of Foreign Affairs tried in the present debate to explain his Government's rejection of negotiations by alleging that Israeli occupation constitutes an impediment—indeed, a prior condition. This claim has no foundation whatever in law, logic or in international conduct. There can be no Israeli withdrawal without agreement between the parties on the line to which withdrawal would take place. The sequence can only be negotiation, agreement, withdrawal, and not the other way around. The refusal to negotiate on the grounds of occupation is unprecedented in history. Moreover, it is to be recalled that when in 1948 the Security Council called upon Israel and the Arab States to negotiate, a situation of occupation obtained as well. At that time, however, it was Israeli territory that was under occupation. Egyptian, Syrian and Jordanian forces occupied large areas of Israel. Yet neither Israel nor anyone else considered it even possible to suggest that the occupation constituted an obstacle to negotiation. All understood that negotiation and agreement was the only way to end the occupation. In fact, it was only after the signature of the Armistice that the armed forces of Egypt, Jordan and Syria withdrew from Israeli territory behind the demarcation lines established by agreement between the parties.

Egypt's objections to negotiations now must therefore be considered as mere pretexts. Israel was ready to conform with international practice and negotiate when its territory was occupied by Arab States. There is no valid reason why Egypt should not conform with the general usage and negotiate with Israel now. The real question is whether the Security Council will encourage Egypt to do it. In 1948 the Council rose above the claims and counterclaims of the parties, above the truce and its violations, and looked to the future and called for negotiations. The Council faces a similar choice today. It could continue to remain enmeshed in the sterility of partisan views or it could elevate itself and call for negotiations. This is the only constructive contribution the Security Council could make to the Middle East situation at this juncture.

6 Vision and Reality of Peace

Excerpts from an address to the Union of Orthodox Jewish Congregations, May 11, 1975.

Freedom is a cornerstone of Jewish civilization. One of the most beautiful of Jewish holydays, Passover, is the Festival of Freedom. For thousands of years we have been celebrating the struggle for freedom, the emergence from Pharaoh's bondage, the joy and glory of liberty. There is a message in the story of the exodus of the children of Israel from Egypt which is particularly appropriate to our times. The redemption from Egypt was not the end. It was only a beginning. It took our forefathers forty years before they reached the Promised Land, and even then the vicissitudes, the challenges, the dangers were far from over. The struggle to preserve freedom, to develop and create in independence continued. Freedom was only the opening of a new chapter. Sovereignty was merely an instrument capable of helping to face the challenges and the difficulties, and the pain and suffering that came with them.

The Talmud says that it was only through suffering that the Jewish people obtained the precious gifts of Torah, the land of Israel and independence. This was true thousands of years ago. This is true today.

When Israel's independence was proclaimed in May 1948, when Israelis danced and sang with joy in the streets of Jerusalem and Tel Aviv, there was a man who did not participate in the festivities. David Ben-Gurion, the father of Jewish statehood, knew that independence was not in itself the solution of the Jewish people's age-long problems.

He knew that the struggle ahead was long and trying. Indeed it was. The struggle is still going on.

In this sense the experience of the Jewish people is not different from that of other nations. The independence and sovereignty of states had always and everywhere to be defended, sometimes for centuries, before they could become firmly established and respected by neighboring peoples. However, there is a fundamental difference between the Israel–Arab conflict and conflicts in other parts of the world.

The war to which Israel has been subjected since its rebirth is not a conflict over territory. Neither is it a clash of economic interests. If it were, peace would have been attained in the Middle East long ago. The Israeli–Arab conflict is an attempt by one party to deny to the other the right to live, the right to exist as an independent nation. The gravity of this is obvious. If this is the nature of the conflict, is peace possible at all? Is understanding between Israel and the Arab States a realistic objective? The answer is yes.

The answer is yes because the conflict in the Middle East is not between the Israeli and Arab peoples. The Israelis, even in the most trying of hours in the Arab war against them, have never felt animosity toward their Arab cousins in general. To the average Israeli, agreement, understanding and harmony with the Arab neighbors is a paramount aspiration and an irrepressible hope. On the other side of the dividing line, there is no inherent, biological Arab hostility toward Israelis. No atavistic hatred toward the people of Israel fills the hearts of Arab people. We know this not from abstract deduction but from the experience of living and working together with a million Arab inhabitants in the Israeli-controlled territories and of contact with more than a million citizens of Arab States who have come since 1967 to the West Bank and to Gaza to visit their relatives and have frequently proceeded from there into the Jewish areas. We know this because we are aware of the sentiments prevailing among the people in the Arab States themselves. Thus the Middle East conflict does not find the Israeli and Arab peoples locked in mortal struggle. The conflict is, above all, the result of the policies and acts of Arab leadership. The tragedy of the Middle East is the tragedy of Arab leadership. A different attitude on the part of Arab leaders would have averted the conflict or, at the very least, brought about its termination at an early stage.

Unfortunately the humanism and liberalism of the leader of the Arab national revival in World War I, Emir Feisal, were succeeded by the fanaticism and extremism of those who followed in the footsteps of the Hitler collaborator Haj Amin el Husseini. Yet if the negative position of Arab leaders is at the root of the conflict, the hope and possibility of changing that position and bringing the war to an end appear as a realistic goal. Policies do change. Attitudes of Governments can be modified. International relations of States, even of those with the most dogmatic regimes, do not remain petrified. The views expressed by Arab leaders themselves toward Israel have seen nuances creep into them through the years.

In 1948 the Arab States which attacked Israel announced that this would be "a massacre of Jews reminiscent of the Mongolian massacres." In the nineteen-fifties and -sixties, Arab leaders boasted that they would "throw the Jews in the sea." On the eve of the 1967 Six-Day War, President Nasser of Egypt announced that "the hour has come to strike a death blow at Israel." Today some Arab statesmen speak of their readiness to sign a peace agreement with Israel. Thus far these pronouncements are mere words. They are still not translated into positive action toward building a durable peace with Israel. However, in what has become the longest and probably most complex conflict of this century, even a change in the terminology employed is significant. The challenge before us is, therefore, not unmanageable; the obstacles not unsurmountable. The problem is how to turn the words of Arab leaders about peace into reality.

We must have no illusions about the difficulties inherent in the effort to bring this about. The future may hold for us more Arab aggression and more bloodshed. However, we can rest assured that the Israeli–Arab conflict does lend itself to a solution, and when the Arab Governments become ready to construct genuine peace with Israel, peace there will be.

If we project our thoughts into the future we can see a peace of equality and harmony, a peace responding to the needs and hopes of the Israeli and Arab peoples alike.

For Israel Sinai has always been not a coveted territory but an instrument for peace. It should be possible to establish in Sinai a boundary of peace providing Israel with security and Egypt with the satisfaction of its sovereign rights.

The voices calling for a new bizarre partition of Jerusalem are becoming less and less numerous. The welfare of the city and its inhabitants, its millennial history and the central role it has always played in the life of the Jewish people make it inevitable that its unity and its integrity as Israel's capital should be preserved. However, Israel recognizes and respects the universal religious interests in the Holy Places situated in the city, and those sites would be under the jurisdiction of their respective religious communities. This is already the situation at present, but the status of the Holy Places could and should be enshrined in formal arrangements.

It should also be possible to work out a peace agreement between Israel and Syria that would take into account Israel's desire never again to expose its border villages to Syrian attacks from the Golan Heights. Under Syrian control the Heights were one vast military camp, with the villages clustering around army installations being inhabited, in large measure, by army dependents. Territorial modifications in this area, agreed between Israel and Syria, should not be impossible.

The future of the West Bank requires a special approach. We live in a world of changing concepts. Yesterday's views may not be valid today. Today's visions may be tomorrow's facts. This is true, for instance, of the idea of State boundaries. The Bible refers to States and empires, but there is no indication that they had well-defined borders. Ancient Israel was sometimes described as being situated between Dan and Beersheba, two localities, but the lines linking them were undefined. Even in this century the significance of borders has undergone changes. Seventy years ago there was no need for a person traveling from one country to another or emigrating to a foreign land to acquire visas. In the period prior to World War II travel across borders became restricted. In the aftermath of that war, however, most people can again travel from one State to another without special permits. Metamorphoses can be discerned also in other concepts such as sovereignty and other rights of States and peoples.

The Jewish people's historic and religious ties to such Biblical sites as Hebron and Jericho are irrevocable. However, the rights of the Arab inhabitants of those areas to political self-expression are equally self-evident. By recourse to nonconformist formulas regarding concepts such as sovereignty and boundaries, Israel and the Palestinian Arab State of Jordan should be able to vindicate the historic and spiritual bonds of the people of Israel with the entire land of Israel, including the right of Jews to settle in every part of their ancestral homeland, while at the same time ensuring the political rights of the Arab inhabitants as full-fledged citizens of an Arab State.

Appendix

Resolution 242 (1967) of November 22, 1967

The Security Council,

Expressing its continuing concern with the grave situation in the Middle East,

Emphasizing the inadmissibility of the acquisition of territory by war and the need to work for a just and lasting peace in which every State in the area can live in security,

Emphasizing further that all Member States in their acceptance of the Charter of the United Nations have undertaken a commitment to act in accordance with Article 2 of the Charter,

1. Affirms that the fulfillment of Charter principles requires the establishment of a just and lasting peace in the Middle East which should include the application of both the following principles:

(i) Withdrawal of Israel armed forces from territories occupied in the recent conflict;

(ii) Termination of all claims or states of belligerency and respect for and acknowledgment of the sovereignty, territorial integrity and political independence of every State in the area and their right to live in peace within secure and recognized boundaries free from threats or acts of force;

2. Affirms further the necessity

(a) For guaranteeing freedom of navigation through international waterways in the area;

(b) For achieving a just settlement of the refugee problem;

(c) For guaranteeing the territorial inviolability and political independence of every State in the area, through measures including the establishment of demilitarized zones;

3. Requests the Secretary-General to designate a Special Representative to proceed to the Middle East to establish and maintain contacts with the States concerned in order to promote agreement and assist efforts to achieve a peaceful and accepted settlement in accordance with the provisions and principles in this resolution;

4. Requests the Secretary-General to report to the Security Council on the progress of the efforts of the Special Representative as soon as possible.

RESOLUTION 338 (1973) ADOPTED BY THE SECURITY COUNCIL AT ITS 1747TH MEETING, ON 21/22 OCTOBER 1973

The Security Council

1. *Calls upon* all parties to the present fighting to cease all firing and terminate all military activity immediately, no later than 12 hours after the moment of the adoption of this decision, in the positions they now occupy;

2. *Calls upon* the parties concerned to start immediately after the cease-fire the implementation of Security Council resolution 242 (1967) in all of its parts;

3. *Decides* that, immediately and concurrently with the cease-fire, negotiations start between the parties concerned under appropriate auspices aimed at establishing a just and durable peace in the Middle East.